WOMEN
BEHIND
BARS

WOMEN
BEHIND
BARS

Gender and Race in US Prisons

Vernetta D. Young
Rebecca Reviere

LYNNE
RIENNER
PUBLISHERS

BOULDER
LONDON

Published in the United States of America in 2006 by
Lynne Rienner Publishers, Inc.
1800 30th Street, Boulder, Colorado 80301
www.rienner.com

and in the United Kingdom by
Lynne Rienner Publishers, Inc.
3 Henrietta Street, Covent Garden, London WC2E 8LU

Library of Congress Cataloging-in-Publication Data
Young, Vernetta D.
   Women behind bars : gender and race in US prisons / Vernetta D.
Young, Rebecca Reviere.
      p. cm.
   Includes bibliographical references and index.
   ISBN 1-58826-371-1 (hardcover : alk. paper) — ISBN 1-58826-395-9 (pbk. :
alk. paper)
      1. Women prisoners—United States.   2. Minority women—United
States—Social conditions.   3. Minority women—United States—Economic
conditions.   I. Reviere, Rebecca.   II. Title.
HV9471.Y68 2005
365'.43'0973–dc22

                                                              2005018306

British Cataloguing in Publication Data
A Cataloguing in Publication record for this book
is available from the British Library.

Printed and bound in the United States of America

      The paper used in this publication meets the requirements
 ∞   of the American National Standard for Permanence of
      Paper for Printed Library Materials Z39.48-1992.

   5   4   3   2   1

Contents

Part 2   Women Prisoners: Special Issues

Part 3   Conclusion

Tables and Figures

Tables

Figure

Acknowledgments

We would like to thank all those who provided assistance during this project. In particular, we appreciate the time and comments of Nora Arnold, Caroline Cottom, Emily Piccirillo, Mary Lynn Reithel, Hannah Schneider, Jessica Schneider, Ira Shorr, Adrienne Small, and Zoe Spencer.

—*Vernetta D. Young*
Rebecca Reviere

Equal Rights or Lost Opportunities?

The end of the twentieth century was a time of unparalleled growth in the female prison population. This period was characterized by social and political developments that drained the resources from urban neighborhoods, increased income disparities between the rich and the poor, and changed the roles and expectations for and of women. More important, however, it was a time when the nation declared "war on drugs," launching policies that had a greater impact on the criminalization and incarceration of women than any others in the nation's history. This confluence of events and trends resulted in a state and federal female prison population that soared from 12,300 in 1980 to 96,000 in 2002, even though women's rate of violent crime actually decreased during this period. Black women are imprisoned at a rate eight times that of white women; Hispanic women are imprisoned at a rate four times that of white women (Amnesty International 1999).

This incredible explosion in the women's prison population comes at a huge cost, not only to the women themselves but also to their families and communities. Many incarcerated women are serving long sentences for small-time drug crimes. They serve these years behind bars in prisons that were designed for and by men, and the implications of this male-oriented design are simple—prisons do not meet the needs of women or the nearly 200,000 children they leave behind. When they return to the community, and most do, they bring home the same sets of problems, as well as new ones. They return to communities where many of their basic rights are taken away; sometimes they even lose their children. Taxpayers pay millions of dollars to fund prison building and maintenance rather than social programs to prevent and treat the problems that send these women to prison in the first place.

In this book we examine the history and the special concerns of women, overwhelmingly women of color, in prison. Because far fewer women are incarcerated and because women as a group have less power and lower status than men, the causes and conditions of their skyrocketing rates of imprisonment have only recently come under scrutiny. The picture that has begun to emerge is one of tremendous disparities. The male-female disparity between the crimes that are punished and the penalties received and between their prison and postprison needs and the services offered to meet these needs is striking. Because of harsh sentencing policies that incarcerate women for years for low-level drug involvement, prisons that do not meet the treatment needs of women, and reentry policies that fail to provide a safety net, these women are punished twice, directly through their prison terms and indirectly through the many policies that do nothing to solve their problems but instead compound their misery.

The neglect of female prisoners results from complex and cumulative factors. It has been possible to ignore female criminals for several reasons: (1) with the small number of women in prison, there was no obvious imperative to develop separate policies; (2) women do not riot or become violent when their demands are not met, making them easier to disregard; (3) the needs and problems of poor, minority women are easy to overlook; and (4) current prisons were developed for men, and policies and programs from men's institutions are often simply stenciled onto women's prisons. But most prisons are built to house violent men; when that template is applied to women, with their different histories and different needs, it simply does not fit. In a male-oriented society, policies and programs created without gender in mind are designed for men by default. Women are marginalized in society; without deliberate design, they become further disenfranchised in prison. Specifically developing environments uniquely suited to the improvement of women's lives has so far proven impossible in prison.

■ **Social Control of the Undeserving**

This is not to suggest that men's prisons are ever particularly conducive to health and rehabilitation. Prisons are designed as institutions of formal social control; they were originally intended simply for the punishment of those who broke the law. Over time the focus changed to rehabilitation, but now the mission is once again to punish. For the most part, members of society accept and applaud this mission of the prison system and call for criminals to get the punishment they deserve: "you do the crime, you do the time." The popular feeling is that having stepped outside the bounds of common decency and proper society, lawbreakers do not deserve privileges or special treatment. Having broken the law, they lose their civil rights. This reasoning is not hard to understand when prisoners are violent repeat offenders.

Once locked away, prisoners are alternately dehumanized and ignored. When they are considered, they are feared and despised as dangerous predators; otherwise, they are forgotten until a sensational story brings them to the public eye. If it is easy to disdain and disregard men in prison, it is even easier to look down on or overlook women in prison. Women who are incarcerated are seen not only as prisoners but also as bad wives, mothers, and daughters; they have both broken the law and stepped outside of their normative roles. In addition, they are primarily poor and dark-skinned. Many are mentally ill; most have been victims of gender-based violence. They are not the women that conjure respect or concern or attention, but they are the women who were locked away in unprecedented numbers during the end of the twentieth century.

> "It would be impossible for me to say imprisonment is *worse* for women than for men. Imprisonment is terrible for everybody. Imprisonment is different for women because women are different from men" (Kathryn Watterson Burkhart 1973, 425).

■ Background to the Buildup

Prisons and the prisoners they house reflect the social and political climate in which they exist and operate. Conditions were ripe during the end of the twentieth century for an explosion in the prison population (Mauer 2001).

The Social Climate

Changes in residential patterns that began after World War II were beginning to reshape major metropolitan areas by the 1970s. As more affluent families bought homes outside the cities ("white flight"), the suburbs became major centers of employment. The poorest were left behind in sections of urban areas that became "slums of despair" (Palen 2002). Unlike the wealthier urban dwellers, the inhabitants of these areas had (and still have) few marketable skills, erratic work records, and high welfare rates. These neighborhoods were characterized by residential instability, poverty, and crime. As manufacturing and blue collar jobs disappeared, few decent employment opportunities were available for those who did not have the advantages of appropriate education, experience, transportation, or computer access.

With this brittle backdrop, crack cocaine entered the scene and wreaked havoc. Drugs and drug abuse have always been around; for example, the 1960s introduced drugs to a broad slice of the population. But the emergence of crack in the 1980s was different and devastating. Simply made by cooking powder cocaine with baking powder, it was a cheap, quick, euphoric high and a marketing marvel. Having few other employment options, many in these "slums of despair" turned to drug dealing as the only viable route to earning money. The

drug trade was accompanied by guns and gangs, and an underground economy
sprang up. The media image of littered streets, broken windows, and hooded
young men on the prowl was frightening to most Americans. The country's
reflex was to erase the problem, and the set of sentencing requirements that
were available made it easy to do just that.

As these urban areas grew more blighted, the wealthiest communities
grew more affluent. During the thirty-year period between 1970 and 2000, income disparity widened between the richest and poorest Americans. In 1979,
the richest 1 percent earned 7.5 percent of after-tax income compared to 6.8
percent for the lowest 20 percent. By 2000, the top 1 percent share of after-
tax income had increased to 15.5 percent, while the lowest 20 percent were
earning only 4.9 percent (Greenstein and Shapiro 2003). The economic chasm
that segregated the US population according to wealth and privilege had profound implications for the poor generally and for lawbreakers specifically.

When society becomes so radically divided, it is much easier to dehu-
manize those who are "different" (Mauer 2001). The frightening depictions of
these urban neighborhoods reinforced this belief. Women during the crack
epidemic were depicted in particularly vile ways; they were called "crack
whores" and "crack moms." Photographs were published of women with babies on their backs performing sex acts to make money for drugs. With these
images in mind, most Americans had no difficulty agreeing with the need for
increasingly harsh punishments.

The Political Climate

This social mix was both a cause of and a reaction to the political climate of
the times. Policies had begun to "get tough on crime" in the 1960s (Mauer
2001). These policies, however, had a fairly small impact on incarceration
rates of women since they did not participate in crime in substantial numbers.
There was another development, however, that had the most direct impact on
women.

The war on drugs began slowly about 1972, and by the early 1980s the
consequences for incarceration rates were evident. Four particular aspects of
this war are relevant here:

1. Drugs were deemed a serious and dangerous public problem—the
    cause of criminal offenses that, as defined by the Drug Enforcement
    Administration (DEA), include the possession, distribution, manufac-
    ture, cultivation, sale, transfer, or the attempt or conspiracy to possess,
    distribute, manufacture, cultivate, sell, or transfer any substance the
    possession of which is prohibited. The health or psychological inter-
    pretations of drug use were disregarded or forgotten. As a result, drug
    crimes became felonies (criminal offenses punishable by death or im-

prisonment for a term exceeding one year) as opposed to misdemeanors (criminal offenses punishable by a jail term not exceeding one year).

2. This definition of drugs as "criminal" was coupled with increasingly aggressive policing, especially in high-crime areas. More police officers on the streets made communities appear safer as drug officers infiltrated drug markets and made arrests in unprecedented numbers. The areas that came under this criminal justice gaze were those already distressed, and the many law-abiding citizens in those neighborhoods welcomed the protection from the chaos.

3. Sentencing policies for felonies were reformed, becoming harsher and less flexible. Box 1.1 gives a brief description of these guidelines. Before these changes occurred, judges had discretion to sentence according to their knowledge of each specific case and defendant. There was obvious racial discrimination in this system, but it did give judges the power to make decisions based on the individual rather than on a strict definition of the crime as presented by the prosecutor. As sentencing went from offender-based to offense-based (Mauer 2001), there were serious deleterious implications for women. Their low levels of criminal involvement and violence and their central roles in their families were no longer considered relevant to their sentencing. They were subject to the same increasingly severe punishment as the person who actually controlled a drug operation—even though they might have only answered the phone in a house where drugs were sold.

Box 1.1   Sentencing Policies

- Mandatory sentencing is a sentencing system in which the judge is **required** by law to impose an incarcerative sentence, often of a specified length, for certain crimes or for particular categories of offenders.
- Sentencing guidelines indicate to judges the expected sanctions for certain offenses.
- Determinate sentencing, also called flat or fixed sentencing, is a sentencing system that fixes the term of imprisonment at a specific period.
- Truth in sentencing is a sentencing system that requires offenders to serve a substantial proportion (usually 85 percent for violent crimes) of their prison sentence before being released on parole.

4. Systemic shifts in funding priorities essentially transferred monies toward drug control, prison building, and maintenance and away from social programs. Funds that once went to support low-income women and their children in the community and to fund educational opportunities have been continually cut back at the same time that funds for the war on drugs increased (Chesney-Lind 1998). For example, in fiscal year 2004, the following received funding from drug control monies: the Department of Agriculture (this includes Women, Infants, and Children programs), Corporation for National and Community Service, District of Columbia Court Services and Offender Supervision, Department of Defense, Intelligence Community Management Account, Department of Education, Department of Health and Human Services, Department of Housing and Urban Development, Department of the Interior, the judiciary, Department of Justice, Department of Labor, Office of National Drug Control Policy, Small Business Administration, Bureau of State, Department of Transportation, Department of the Treasury, and the Department of Veterans Affairs ("National Drug Control Strategy" 2003). Monies funneled to fight drugs are no longer available to help women and their families avoid or treat their drug problems or to help them reintegrate successfully into the community after prison. With the war on terror joining the war on drugs, poor women and their children face even more drastic cutbacks and a smaller social safety net.

Sociopolitical factors coupled with economic transfers were crucial to the spike in the general incarceration rate. But there was an additional set of circumstances unique to women that made them more vulnerable to arrest and incarceration than ever before. Changing roles, increasing numbers of female-headed households in poverty, and the ever-present violence toward women made the allure of drugs as escapes and avenues to income compelling.

The Climate for Women

By the 1970s, the notion of "women's liberation" had reached center stage in the United States. Women's attitudes about their rights and opportunities and the general public's perceptions of women had changed dramatically. Increasingly, women saw themselves and were seen as equal to men; women were ready, able, and determined to do everything men did. At the same time, the criminal justice system began to react to women differently. Punishment originally assigned to men was increasingly seen as appropriate for women. (African American women have always received harsher punishment than white women. See Chapter 2 for more details about racial differences in punishment.)

During this period there was also a marked increase in the number of female-headed households. This phenomenon was the result of social changes such as increases in the number of divorces, decreased use of adoption for extramarital pregnancies, and the growing acceptance of out-of-wedlock births. Although the stigma of single motherhood was reduced, the financial burden was tremendous. Female-headed households have always been more vulnerable to poverty than households with two adults. (For example, in 2000, 26.5 percent of all female-headed households were below the poverty line [US Census Bureau 2002]). Raising children alone is difficult; raising children alone with minimal resources is daunting and extremely stressful. For some women, a readily available coping mechanism for stress was the use of illicit drugs.

Women's high rates of physical and sexual abuse also made them more vulnerable to the escape of drugs. Women have always been subject to male violence. Their fathers, stepfathers, husbands, and lovers beat and rape them with virtual impunity. Crimes that would be severely punished if perpetrated on a stranger are overlooked when the victim is a female intimate. This gender-based violence erodes a woman's self-confidence and envelops her in fear and hopelessness. When women are victims of abuse, their lives are a crime scene already; to engage in illegal behavior themselves is not a step out of line with their existing realities. And drugs offered a break from their misery and pain and a chance to make some much-needed money.

These historical trends converged, and in this book we show a snapshot of a particular time in the history of the criminal justice system. The intersection of concentrated poverty, harsh drug penalties, and new roles and responsibilities for women meant that women were suddenly engaged in punishable crimes on a broad scale. And those punished were, and are, overwhelmingly women of color. Historically, the inequalities in prison parallel the inequalities in society. The sexism, racism, and classism that exist in the larger community also exist in the criminal justice system. With scarce resources and little support, some women have few alternatives in a society that favors punishment over prevention. For many, prisons become the social program of last resort (Church and Browning 1990).

A Prison System Unprepared

Prison conditions for women have never been comfortable and therapeutic, but an annual report from the early 1900s describes a very different prison than what we see today. "Outdoors the women have carried water, chopped wood, mowed the yards, cared for the roads and paths, weeded, dug potatoes, gathered and prepared vegetables, picked and canned blueberries, cared for pigs. . . ." A later report from that same prison went on, "The work helps to build bodies and to strengthen high-strung nervous creatures that come to us worn out by their habits of late hours, improper eating and vile indulgence" (quoted in Rierden 1997, 47). In addition, "these buildings with soft chairs, couches, and a fireplace, picture windows and open-out windows for each inmate's room, give the appearance of a convalescent hospital" (Ward and Kassebaum 1965, 7).

At the end of the twentieth century, sentencing changes rapidly escalated the number of women sentenced to prison. Prison officials, largely unprepared for the sudden influx, scrambled simply to make space. As prison construction tried to catch up with the growing prison population, there was a dramatic change from the earlier picture of more "homey" conditions. These women were now crowded, sometimes six to a cell, into prisons designed for a smaller number of women. Today, many maximum security inmates are locked in their cells much of the time, eat army-style rations, and rarely see the sun (Murphy 2004). They must buy their supplies in overpriced commissaries; work for pennies an hour to maintain the prison; and have access only to food that is high in fat, sodium, and sugar (Chandler 2003). Women are punished by far more than simple incarceration; they are punished with overcrowded, exploitive, and unhealthy living conditions.

■ The Importance of Policy

Policies are "authoritative decisions that are made in the legislative, executive, or judicial branches of government. These decisions are intended to direct or influence the actions, behaviors, or decisions of others" (Longest 1998). Although this book is not about policy per se, prisons do reflect the policies of society. They are agents of social control, and thus the laws of society determine what behaviors are punishable by imprisonment. Now most women end up in prison because of drug laws instituted in the 1970s, 1980s, and 1990s. These laws were intended to catch major drug lords, but instead small-time using, running, and dealing women were hauled in. Drug laws and policies are particularly salient because they affect women directly through sentencing requirements that mandate long sentence terms and indirectly through policies that are not explicitly related to criminal justice. The indirect effects come from the many agencies that are involved in "deterring" drug trafficking and that control options women have when they return to the community. Women convicted of drug crimes may find they have lost their children, homes, and opportunities for income and education—they are punished again for their drug crimes.

The policies of the prisons themselves shape what structure, rules, and sanctions govern the lives of prisoners once they are behind bars. Policies within prisons determine the treatment that women receive and the programs that are available. Relationships with family, drug treatment, and physical and mental health care are all governed by the prison. Because there has only been lip service paid to women's concerns, the programs that should and could help women are barely adequate. On every front, the consequences of these policies are harsher for women than for men. Policies begin on paper, but they become manifest in the lives of individuals; the picture of sentencing and drug policies is the faces of suffering dark-skinned women.

■ The Diversity of Women

We recognize that to talk about "women" in prison assumes a monolithic group, and the above discussion implies that only poor urban women break the law and that drug crimes are the only route to prison. Clearly that is not the case; many different types of women enter prison for many different reasons. For example, Jean Harris, a graduate of Smith College and headmistress of a private school in Virginia, was sentenced to fifteen years to life for murdering her physician lover. Martha Stewart, the lifestyle maven, was sentenced to five months for obstruction of justice and lying to investigators about a stock deal. Women steal cars, embezzle, and commit murder.

But there is a modal woman, a typical woman who ends up behind bars. Most women in prison are dark-skinned, poor, unskilled mothers who are incarcerated for low-level drug involvement. They have been physically and sexually abused by the men in their lives, some since childhood. Many have complex collections of mental health and medical conditions and substance abuse problems. Relatively little has been written about subgroups of incarcerated women. We know almost nothing about Hispanic women (McQuaide and Ehrenreich 1998) and even less about Native American and Asian American women who are incarcerated. A major barrier to understanding and addressing the unique difficulties of women in prison is the remarkable lack of available data.

■ Data Sources

Most of the available statistics on women in prison come from the federal government. The National Institute of Justice (NIJ) is the research, development, and evaluation agency of the US Department of Justice and is dedicated to researching crime control and justice issues. The director, appointed by the president and confirmed by the Senate, establishes the institute's objectives, guided by the priorities of the Office of Justice Programs, the US Department of Justice, and the needs of the field. Within the NIJ, the Bureau of Justice Statistics gathers and disseminates most of the information, including data from various state departments of corrections. Clearly the political interests of each administration determine which statistics are gathered and disseminated to the public. For example, in the pro-marriage Bush administration of 2004, the first comprehensive study of the relationship between marriage and low drug use was released.

For most researchers data are available only when released by these governmental agencies and only in the forms that they present. For example, many past and present reports give information only on "prisoners" and do not differentiate between females and males. It is even rarer when statistics are broken down into gender and race groups; for example, a report may give the percentage of women in prison who have received drug treatment but not the percentage of black, white, or Hispanic women who have received treatment. We know even less about social class or education of prisoners.

The lack of in-depth and current data makes painting a detailed picture of the complicated issues facing women in prison prohibitive. However, several nongovernmental organizations, such as Amnesty International and the Sentencing Project, collect information on women in prison. There are many such progressive groups involved in reporting and rectifying various aspects of incarceration issues and policies. Although these organizations may not have the broad overview of the federal data sources, they give a more human picture of certain aspects of women's imprisonment. For example, much of what is known about the mental health problems and treatment of women in prison comes from Amnesty International's groundbreaking study, *Not Part of My Sentence* (1999). Justice Now, based in San Francisco, has contributed greatly to the understanding of end-of-life issues for women dying in prison. Families against Mandatory Minimums has published widely on the harmful impact of sentencing policies for women and their families.

■ Organization of the Book

We begin with a history of the penal system of the United States in Chapter 2. Women have been punished for the same and also for different crimes than men. In addition to punishment for theft, for example, women were subject to humiliation for having overstepped their roles as women, wives, and mothers. As the prison system developed, institutions for women were always the afterthought. They were allocated scant resources, but ironically, because there were so few incarcerated women, some early prisons managed to be less stark than they are today. Universally higher rates of incarceration for minority women have always meant that they were subject to more severe and abusive punishment. Chapter 3 discusses prisons and prisoners as they exist today and how they have changed over time.

The next five chapters (Chapters 4 through 8) present a specific set of concerns relevant to the lives of incarcerated women. Specifically, we examine drugs, health, family, death, and reentry. Men also deal with these same concerns, but our purpose is to examine these issues from a woman's perspective. We demonstrate that, in essence, these women are punished twice. They are first punished by their sentence, and then they are punished again because the policies that govern their prison and postprison lives were not designed from the standpoint of women's needs and responsibilities. From every angle, we see that when policymakers do not explicitly consider women, women suffer. Opportunities to establish a path to health and productivity for these women are lost.

In Chapter 4, we begin with drugs as the entry point and main problem for most women in prison. The laws governing the use of, sale of, and conspiracy to sell illegal drugs, or legal drugs illegally, have punished women disproportionately. The "gender-neutral" sentencing requirements failed to recognize the nonviolent, low-level drug involvement of most of these women. Further, women's unique life histories have made them more vulnerable to substance abuse while making treatment less accessible.

Chapter 5 discusses women's larger and distinct burden of physical and mental health disorders—problems that have become more obvious as more women are incarcerated. The realities of older women's lives help to elucidate many of the essential difficulties that all women face. Health care is identified as a priority in the prison system, yet women have more and different health issues than men, and most prison health care has not been designed with women in mind. As a result, lawsuits have reformed prison health care more than advance planning or common sense.

Chapter 6 describes the caregiving dilemmas that face women in prison. Family issues are always particularly relevant for women, but they are further highlighted with the rising number of mothers being imprisoned and separated from their children for long periods. The problem of what to do with the children is one that incarcerated males seldom have to face. The double punishment and lost opportunities of new policies become painfully obvious as many mothers lose custody of their children altogether.

In Chapter 7, we examine death and dying in prison. Most incarcerated women do not die as a result of the criminal justice system; it is rare when a woman is executed. But as more women enter prison and remain for longer times, more will face their own deaths, and many will face the death of a loved one.

Chapter 8 traces the hardships women face when they leave prison. Most women will return to their communities when they complete their sentences. Reentry, however, is not the joyful reunion imagined as women accused of drug crimes lose rights and opportunities. And regardless of type of crime, work and family transitions are difficult.

In the final chapter, we summarize our findings and look to the future. The double burden of punishment faced by women, particularly minority women, drains their strength, dilutes their opportunities, and destroys their families. Policies must change to recognize that women returning to the community have different needs than men; the same strategies that work for men do not work for women. Equal rights are not enough for women who shoulder a double burden.

■ Conclusion

Women in prison are punished once because of the restricted life behind bars. They are punished again because they are the afterthought in an overburdened system scrambling to keep up with unprecedented growth. The laws that put women there and the policies that govern what happens within prisons and what happens to them and their families on their release subject women to the unintended catastrophic consequences of policies developed without consideration of women's unique backgrounds or needs.

This is a significant period in the history of women's prisons. Because of the extreme costs, both financial and familial, states and citizens are beginning to sense a need for reform and to realize that these policies have not made society safer and in the process have cost millions and millions of dollars. Yet even if there were a change in these drug policies and the related prison buildup, the impact would not be quickly felt. The lives of women and their families that have been irreversibly damaged will never be reclaimed. For many of these women, the second punishment is far worse than the first.

PART 1

Women in the Prison System

A Brief History
of Punishment

Historians have noted that although the overall punishments of women and men were similar; the exceptions were largely to women's disadvantage and involved punishing them for crimes against their husbands, violating the standards for sexuality, or both. (Belknap 2001, 156)

Much has been written about punishments during the Elizabethan period in England (1558–1603). What stands out most is the range of penalties imposed from the severe infliction of physical pain to the more poignant meting out of public humiliation. Offenders were subject to death by burning, boiling, beheading, pressing, drawing and quartering, and hanging alive in chains; they were punished through the use of the ducking stools, the branks, the stocks, and the pillory. All were public punishments. Of course, the specific method of punishment depended on the crime, with treason and offenses against the state punished more harshly than other offenses. Even more so, the manner of the punishment depended upon the country of origin, status, and sex of the offender. For example, the ducking stool and the brank were mainly used to punish women who were charged as scolds or with gossiping. What's more, allegations of adultery were almost always waged against women, with penalties ranging from beheading and dunking repeatedly until dead to transportation or deportation.[1]

Punishment in the United States mirrored in many ways those techniques practiced in England. Kathryn Preyer (1982) reported that colonial America adopted a range of punishments: capital punishment, or death; corporal punishment, which involved the infliction of pain on the body; and noncorporal punishment. Included in almost all these punishments was the element of public humiliation. These punishments remained in place throughout the eighteenth century. The colonists also adopted the practice of differential treatment based on gender and types of offenses. Clarice Feinman (1983) reported that women were punished more harshly than men for certain offenses, especially adultery, and that women could be punished by the church as well as the state for the same offense. She also noted that public humiliation was more common in the punishment of women than of men (Dobash, Dobash, and Gutteridge 1986; Feinman 1983).

During this period white women were protected through the "cult of true womanhood," which identified piety, purity, submissiveness, and domesticity as the values exemplified by true women (Welter 1966). Living up to these ideals distinguished her as an upstanding pillar of the community. However, if these women violated accepted values, they were subject to harsh punishment. Moreover, criminal violations labeled white women as less than ideal and therefore subject to a range of corrective actions. Public humiliation, a punishment in which a person is stripped of her identity as a true woman, proved effective for white women but was meaningless for black women who, because of their slave status, were never viewed as true women.

In the nineteenth century corporal punishments gave way to the increased use of custodial handling of law violators. Jails, which originally held pretrial detainees and those sentenced for minor violations, were quickly becoming overcrowded. These local city and county facilities turned into state penitentiaries and reformatories. The penitentiaries, which were established first, focused on punishment through isolation from the outside world and other prisoners. The reformatories were founded much later and stressed the reformation and reintegration of the prisoner.

Women who violated the law were initially housed in the same institutions as male violators. Later, women were moved into a separate section or wing of the male institutions and were then housed in separate buildings on the same grounds as the male institutions, until finally, women were housed in totally separate institutions.

In this chapter we provide an overview of the early punishment of women as criminals in the United States, discuss changes in the nature of the prisons for women and the types of offenses for which women were sent to prison, and present an illustrative case study of the Maryland penitentiary.

■ Early Punishments

Seventeenth-century American settlers were a mixed group. Some had come to the Americas with land grants in hand to seek their fortunes. Others had come to escape the punishment and harsh conditions in the jails and the workhouses in their homeland. They sought the promise of freedom. According to L. Mara Dodge (2002, p.13), one-quarter to one-third of the convicted felons who were transported from England to the Americas and Australia were women who, in their native countries, were destined to be "whipped, pilloried and hung next to men." In America, these new colonists served as indentured servants. In exchange for their passage to the colonies and food, clothing, and shelter, these servants contracted to work for an employer for five to seven years.

Russell Menard stressed the importance of including both Native Americans and African Americans in the early history of the American population, because history often overlooks the fact that North America was already an inhabited land when the colonists arrived. Native Americans were the original inhabitants of the Americas and remained the majority until well into the colonial era (Menard 1993). The numbers of Native Americans eventually decreased as a result of diseases carried by the settlers, the use of alcohol, and war.

In the case of African immigrants, the colonist began the "importation" of Africans very early in the colonial era, around 1619, and this segment of the population continued to increase. African immigrants served as indentured servants during the early colonial era, but their status changed as the demand for labor increased and the institution of slavery was introduced. By 1790 slaves accounted for about 92 percent of the total black population (1790 Census Page, www.cviog.uga.edu/Projects/gainfo/1790cen.htm). All three segments of the population came into contact with the legal structure of the colonial government.

Capital Punishment

When the settlers arrived in the colonies, they had left behind a country, England, in which over 200 crimes were punishable by death. Although the colonists followed the laws of England, they did not adopt all the methods of punishment or all the capital offenses. The number of capital crimes adopted by the colonies varied. New York instituted the Duke's Laws of 1665, which included striking one's mother or denying the "true God" among the list of capital offenses, as well as premeditated murder, killing someone who had no weapon of defense, killing by lying in wait or by poisoning, sodomy, buggery, kidnapping, perjury in a capital trial, and traitorous denial of the king's rights (Randa 1997). However, by 1780 the Massachusetts colony had reduced from fifteen to seven the number of offenses punishable by death in that jurisdiction. Similarly, by 1796 New York had reduced the number of offenses punishable by death to two (Mackey 1982). By the end of the eighteenth century, Virginia and Maryland had also moved to reduce the number of capital crimes in their respective jurisdictions (Preyer 1982; Mackey 1982).

England had employed a number of approaches to capital punishment, including stoning to death, breaking on the wheel, burning to death, and hanging. The breaking on the wheel involved weaving the limbs of a person through the spokes of a wheel after of the joints had been smashed. The offender, left upon the wheel to suffer in the heat or the cold, would be the target of scavenging birds. The colonists adopted a number of these approaches, especially burning and the wheel. For example, Julius Goebel and T. Raymond Naughton

(1944) reported that a black woman, convicted in the murder of a family, was sentenced to be burned to death in New York in 1708. However, these approaches to capital punishment were rarely used, because the primary method of capital punishment in the colonies was hanging. This method was used until the introduction of the electric chair in 1899 (Gillespie 1997). According to Victor Streib (2003), women as well as men were executed in the early days of the colonies. In 1632, Jane Champion became the first woman to be executed. She was hanged in James City, Virginia, for an unknown crime (O'Shea 1999).

V. Schneider and John Smykla (1991) reported that in colonial America, women represented 2.5 percent of all persons legally executed. Most of the women executed were black. Kathleen O'Shea (1999) recorded thirty-eight executions of women from 1632 to 1898. Thirty-one were black, six were white, and one was Native American. O'Shea also reported that murder and witchcraft were the two most common crimes resulting in executions. White women were more likely to be hanged for witchcraft than were any other racial group. Furthermore, those who were accused of witchcraft were more likely to be older and unattached (Kurshan 1996). The execution of women for witchcraft began in 1647 with the hanging of accused witch Alice Young. Graeme Newman (1978) reported that a total of thirty-five alleged witches were hanged during colonial times and that half of them were hanged in Salem, Massachusetts.

Furthermore, hangings were treated as sport, and hangings of women were exhibitionist. According to Graeme Newman (1983), before being executed, women were paraded in thin gowns. The early executions were public, but by 1834 Pennsylvania took the lead in moving these executions away from public view to the inside of the correctional facility. Other forms of punishment, both corporal and noncorporal, were also public. In reviewing punishment in Massachusetts, Linda Kealey (1986, 172) used the following quote from Samuel Breck to demonstrate the public and shaming nature of punishment:

> The large whipping post . . . was placed in State Street, directly under the Windows of a great writing-school which I frequented, and from them the scholars were indulged in the spectacle of all kinds of punishments, suited to harden their hearts and brutalize their feelings. Here women were taken from a huge cage, in which they had been dragged on wheels from prison, and tied to the post with bare backs, on which thirty or forty lashes were bestowed amid the screams of the culprits and the uproar of the mob. A little farther in the street was to be seen the pillory, with three or four fellows fastened by the head and hands, and standing for an hour in that helpless posture, exposed to gross and cruel insult from the multitude, who pelted them incessantly with rotten eggs and every repulsive kind of garbage that could be collected.

Punishments in the United States have been both judicial and extrajudicial. The majority of extrajudicial punishments have been lynchings. Lynching in the United States began with the founding of the country and expanded to the frontier. After the Civil War, the targets were primarily blacks in the South. One woman in particular was instrumental in bringing this issue to public attention (see Box 2.1). Capital punishment is discussed in greater detail in Chapter 7.

Box 2.1   Ida B. Wells-Barnett, 1862–1931

A famous educator, journalist, and suffragette, Ida Bell Wells-Barnett is probably best remembered for her tireless work to abolish lynching.

Even though her parents were slaves, Wells-Barnett attended university. After her parents died, she began teaching school to support her siblings when she was only fourteen years old. She moved to Memphis, Tennessee, to teach, but because she was outraged by her treatment and that of other African Americans, she began to write outspoken editorials for the local newspaper. When her fiery articles came to the attention of the Memphis School Board, her teaching contract was not renewed.

Her interest in inequality became focused when three of her friends, prominent African American businessmen, were lynched. Part owner of a newspaper, *The Free Speech and Headlight,* Wells-Barnett wrote a series of editorials condemning lynching and the system that allowed and supported the practice. Her office was sacked, and she moved to New York. She traveled and lectured throughout the United States and Britain on antilynching activities. She never forgot her crusade against lynching, and in 1895 Wells-Barnett published *A Red Record,* an account of blacks lynched in the United States. Women were not immune to the possibility of lynching; during the 1800s and early 1900s roughly eighty women, mainly black, were hanged (O'Shea 1999).

Wells-Barnett continued her work for equality throughout her life.

Source: "Ida B. Wells, A Passion for Justice," www.library.csi.cuny.edu/dept/history/lavender/wells.html.

Corporal Punishment and Women

Corporal punishment, the infliction of physical pain directly on the body, was an early approach to the punishment of criminals. Several forms of corporal punishment were adopted by the colonies, including the pillory, which consisted of an upright board with three openings, one for the head and two for the hands (see Box 2.2). The ears of the offender were nailed to the wood on

Box 2.2 Early Corporal Punishments

Above Left: The pillory consisted of a wooden board with holes for the head and hands. Sometimes the ears were nailed to the wood. *Above Right:* Branding and maiming included lopping off ears, slitting nostrils, and searing a brand or gash on the forehead or cheek. *Left:* In bilboes, the offender's legs are placed in sliding shackles and padlocked to a long iron bar.

continues

Box 2.2   continued

Left: The branks consisted of an iron curb for the tongue held in place by a frame around the head. Some added a spiked or flat piece of iron placed in the mouth over the tongue. *Right:* The offender is tied to a post and then struck a number of times on the back with a whip.

Source: Alice Earle. 1969. *Curious Punishments of Bygone Days.* Montclair, NJ: Patterson Smith.

either side of the head. Raphael Semmes (1938, 30) reported that in Maryland in 1648,

> Blanche Howell was said to have committed "a wilful and voluntary perjury therein." In the name of the Lord Proprietor, his Lordship's attorney asked that Blanche should be brought "to condign punishment." Although the woman denied the charge, a jury found her guilty. Thereupon the judges of the provincial court ordered that she should stand nailed "in the pillory and loose both of her ears, and this to be executed before any other business in court be proceeded upon."

In 1827 the pillorying of white women was prohibited in Illinois (Dodge 2002). Although the use of the pillory faded in most places by 1839, its use was still allowed in Delaware until 1905 (Moynahan and Stewart 1980).

Other techniques of corporal punishment widely used in the United States were also adopted from Europe. They included being whipped while tied to a post; branding and maiming (cutting off of ears); forcing the accused to wear branks, gags, or bridles; and laying by the heels (bilboes). The whipping post was the most frequently imposed corporal punishment (Preyer 1982). It was used widely until the late 1700s. Punishment at the whipping posts was more likely to be imposed on servants. However, the number of lashes administered depended on the type of offense.

According to Preyer (1982), crimes of immorality were punished by up to forty lashes, whereas crimes of insubordinate behavior, mutiny, or falsely accusing the mistress of acts of unchastity were punished by 100 lashes on the bare back. It is important to recognize that each of these crimes was linked to the race of the female offender. To begin with, black women were punished more harshly than white women. Furthermore, crimes of immorality were serious violations for white women but not for black women. For a white woman, such violations were contrary to the "cult of true womanhood" and therefore placed her outside the protective blanket that was otherwise accorded her status as a woman. In the case of black women, the denial of their humanity under the institution of slavery also made questions of morality or immorality nonsensical. Black women, however, were more likely to be under the rule of a mistress and, because of their status as slaves, were subject to very harsh punishment for disparaging the mistress. In the event that a white female indentured servant accused her mistress of misconduct, it is unlikely that the penalty would have been so severe.

By the twentieth century, only Maryland and Delaware still used whipping. Maryland discontinued its use in 1949 and Delaware in 1952. Although women were not subject to whippings in Maryland, they were in a number of jurisdictions. Alice Earle (1969) reported that although most whippings were for public view, in Rhode Island only women could see women being whipped. These whippings were carried out in the jail yard.

A number of these punishments were specific to the type of offender. Newman (1978) reported that the bilboes were used extensively in Virginia and other slave states for the shackling of slaves for the night. The branks, metal headgear fastened over the head of the offender with a tongue piece adorned with sharp spikes and designed to inflict injury if the person tried to move his or her tongue while wearing it, was usually reserved for female offenders (Burford and Shulman 1992).

Specific punishments were also meted out by type of offense. Again, Newman (1978) reported that the pillory was used especially for economic crimes such as counterfeiting, forestalling, and frauds of any kind, whereas the bridle was used against females and males for swearing and drunkenness.

The crimes that resulted in punishment differed for men and women. Adultery was one of the worst crimes that a woman could commit in early colonial

America because of the importance of inheritance rules (Merlo and Pollock 1995). In addition, in some instances the punishments differed for men and women convicted of the same crime. Paul Keve (1986, 8) reported on the following case in Accomack County of a "couple charged with fornication; the man was required to pay a fine and do penance in church while the woman, who apparently was a servant without money for payment of a fine, was ordered to received thirty lashes and to be shipped out." Women were also punished for crimes that only applied to women, such as being a "common scold," which was often defined as a woman who berated her husband or was too vocal in public settings. This offense could be punished by a variety of corporal or noncorporal methods.

The use of corporal punishment of offenders gradually decreased over time. By the late eighteenth century, these types of punishments were replaced by custodial punishments in most places.

Noncorporal Punishment

A significant proportion of the early noncorporal punishments were aimed at public humiliation. The ducking stool, stocks, the gallows, and the use of gags and placards were included in this list. Even though many of these noncorporal punishments involved some degree of physical discomfort, the primary focus was to undermine the person's self-respect and dignity before members of the community. The ducking stool, which consisted of a chair attached to the end of a plank, was used in the late 1700s and early 1800s (see Box 2.2), but its use ended by the late 1800s (Earle 1969; Andrews 1899). In this kind of punishment, the offender was tied to the chair and ducked into the water. According to Newman (1978), this form of punishment was widespread in Virginia, the Carolinas, and Pennsylvania. It was used for public punishment of those characterized as "scolds," defined as people who constantly find fault, often with loud and abusive language. Almost all scolds were women (Newman 1978). The state of Virginia's use of ducking was outlined in Dale's Laws: "Whereas oftentimes many babbling women often slander and scandalize their neighbors, for which their poor husbands are often brought into chargeable and vexatious suits and cast in great damages, be it enacted that all women found guilty be sentenced to ducking" (www.getchwood.com/punishments/curious/chapter-2.html).

The stocks were used mainly in the seventeenth century to punish those convicted of "petty offenses such as slandering, signing a rebellious petition, bigamy, stealing yarn, stealing an Indian child, lying idle, drunkenness, vagrancy, petty theft, swearing, and resisting a constable" (Newman 1978). The stocks were used to punish women, although Earle (1969) reportedly did not find very many examples of women receiving that sentence.

Sitting in the gallows, gagging, and standing in a public place wearing a placard proclaiming the offense were all punishments aimed at public humil-

Box 2.3   Noncorporal Punishments

Above Left: An offender is tied to a chair placed at the end of a plank over a body of water. The offender is ducked into the water repeatedly. *Above Right:* The stocks consisted of a wooden frame with holes for confining the offender's ankles and wrists. *Left:* An offender wears a placard indicating the nature of the offense.

Source: Alice Earle. 1969. *Curious Punishments of Bygone Days.* Montclair, NJ: Patterson Smith.

iation. Central to these practices was what Kealey (1986) called wearing the "badge of their infamy." For example, the wearing of a placard with the letter "A" announced to all that the offender had been deemed an adulteress.

Three other noncorporal punishments imposed in the early colonies were hard labor, banishment, and fines. Both men and women were sentenced to hard labor. In Maryland, sentences were limited to a maximum of seven years. In addition, the type of hard labor differed for men and women. Men were sentenced to work on the public roads, repairing or cleaning the streets, whereas women were sentenced to picking oakum, beating or hackling hemp or flax, manufacturing wool, knitting, or sewing, all out of public view (Chapter 57, Maryland Acts of 1793). Upon close inspection, the tasks for women, which on their face sound somewhat benign, involved tremendous effort. Picking oakum involved untwisting and picking apart old ropes to obtain the fiber for use in caulking, and hemp and flax are both tough fibers that are difficult to cut, especially with the rudimentary "machinery" provided to the women.

Banishment, which was aimed at removing unwanted people from the state, was used against religious dissenters but also against other offenders, especially free blacks. Anne Hutchinson, a religious dissenter, was brought to trial, charged with holding disorderly meetings, and branded a heretic and a leper because of her beliefs. She was excommunicated from the Puritan Church and banished from the Massachusetts colony in 1638.

In Maryland, banishment was included in the Acts of 1809, specifically in An Act Concerning Crimes and Punishments, which provided that for all crimes except those punishable by hanging, the court could substitute whipping not exceeding 100 lashes, or banishment from the state by transportation and sale into some foreign country, or confinement in the penitentiary in the case of slaves (Maryland Acts of 1809, chap. 138). Information on the number of free blacks actually banished was not available (McDonald 1974; Brackett 1889). According to Edgar McManus (1993), those convicted of perjury and adultery were prime targets for banishment. These offenders were banished to the western territories or to "Barbados or some far away place" (Newman 1978).

In 1825 the General Assembly of Maryland passed a supplement to the Act of 1809. This new legislation provided that no black person be sentenced to the penitentiary but rather be sentenced to whipping, not to exceed forty lashes, or banishment from the state (Laws of Maryland 1825). This was followed in 1826 with another supplement to the Act of 1809, which provided that after free negroes or mulattoes either served a prison term or was pardoned, they must leave the state within sixty days or be subject to enslavement (Laws of Maryland 1826). Many black families in the state included both free and slave members, with free blacks often saving money to buy the freedom of enslaved family members. Unwilling to leave family members behind, some jeopardized their free status by remaining in the state after their release from prison. Banishment remained on the books through the 1830s.

The final noncorporal punishment imposed was the fine. Preyer (1982, 350) reported that it was "overwhelmingly the most common of the non-capital punishments." A number of offenses could be punished by a fine or corporal punishment or both. In other instances the payment of a fine allowed offenders to avoid corporal punishment. Whether to impose a fine and the specific amount of the fine were both at the discretion of the judge. Oftentimes the nature of the punishment depended on the characteristics of the offender. Offenders of a higher social class were more likely to be fined than those of the lower classes; depending on the type of crime committed, men were more likely to be fined than women; and slaves were more likely than nonslaves to have received corporal punishment than fines. Kealey (1986, 173) reported that from 1750 to 1796, monetary punishments accounted for 45 percent of the total punishments handed down in Massachusetts. Fines accounted for almost 79 percent of punishments for state and public order crimes, 57 percent of person crimes, 46 percent of fraud crimes, and just about one-third of the punishments for moral and property crimes.

Toward the end of the eighteenth century, the nature of acceptable punishments changed. The use of corporal punishment and those noncorporal punishments aimed at public humiliation lost support. Custodial handling of law violators, which had become a part of the local punishment arsenal, was adopted at the state level in the form of prisons, penitentiaries, and reformatories.

■ Incarceration

Punishing law violators by restricting their freedom has a very long history. Since its introduction in the United States, custodial punishment has changed form and philosophy. The pattern of adoption moved in stages from jails to penitentiaries to reformatories.

Jails

The first jail in the United States was established in Jamestown, Virginia, in 1608, the same year that the colony was established. The colonists based these jails on the commonly used English institution, the gaol. Generally constructed shortly after local governments were established, they were used to provide pretrial detention and to hold those awaiting dispositions after trial (Lewis 1922). James Moynahan and Earle Stewart (1980) reported that these facilities had no cells. Inmates were housed in small rooms holding between twenty and thirty men, women, and children without regard for sex, age, or seriousness of offense.

As crime increased in the colonies and corporal punishment came under attack, the population of the jails changed. These institutions were used to hold those convicted of minor offenses like vagrancy, drunkenness, prostitution, and begging (Moynahan and Stewart 1980; Rothman 1971). They also handled those not punished publicly. Later these facilities were used to detain the mentally ill, as well as political prisoners, religious offenders, and debtors.

Maryland provides a contrasting example because the colony of Maryland existed from 1634 to 1662 before the Maryland General Assembly passed an order to build a jail at St. Mary's City (Richardson 1903). An act to construct a second jail was passed in 1666. Semmes (1938, 33) reported that the jail was to hold "all criminals who had committed some offense, the punishment for which might be death, or the taking of 'member,' and also all persons who failed to pay their debts, unless the county where the debt was incurred already had a place for confining debtors." The first jail to exclusively house convicted offenders serving a sentence opened in Philadelphia in 1790.

The Advent of the Penitentiary

The early history of prisons in the United States was marked by the idea that criminals should be placed in institutions where they would have opportunities for work and penitence. However, there was considerable debate over the form of this work and penitence. In 1787 the Philadelphia Society for Alleviating the Miseries of Public Prisons advocated the replacement of capital and corporal punishment with incarceration. The system that developed, later called the Pennsylvania system or the silent system, required that each inmate be held in isolation from other inmates and that all activities, including craft work, take place in the cells. This system was used as early as 1790 in the Walnut Street Jail in Philadelphia. It was put into full operation with the opening of the Eastern Penitentiary in Philadelphia, Pennsylvania, in 1829. Other states adopted this approach to incarceration. All felons convicted in the state were sent to the institution, regardless of age, offense, conviction status, or sex, and were housed in the same institution. Men and women were initially housed in adjoining cells. As a result women, like men, suffered from filth, overcrowding, and hard conditions. For example, Nancy Kurshan (1996) reported that in the New York City jail, seventy women were confined to forty-two one-person cells.

Auburn State Prison, built in New York State in 1816 and turned into a penitentiary in 1819, adopted a plan of congregate work in the prison shops and yards during the day, silence all day and night, and confinement in separate cells at night. This system was in full operation in 1823. However, this practice of providing inmates with separate cells was not extended to women until much later (Zedner 1995). Women sent to this institution were housed in a windowless attic room. There was no female supervision for the approximately thirty women. Moreover, their daily routine included the delivery of food and water and the pickup of refuse (Lewis 1922; Rafter 1985).

Soon after the introduction of the state prison, a number of jurisdictions moved to confine women in separate quarters or wings in men's prisons. Lucia

Zedner (1995) attributed this change to a law passed in 1828 that mandated the segregation of male and female prisoners in all county prisons. Dodge (2002) noted that because the women were seen as social outcasts and pariahs, there were few attempts made to care for them. These spaces soon become over-crowded. The women were idle and lacked supervision. Kurshan (1996) re-ported: "There existed a policy of calculated neglect of women in 'men's' pris-ons, when sexual abuse often resulted in pregnancy and the floggings sometimes caused death (Feinman 1983, 13). The 1826 case of Rachel Welch, a prisoner at Auburn State Penitentiary who became pregnant while confined to solitary and was flogged after childbirth by a prison official, has been used by many as an example of sexual abuse in mixed-sex institutions (Kurshan 1996; Freedman 1981). Reports also indicated that, unlike the men in these in-stitutions, women did not have access to physicians, programs, dining halls, exercise yards, or workshops (Rafter 1985; Kurshan 1996).

Across the United States, prison conditions caused problems for women. Focusing on the conditions of black women in western prisons, Anne M. But-ler (1989) reported that between 1866 and 1872, there were sixty-seven women in the Louisiana state prison system and that sixty-four of these women were black or mulatto. During this same period, the Texas prison sys-tem housed a disproportionate number of black women, who suffered physi-cal and sexual abuse at the hands of male inmates and prison staff members (Butler 1989). This same pattern was reported in Kansas, Nebraska, and Mon-tana. Surprisingly, the registry from the Nebraska penitentiary listed fifty-one black female prisoners, nine white female prisoners, one Native American fe-male prisoner, and one Hispanic female prisoner (Butler 1989, 32). Nebraska did not gain statehood until 1867, but blacks had started to establish them-selves in the territory after the Civil War. This migration stemmed from an ef-fort to escape the violence of the South during reconstruction and to find em-ployment opportunities.

Maryland: A Case in Point

Maryland, one of the original colonies, was divided on the institution of slav-ery. The state had strong industrial and agricultural interests. At the turn of the nineteenth century, the slave population outnumbered the free black popula-tion by a ratio of three to one (Walsh and Fox 1974). However, by 1860 there were nearly equal proportions of free blacks and slaves in the state. Using Maryland as our case study will allow us to look at the treatment of women by race and status (free or slave) in a state with a unique racial composition. In addition, Maryland had one of the earliest state prisons, authorized by the Acts of 1804. It opened in Baltimore on September 13, 1811.

The Maryland Penitentiary adopted aspects of the Pennsylvania model implemented at the Walnut Street Jail in Philadelphia. This model emphasized solitary confinement under a strict rule of silence. Inmates were supposed to be separated and were required to engage in daily labor in their cells.

Women were admitted to the penitentiary in 1812 and housed in the same building as men. However, the rules governing the management of the penitentiary stipulated that prisoners must be separated by sex (Wade 1964; Shugg 2000). And although the substance of that policy placed Maryland in the forefront of the movement to separate prisoners by sex, it does not appear the policy was enforced. In fact, Marvin Gettleman (1992) described the strict separation of prisoners by sex as "almost impossible."

The institution consisted of nine cells measuring 8 feet by 16 feet. Unlike the male inmates, who were isolated from other inmates, females were housed in congregate cells located in a separate ward of the dormitory wing of the penitentiary (Shugg 2000). Thus the Pennsylvania system that was adopted for the male prisoners was not used for the female prisoners. According to Orlando Lewis (1922), the female wing of the Maryland Penitentiary consisted of six rooms on the southern side of the second story of the prison and nine solitary cells in the northern end of the third story.

Upon its opening in 1811, the prison housed twenty-nine men. In 1812, thirty-two women entered the prison, comprising 34 percent of the total prison population. By 1813, women accounted for 58 percent of the total prison population. That was the only year in which female inmates outnumbered male inmates (by 1.4 to 1). As early as 1822, the Maryland Penitentiary hired its first matron, Rachael Perijo, to provide industrial, educational, and religious training to the female prisoners (Freedman 1981). By January 1825, females accounted for 20 percent of the total prison population, and almost all these female prisoners were black.

Nicole Rafter (1985, 10) reported that women rarely made up more than 10 percent of state prison populations. That was not the case in Maryland. Overall, from 1812 to 1869, females accounted for close to 17 percent of the total prison population, almost twice that of other state prison populations. From 1812 to 1816, females accounted for more than one-third of the Maryland state prison population. Seventy-two percent of the female inmate population were black; the remaining 28 percent were white. That is, a much larger proportion of the female inmate population (72 percent) was black than the male inmate population (44 percent).

According to Vernetta Young (2001), in Maryland over one-third of the white female inmates were born outside the United States, primarily in Ireland and Germany. She concluded that the majority of the female inmate population were not native white Marylanders but were more likely to be black or foreign-born. As indicated earlier, there were a significant number of Native Americans in the colonies. Over time the numbers of Native Americans decreased as a result of sickness and warfare. No Native American female inmates were identified in Maryland prison records. It is possible that Native

American females failed to violate the law. However, it is even more likely that they were excluded from the state criminal justice system and handled by tribal councils.

In 1829 a new wing of the penitentiary containing 320 separate cells was completed (Lewis 1922). This section of the institution was based on the Auburn, or New York, system, also called the congregate system. It was designed so that each inmate would be held in solitary confinement during the night but would work with fellow prisoners during the day under a rule of silence. Introduced with the opening of the Auburn State Penitentiary in 1819, the congregate system was widely adopted by state prison systems.

The competing ideologies of the Pennsylvania and the Auburn systems, which provided the cornerstone of the early history of prisons for men, were debated throughout the country. However, this debate failed to influence the treatment of women in prison. Women were small in numbers and were primarily warehoused in whatever space was available (Rafter 1985). But in 1837 the Maryland State Penitentiary was rebuilt so that the Philadelphia system of total isolation could be extended to the women's section of the institution. Women remained on the grounds but were separated from male prisoners until 1921. In 1941 most of the women in the Maryland Penitentiary were transferred into their own facility, the Maryland House of Corrections. By 1947 all female prisoners had been removed.

The Move to Separation

The movement to establish separate prisons for women began in the early 1800s but met with much opposition. According to Estelle Freedman (1981, 47), the "promiscuous and unrestricted intercourse" evidenced in the Philadelphia jails in 1826 led to the separation of the sexes there. As the number of female prisoners increased, the concern over the treatment of women in facilities created and managed for male prisoners and run by male guards and administrators also increased.

Kurshan (1996) reported that in the 1820s at Auburn State Penitentiary in New York, at least twenty-five women were placed in a one-room attic with sealed windows, whereas in 1838 in the New York City Jail, there were forty-two one-person cells for seventy women. The overcrowding of the separate units for women and the conditions reported therein contributed to the call for change in the housing of female prisoners.

According to Dodge (2002), an 1840 survey of state penitentiaries indicated that twelve out of fifteen state penitentiaries housed female prisoners. The movement of female prisoners from male institutions to separate women's prisons established with women in mind was a gradual process. Although the penitentiary movement began at the turn of the nineteenth century, it took three decades before a separate building devoted to female prisoners was opened.

The first prison building in the United States devoted entirely to women was Mount Pleasant Female Prison in Auburn. It was established in 1835 by the New York State legislature and opened in 1839 in Ossining. The board of inspectors of Sing Sing managed Mount Pleasant as part of the Sing Sing complex. Mount Pleasant was a three-story building with twenty-four cells on each story with its own staff. The facility included space for chapel services, lectures, a workshop, and two separate punishment cells (Rafter 1985).

Eliza Wood Farnham was hired as a prison matron in 1844 and was supported in her work by a number of assistant female matrons (see Box 2.4). Farnham introduced a number of changes, including the relaxation of the rule of silence, the provision of novels to the prison library that inmates could take to their cells, and the construction of a nursery (Rafter 1985; Bacon 2000). Zedner (1995, 343) reported that before the nursery at Mount Pleasant was opened, every baby born at nearby Sing Sing had died.

Box 2.4   Eliza Wood Farnham, 1815–1864

One of Farnham's earliest published works was a 1843 essay opposing political rights for women. She argued that having rights such as the vote would reduce the influence of women. In 1844 Farnham was appointed matron of the women's division of Sing Sing prison. She eliminated the ban on speaking among inmates and set up a system of discussions, privileges, and useful training. She introduced an educational program that included history, astronomy, geography, physiology, and personal hygiene. Farnham also inaugurated a classification system that allowed her to give differential treatment to inmates based upon their behavior and needs. The introduction of this unorthodox approach to prison management led to her forced resignation in 1847. One year later, after the death of her husband, she went to San Francisco with a group of unmarried women to bring refinement to the city. For the next decade, Farnham moved between New York and California, ferrying women seeking homes to the West. In 1861 she became matron of the female department of the Stockton [California] Insane Asylum. She joined the Women's National Loyal League in 1863 and volunteered for service as a nurse in the aftermath of the Battle of Gettysburg.

Source: Adapted from *Encyclopedia Britannica.* 1999; Mark Colvin. 1997. *Penitentiaries, Reformatories, and Chain Gangs: Social Theory and the History of Punishment in Nineteenth-Century America.* New York: St. Martin's Press.

In 1843 women at the Mount Pleasant Female Prison rioted almost continuously in response to crowded conditions (Zedner 1995). Amid angry opposition from the board of inspectors, who did not approve of the changes Farnham had introduced, she continued her efforts to institute reform but was forced to resign in 1847. Others attempted to continue her work, but the reform measures were gradually phased out. Faced with overcrowding, poor management, and a monotonous prison regime, women inmates acted out. At Mount Pleasant this behavior was punished with the use of straitjackets, the gag, and the "shower bath," which involved cold water being sprayed on the inmate from above. The institution continued to house women but was at nearly twice its capacity by 1865 (Zedner 1995). Funds for the necessary expansion of the facility were not forthcoming, so the state closed the prison in 1865 and sent the inmates to local prisons.

Separate Women's Prisons

Dodge (2002) noted that the campaign for separate and autonomous women's prisons began again in earnest after the Civil War under the leadership of Elizabeth Chace, a Quaker activist from Rhode Island. Chace was dismayed by the widely held perception that the reformation of women was hopeless and campaigned for a new approach to the treatment of female prisoners. She contended that a separate facility would give those who believed that female prisoners could be rehabilitated an opportunity to provide the needed treatment. This in turn would cause female prisoners themselves to believe in the potential they had to change their lives.

The first US correctional facility (prison) exclusively for women opened not in the Northeast, where most of the early innovations in corrections began, but in the Midwest. Ellen Swain reported that in 1868 at the request of Governor Conrad Baker, Charles and Rhonda Coffin, a Quaker couple active in prison reform efforts, visited Indiana's two state penitentiaries "to assess conditions and recommend improvements" (2001, 193). The Indiana State Prison for men at Jeffersonville, established in 1860, also housed female prisoners until the female prison opened. The Coffins relayed to Governor Baker the reports of sexual and physical abuse they heard from the inmates, male and female, at the state prison in Jeffersonville. Freedman (1981) reported that according to a young male prisoner, the prison chaplain, and information gathered as a result of a legislative investigation, the Indiana State Prison could realistically be classified as a "vast bawdy house" in which the women were treated as prostitutes and subject to beatings, rape, and other forms of inhumane treatment. Rhonda Coffin proposed that the state establish a separate female prison operated by women, believing that this was the only way to end the abuses women were subjected to in the male prison (Swain 2001).

As prison populations increased beyond capacity, the problem of segregating the women from the men became more difficult. Numerous scandals roused popular indignation in several states, adding incentive to the move for complete separation. Thus Indiana's success in building the first entirely separate institution for women was the fortuitous result of a series of scandals, rather than the work of reformers. Yet it takes leaders to direct public indignation. (McKelvey 1968, 77)

Construction of the institution was authorized by the Indiana legislature in 1869. Contrary to Coffin's wishes, however, the institution was to be directed by a visiting board of men and women and a manager's board comprised only of men (Swain 2001). The Indiana Reformatory Institution for Women and Girls opened in 1873 (Lekkerkerker 1931). Rhonda Coffin was appointed to the first board of visitors, and Sarah Smith, also a Quaker, was the new matron. It was 1877 before Coffin was successful in her attempts to garner support for a new female board. Once the legislation passed, the governor appointed Coffin to the board, and she later became board president. As a result of the work of these early reformers, the Reformatory Institution became the first prison for women staffed by women (Feinman 1983; Swain 2001).

The institution was housed in a congregate building located on 8 acres of land on the outskirts of Indianapolis. Each inmate had a separate room. There were also common living and dining rooms, a school, workrooms, and a chapel. Eugenia Lekkerkerker (1931) reported that originally the women's prison was to handle only felons over eighteen years of age. However, because there was no other facility except the jail for younger girls, the reformatory opened as a model prison for young girls sixteen and over and for older women. These two groups of offenders were separated. The wing housing adult felons accommodated between forty and sixty people. The juvenile wing housed approximately 200 girls who had been convicted of minor offenses or who were incorrigible or neglected by their parents (Freedman 1981). Lekkerkerker (1931) reported that in 1889 the name of the institution was changed to the Indiana Reform School for Girls and Women's Prison in an effort to protect the younger girls from the stigma of prison.

The Indiana facility was soon followed, in 1877, by a similar reformatory that opened in Framingham, Massachusetts. Lekkerkerker (1931) reported that the Massachusetts reformatory was better equipped and better known than its predecessor. The movement to establish an institution for women began in the mid-1860s as a result of the efforts of Hannah B. Chickering, Ellen Cheney Johnson, and Dorothea Lynde Dix (see Box 2.5). These women lobbied for a survey of the condition of female offenders in Massachusetts, the results of which were presented in 1869 in Boston at a conference of penologists. They reported that men, women, and children, those convicted of all manner of offenses, as well as those who were being held as material witnesses, were in-

Box 2.5   Dorothea Lynde Dix, 1802–1887

Brought up in an educated family, raised by her grandparents, and sickly, Dix began teaching school at age fourteen without any formal education. She also published books and ran a school for girls, but her life's passion was sparked when she began teaching Sunday school to the girls in the Cambridge, Massachusetts, jail. Wandering around the institution after the lesson, she was appalled that the cells were bare and unheated despite the cold weather. When she asked, the jailer told her that lunatics did not feel the cold; Dix brought the situation to the attention of friends, contacts, and eventually the court. The inmates got heat.

This success emboldened her to take on the mission that would occupy most of her life, make her reputation, and improve her health— the mission to establish separate, safe, and healthy environments for the mentally ill. Her observation that insane persons, hardened criminals, and paupers (terms that were popular then) were housed together without any of the typical moral or medical treatments of the time left her adamant about society's responsibility toward the most helpless.

Because she wanted facts to support her lobby for change, she began traveling, first to every almshouse, workhouse, and prison in Massachusetts and then around the United States and to Europe. Her visits uncovered shocking situations—a woman chained to a wall for months, a man confined to a cage for fourteen years, someone housed with a corpse— that convinced her that "furiously mad persons," as well as prisoners and the poor, had a right to be treated with dignity. In addition to her work for the mentally ill, she called for prison reform, believing that prisons should isolate prisoners; provide refuges for juvenile offenders; and offer moral, religious, and general instruction. Her reform efforts were critical to the development of separate institutions for the mentally ill.

After working as superintendent of women nurses for the Union during the Civil War (she would only hire "very plain-looking women"), she spent the last years of her life living in an apartment on the grounds of the New Jersey State Lunatic Asylum.

Sources: Helen E. Marshall. 1937. *Dorothea Dix: Forgotten Samaritan.* New York: Russell and Russell; Margaret Muckenhoupt. 2003. *Dorothea Dix: Advocate for Mental Health Care.* Oxford: Oxford University Press.

discriminately mixed together in the prison (Lekkerkerker 1931; Janusz 1991). This meeting ended with the adoption of a resolution to push for the establishment of a separate prison for women and a reformatory for older delinquent girls who were being housed in the adult facilities (Lekkerkerker 1931).

According to Lekkerkerker (1931), legislation passed in 1870 in Massachusetts incorporated the indeterminate sentence, a system in which a sentence with a minimum and maximum term of confinement is imposed, and the classification of female offenders according to their offenses. However, this action met with opposition both outside and inside the state.

> It was contended by prison officials that they needed their women prisoners to do the household chores in the prison, for which they would otherwise be obliged to hire outside help. Private contractors who had women prisoners working for them opposed the new propositions because they feared that a change of system would deprive them of the profits which the work of the female convicts secured them. (Lekkerkerker 1931, 92)

Nevertheless, the "experiment" proceeded, with the Greenfield, Massachusetts, jail serving as the facility selected to house women exclusively under female supervision. Unfortunately, the experiment was abandoned because the courts moved to sentence men and boys to the jail and county authorities were reluctant to transfer female prisoners because of the expense.

Another bill was introduced in 1874 to establish a separate prison for women, and in 1877 the Massachusetts Reformatory Prison for Women opened on a 30-acre tract of land near the Sherborn-Framingham border. This institution was to handle all women serving a maximum term of not more than two years, that is, misdemeanants, including those convicted of vagrancy, prostitution, adultery, fornication, disorderly conduct, and drunkenness (Lekkerkerker 1931; Janusz 1991). Those women convicted of more serious offenses were still sentenced to the male prisons in the state. Originally designed with 500 single-prisoner rooms, the prison as built had 300 rooms along the walls of five three-story buildings. A classification system based on behavior was in place, and prisoners were housed in quarters corresponding to their status. For example, those who were the least recalcitrant were placed in rooms with windows facing the garden or lawn, whereas those who were more recalcitrant were housed in bare, unattractive cells. Schoolrooms, a chapel, hospital, and space for recreation and for gardening were all available on the grounds. The staff was almost all female. A number of work assignments were available, including cane seating, machine knitting, needlework, mending, and laundry.

Luke Janusz (1991) reported that the first superintendent, Eudora Atkinson, imposed severe discipline on the prisoners (see Box 2.6). For example, women were punished with isolation for minor infractions: isolation on bread and water for taking extra food to feed her baby and seven days for insolence (Janusz 1991, 10). The second superintendent, Dr. Elizabeth Mosher, emphasized medical treatment and counseling over harsh discipline. She lobbied for the construction of a nursery with rooms for mothers and their babies and encouraged the other prisoners to visit and help to care for the babies (Janusz 1991). Mosher left the position in 1880 and was replaced by Clara Barton,

---

Box 2.6   Eudora Atkinson

Atkinson was the first superintendent of the Massachusetts Reformatory Prison for Women. She served from 1877 to 1880. The female inmates in the reformatory consisted of prostitutes, whom Atkinson felt were redeemable, and vagrants who were "seasoned" and whom she believed corrupted the newly fallen women. Atkinson believed in the benefits of punishment, usually solitary confinement, and in the teaching of domestic skills, which would help the women get jobs upon release. She argued that the sentences, usually less than one year, were too short for real reform to occur. Atkinson resigned in 1880.

Source: Rebecca Burkholder. 1988. *Massachusetts Reformatory for Women: The Superintendents 1877–1930.* www.law.georgetown.edu/glh/burkholder.htm.

---

who served as superintendent for only one year. Barton failed to punish any one of the 300 women housed in the facility. She resigned and went to work with the Red Cross because she felt that the disciplinary measures favored by the Massachusetts Prison Commission were antithetical to the reformation of the inmates, who had not been convicted of "real" crimes. Ellen Cheney Johnson, a past member of the Massachusetts Prison Commission, replaced Barton. Johnson reinstated punishment and introduced a merit system based on four stages of incremental privileges (Janusz 1991). She served until her death in 1899.

Dodge (2002) noted that although the early separate institutions for women in Indiana and Massachusetts introduced all-female staffs, they nevertheless maintained the traditional cellblock design. Institutions that opened later, however, more specifically those in Hudson and Albion, New York, were modeled after juvenile reformatories and incorporated cottage units.

Even though the reformatories handled both felons and misdemeanants, the women who were being sent to the reformatory were minor offenders. Dodge (2002) reported that with the advent of state penitentiaries, women were committed for up to several years, whereas before they were sentenced to jail for rather short sentences, from a few weeks to a few months. According to Lekkerkerker (1931, 94), there was concern that many of these women did not belong in the reformatory but in an almshouse, an asylum, or an institution for the mentally defective. This posed problems for the management, who were intent on providing a program of reform. In 1879 the Massachusetts law was changed so that women who were reconvicted for drunkenness were sentenced to an indefinite period not to exceed two years. In addition, another law passed that same year allowed the "indenture" of prisoners for domestic service. The full use of the indeterminate system did not operate in the Massachusetts women's reformatory until 1903, when all sentences for felonies were for a maximum of five years and those for misdemeanors were for a maximum of two years. Finally, in 1907 the female department of the state prison was abolished (Lekkerkerker 1931).

Lekkerkerker (1931) reported that between 1887 and 1901, three women's reformatories opened in the state of New York. The first reformatory, the New York House of Refuge for Women, opened in Hudson but was turned into an institution for delinquent girls in 1904. The second refuge house opened at Albion in 1893. The third, totally separate institution for women in the state was opened at Bedford Hills, New York in 1901 (see Table 2.1). The New York institutions held women between ages fifteen and thirty who were convicted of misdemeanor offenses. First-time felons were admitted in 1900, and the indeterminate

Table 2.1   Early Women's Prisons

State	Name of Institution	Date
Indiana	Indiana Reformatory Institution for Women and Girls	1873
Massachusetts	Massachusetts Reformatory Prison for Women	1877
New York	House of Refuge for Women, Hudson	1887
New York	House of Refuge for Women, Albion	1893
New York	Reformatory Prison for Women, Bedford Hills	1901
New Jersey	State Reformatory for Women	1913
Maine	Reformatory for Women	1916
Ohio	Reformatory for Women	1916
Kansas	State Industrial Farm for Women	1917
Michigan	State Training School for Women	1917
Connecticut	State Farm for Women	1918
Iowa	Women's Reformatory	1918
Arkansas	State Farm for Women	1920
California	Industrial Farm for Women	1920
Minnesota	State Reformatory for Women	1920
Nebraska	State Reformatory for Women	1920
Pennsylvania	State Industrial Home for Women	1920
Wisconsin	Industrial Home for Women	1921
Rhode Island	State Reformatory for Women	1923
Delaware	Correctional Institution for Women	1929
North Carolina	Farm Colony for Women	1929
Connecticut	Correctional Institution for Women	1930
Illinois	State Reformatory for Women	1930
Virginia	State Industrial Farm for Women	1932
North Carolina	Correctional Center for Women	1934
California	California Institution for Women	1936
Kentucky	Correctional Institution for Women	1938
South Carolina	Harbison Correctional Institution for Women	1938

Source: Estelle Freedman. 1981. *Their Sisters' Keepers: Women's Prison Reform in America, 1830–1930.* Ann Arbor: University of Michigan Press.

sentence was reduced from a maximum of five years to a maximum of three years.

Zedner (1995) noted that the establishment of the reformatories was largely the result of a change in the conceptions of the female offender.

> Whereas women had previously been thought more depraved and more thoroughly corrupt than men, increasingly they were seen as "wayward girls" who had been led astray and who could, therefore, be led back to the paths of "proper" behavior: "childlike, domestic, and asexual." This view was greatly encouraged by the fact that many reformatories refused to take experienced, hardened offenders, preferring those who had only "recently begun lives of crime" over those who had "spent years in prisons and almshouses" and had "lost ambition for better lives."

With the change in the conception of female offenders came changes in the treatment of these offenders. Zedner (1995, 354) reported that at the Indiana reformatory, women "dressed in gingham frocks and ate at tables set with table-cloths and decorated with flowers." The women were also taught reading, writing, and health care, along with cooking, cleaning, and serving. The reformatories employed a number of women in areas that had previously been the purview of males, such as managing the institutions and providing medical and social services and security. The advent of the reformatory also marked the near systematic separation of women offenders by race (Rafter 1985).

Katherine Davis, the superintendent at Bedford Hills, refused to segregate women by race, making that institution a model of another sort. However, once Davis left the institution, it followed the practice of racial segregation that operated in most other women's prisons (Rafter 1985). Davis also introduced social and psychological studies of prisoners. Moreover, the establishment of the New York Bureau of Social Hygiene was a direct result of this movement. In addition to the cottage plan, the indeterminate sentence, and the parole system, the New York institutions for women ranged ahead in the provision of educational and physical training for prisoners (Lekkerkerker 1931).

Blake McKelvey (1968) noted that a number of states continued to house women inmates in a dormitory or small cell house within the state prison under the supervision of a matron. The establishment of separate institutions like those in New York and Massachusetts happened gradually. Institutions opened in the District of Columbia (1910), Ohio (1916), New Jersey (1913), and Minnesota (1920), until by 1917 there were nine states with women's reformatories or industrial homes (Lekkerkerker 1931; Mann 1984). According to Lekkerkerker (1931, 111), "the social hygiene movement and the war measures regarding the repression of prostitution and the prevention of venereal diseases stimulate[d] somewhat the activity during the years 1917–1922."

Some of the institutions established for women were custodial, whereas others were reformatories. The custodial institutions had cells, whereas the reformatories had private rooms. The custodial institutions were primarily designed to warehouse the prisoners, whereas the reformatories focused on rehabilitation. The population of these two types of facilities differed by race, with black women more likely to be confined to the custodial institutions and white women more likely sent to reformatories. Rafter (1985, 153) reported that black women were not received at the New Jersey Reformatory when it opened in 1913 because they could not be separated from the white female prisoners. Consequently, black female prisoners were not admitted until 1915 when monies had been allocated by the state to build a separate cottage for blacks that would not be placed in close proximity to the housing of white female prisoners. This practice of racially segregated units operated in women's prisons until the 1960s.

The reformatory movement met with disillusionment as the institutions became repositories for those convicted for public order offenses (Rafter 1985; Zedner 1995). Increased numbers of women convicted of prostitution and alcohol and drug addiction were housed in these reformatories. The capacity to provide rehabilitative programming was outrun by the inability to house the ever-growing and changing population of offenders. According to Zedner (1995), by the mid-1930s the reformatory movement had declined, and the institutions operated very much like custodial prisons.

Federal Institutions

On March 3, 1891, the US Congress passed An Act for the Erection of United States Prisons and for the Imprisonment of United States Prisoners, and for Other Purposes, authorizing the construction of three penitentiaries. Until that time, federal prisoners had been held in state penitentiaries and county jails. But by the 1880s, the number of federal prisoners in state penitentiaries numbered more than 1,000, with an additional 10,000 housed in county jails (Tappan 1960). By 1895 the number of federal prisoners in state prisons had increased to just over 2,500, and those in county jails topped out at 15,000.

Female federal prisoners were housed at the Fort Leavenworth facility in Kansas. The small number of female convicts led Ellen Foster, special agent for the Department of Justice, to request that a cell house at Leavenworth prison be designated for the female inmates. The construction of a cellblock with a capacity to house thirty women was approved in 1910, but the unit was never completed (Keve 1991). Over the next decade, the number of federal female prisoners increased from thirty to 150. These inmates were shuttled between federal institutions for males, St. Elizabeth's Mental Hospital in Washington, D.C., and state penitentiaries. Mabel Walker Willebrandt, the first appointed female assistant attorney general, took on the issue of a federal prison for females when she took on her new post in 1923. An authorizing bill was passed by Congress in June 1924, and construction monies were appropriated in March 1925 (Keve, 1991).

The first federal prison for women, the Federal Correctional Institution for Women, opened in Alderson, West Virginia, in 1927, three years before the Federal Bureau of Prisons (FBOP) was established and two years after Mary Belle Harris was sworn in as the first superintendent (Rogers 2000). Harris had earned a PhD in Sanskrit from the University of Chicago. She taught Latin at Bryn Mawr, was a singer and organist, and served as superintendent of both the Women's Workhouse on Blackwell's Island, New York, and the New Jersey State Home for Girls (Keve 1991). Harris helped in planning the construction, equipping, and staffing at Alderson.

The facility, which was built at a cost of $2.5 million, covered 515 acres and consisted of fourteen cottages, each with a kitchen and rooms for about thirty women (Heffernan 1992). This new 500-bed facility was built in a horseshoe pattern. It removed female federal offenders from the local jails and state prisons and the D.C. Women's Reformatory where they had been housed previously. At the time of the Alderson prison's opening, FBOP had eleven federal prisons in operation, but by the end of the year the agency operated fourteen institutions for "just over 13,000 inmates with just under 4 percent women" (Heffernan 1992). According to Esther Heffernan (1992, 22), "in the first year of operation before its formal 'opening' on November 14, 1928, 174 women had been sent to Alderson from state prisons and jails, 119 of whom were drug law violators, while only 1.5 had violated prohibition laws." The drug law violators were charged under the first major federal antinarcotics legislation, the Harrison Narcotics Act, which was passed in 1914. This legislation targeted heroin and marijuana.

The cottages at the institution were segregated by race, as were the educational classes begun by Harris. These classes included English, arithmetic, typing, stenography, agriculture, and home economics. Inmates also participated in clubs, hobbies, dances, contests, and a system of self-government (Rogers 2000).

A look at the survey indicates that from 1927 to 1928, the number of female inmates under federal jurisdiction more than doubled. The next year, 1929, saw another doubling of the number of female inmates. In just three years, the number had increased by 46.7 percent.

By 1936 Alderson was overcrowded, with more than 200 women boarded out at nonfederal institutions under contract (Heffernan 1992). A new jail was planned for Terminal Island in California that would accommodate twenty-four women in a wing of a facility built to house 600 men. Just two years later, there were twenty-four institutions under FBOP with a total population of 24,360 inmates. A new federal reformatory for women was officially opened on October 10, 1940, in Seagoville, Texas. It was an open institution with a capacity for 400 women built on a cottage plan similar to that of Alderson (Heffernan 1992). This institution had a very short history. In March 1942, Seagoville became a federal detention station for Japanese, German, and Italian families. The inmates were returned to Alderson, and it again became the only federal institution for women offenders. The May Act, prohibiting prostitution in military establishments, had been passed in 1910. It was used once again during World War II to keep women away from military bases. As a result, "Alderson became the temporary home for several hundred women arrested for prostitution in military areas. In 1945, it was reported that 52 percent of the women committed to Alderson that year suffered from venereal disease" (Heffernan 1992, 26).

In 1977 women were being sent to two federal prisons, one the all-female Federal Reformatory for Women at Alderson, and the other Terminal Island in California, a predominantly male prison with a women's section. By March 1979 there were four federal prisons housing women felons (Mann 1984). Toward the end of the 1980s, federal female prisoners were housed in three separate institutions and eight coeducational facilities. With the number of female inmates increasing at the federal level from 1,400 in 1980 to over 9,000 in 1998, the number of women-only federal prisons also increased to fifteen (US GAO 1999).

In 1977 there were twenty-eight state prisons for women and twenty-four other state prisons with women's sections. There were also about 1,400 local jails in which women were authorized by local ordinance to be held, but only about a half dozen that were all-women facilities. The number of facilities established to handle female prisoners has increased. But after more than a century of separate prisons for women, in March 1979, there were four federal prisons and forty-six state prisons for women. According to Coramae Mann (1984), thirty-four states, Puerto Rico, and the District of Columbia had separate institutions for women, and sixteen other states housed women separately in male prison facilities. A number of states had very small populations of convicted female offenders, and those offenders were placed in city or county jails. Other states contracted with neighboring jurisdictions for the incarceration of their female prisoners. Joan Potter (1978) reported that female felons from Idaho were sent to Oregon; those from New Hampshire, Rhode Island, and Vermont were incarcerated in Massachusetts; those from Montana, North Dakota, and Wyoming were housed in Nebraska; and those from Hawaii who had more than two years to serve were transported to mainland federal prisons.

■ Conclusion

As we evaluated the history of women and imprisonment in the United States, it became clear that, as with the condition of women in a number of other social and political arenas, it has been a challenge for both prisoners and the administrators of the prisons to equitably negotiate the gendered differences that exist within this system. Although in some instances this necessitates differential treatment based on the differing needs of men and women, in other situations it requires that each group be treated in a comparable, if not equitable, manner. In addition, we also came to understand that differences of race and class exist within each gender. This history highlights the failure to take into account the social and political nature of differences that subsequently affect the treatment of women in the penal setting.

Society's treatment of women for what it has judged to be their crimes has also changed. We see that early in the history of the punishment of women in the United States, the punishment imposed depended upon the demographic characteristics of the women and the specific types of crimes they were alleged to have committed. White women were more likely than black women to be punished for offenses, like adultery, that seemed to violate perceived sex-role expectations. Over time, the nature of the offenses leading to punishment changed, but racial differences remained in the type of offense likely to lead to punishment.

The type of facility used to punish women also differed by race, with black women more likely to be punished in custodial institutions, whereas white women were more likely to be punished in reformatories. Of course, as states moved to merge the two types of institutions, this outward difference in the treatment of women prisoners by race was no longer as visible. But as we shall see later, the impact of correctional policies and incarceration still differentially affected women by race and ethnicity.

■ Notes

1. A number of sources were consulted to provide information on punishment during the Elizabethan period. These include "Crime and Punishment in Elizabethan England," EyeWitness to History, www.eyewitnesstohistory.com/punishment.htm (2001); *Crime and Punishment in England: An Introductory History* by John Briggs, Christopher Harrison, Angus McInnes, and David Vincent; and *The Punishment Response* by Graeme Newman.

Evolving Prisons and the Changing Face of Female Prisoners

As indicated in Chapter 2, at the end of the twentieth century just over two-thirds of the states had prisons for women, with other states still holding women prisoners in the women's sections of the larger male institutions. However, as we enter the twenty-first century, the corrections industry in the United States is a mixture of secure facilities and community facilities. These institutions are run by both public and private entities. In this chapter we will look closer at the development of prisons over time and examine projections for the future.

It is also important to look at whom these institutions were built to house, both in terms of demographics and in terms of types of offenses. The second part of this chapter will focus on the prisoners: Who were they? Has their demographic profile changed over the last two centuries? Have the types of offenses leading to their incarceration changed?

■ Prisons: Yesterday, Today, and Tomorrow

The Establishment of Prisons for Women

The history of the development of prisons for women has been gradual. Recall that the first separate institution for women was opened in 1873 in Indiana, and it housed between forty and sixty people. At the close of the nineteenth century, Indiana and New York maintained the only separate prisons for women in the United States (see Table 2.1). In 1920 five prisons for women were opened: one each in Arkansas, California, Minnesota, Nebraska, and Pennsylvania. According to the Southern Legislative Conference (SLC) report (2000), seventeen states opened women's prisons or reformatories between 1900 and 1935. Not until 1940, almost seven decades from the establishment of the first prison just for woman, were there separate women's prisons in about one-half of the states in the United States (twenty-three states) (Kurshan 1996). Although most of these institutions were located in the Northeast, the remaining prisons for women were scattered across the country. Three states (Connecticut, North Carolina, and California) had two separate institutions for women by 1940, with a record two to three facilities being opened each decade from 1930 to 1950 (SLC 2000).

Rafter (1985) reported that by the 1980s, thirty-four women's prisons or units had been built. The boom in the growth of women's prisons that began in the 1980s continued into the 1990s. There were seventy-one female-only facilities by 1990 (SLC 2000). Texas had three institutions in 1981 and built an additional three by 1995; California had two and built an additional two by 1995. Since the mid-1980s, the state of California alone has built twenty-one prisons. New York and Florida each built one prison during that period. By 1995 there were 104 female-only facilities (SLC 2000) in the United States, and four additional institutions were added by 1997, for a total of 108.

As Figure 3.1 indicates, there have been spurts and sputters in the growth of prisons for women from 1900 to 1997. Some states built their first separate prison for women as recently as the 1970s. However, by 1997, there were at least 108 secure facilities housing female state-sentenced offenders in the United States. According to the 1997 survey of women's prisons conducted by the National Institute of Corrections (NIC) Information Center, each of the fifty states had at least one facility for female inmates as of December 31,

Figure 3.1   Female Prisons, 1900–1997

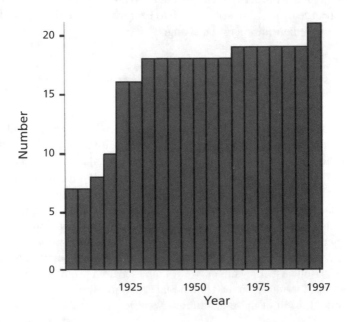

1997 (Thigpen and Hunter 1998). And although twenty-one states had only one female facility, an additional nineteen states housed women offenders in more than one women's prison. Add to this the fact that six states housed women offenders only in co-correctional institutions and four states housed women in a combination of single-sex and co-correctional facilities.

As indicated above, because most states had only one prison for women, there was little choice as to which state facility women would be assigned after sentencing. Amy Craddock (1996, 87) reported that

> classification assigns the inmate to an institution with the appropriate secu-rity level, designates appropriate housing placements and identifies custody supervision requirements within a given institution, and makes medical, mental health, vocational, educational, and work assignments based on in-mate needs and available resources. . . . classification of women inmates may not have seemed a very important issue because most states had only one women's institution, with very little variety in housing and often few program placement options.

Patricia Van Voorhis and Lois Presser (2001) reported that most states used a classification system for women. Unfortunately, these systems were devel-oped for male prisoners rather than female prisoners. The use of these classi-fication systems posed problems for women, who have very different medical, mental health, and vocational needs than men. But most states have only one prison for women, thereby making the classification of these offenders by se-curity level virtually impossible. (See Box 3.1 for a typical breakdown of se-curity levels.)

Since the 1997 National Institute of Corrections survey, a number of in-stitutions for women have opened in the United States. In 1998 the Ronald McPherson Correctional Facility opened in Arkansas. Privately managed by Wackenhut Corrections Corporation, this institution houses all adult women inmates—minimum, medium, and maximum security levels. It has a design capacity of 600, and as of November 11, 2004, it had a population of 989 (Shurley 2004). Florida opened two additional facilities in 1999, the Dade Correctional Institution in Florida City and the Hernando Correctional Insti-tution in Brooksville. The Dade institution had a maximum capacity of 713 and housed all levels of custody. The Hernando institution, with a maximum capacity of 341, was the first institution for female youths (ages 19–24) in the state of Florida. Oklahoma, which incarcerates more women per capita than any other state, opened one additional facility in 1999, the Mabel Bassett Min-imum Unit in Oklahoma City. This allows the Oklahoma Department of Cor-rections more flexibility with regard to classification. Note that as of May 22, 2000, the minimum unit was at 100 percent capacity with 160 inmates. Ten-nessee runs two prisons for women, the Tennessee State Prison in Nashville and the Mark H. Luttrell Correctional Center in Memphis, and is looking to

---

Box 3.1   Inmate Security Classifications

1. Community: inmates who are eligible for placement at a community residential facility or in community work release.
2. Minimum: inmates are eligible for assignments outside the secure perimeter of an institution. Depending on the type and location of work on institutional property, the type of supervision ranges from a requirement that the inmate(s) be kept under sight and sound supervision at all times to intermittent supervision with a physical check by the supervisor at least every thirty minutes. For minimum custody inmates who work off institutional property in the community, continuous sight and sound supervision is required.
3. Medium: inmates do not require armed supervision when outside a secure perimeter but require direct sight and sound supervision. Inmates who qualify for medium security classification have demonstrated some degree of trustworthiness. These inmates are eligible for placement at a work camp with a secure perimeter but are not eligible for placement in an outside work assignment without armed supervision.
4. Close: inmates must be maintained within an armed perimeter or under direct armed supervision when outside a secure perimeter. Close custody assignments are based on an inmate's sentence and the related risk of escape. Although close custody inmates may demonstrate some degree of trustworthiness, their sentence structure requires a higher level of security.
5. Maximum: inmates under a sentence of death. These inmates are housed in specially designated facilities in one-person cells.

Source: Department of Corrections Inmate Classification, http://www. oppaga.state.fl.us/profiles/1039/.

---

build a third site in eastern Tennessee. Finally, the Ohio County Correctional Center opened in Wheeling, West Virginia, in 1998. It was the only all-female facility in West Virginia until it was replaced by the Lakin Correctional Center for Women in West Columbia, which opened in 2003. This institution has a capacity of 240 and houses minimum to maximum security levels.

Finally, five states (Arkansas, Florida, Kentucky, Nevada, and New Mexico) contracted with private companies to provide facilities for women in 1997. The rapid growth in the jail and prison population in the 1980s and 1990s led to a corresponding increase in the number of private prisons. Scott D. Camp and Gerald G. Gaes (2002) identified the ten largest private prison vendors. Corrections Corporation of America in Nashville, Tennessee, and Wackenhut Corrections Corporation in Boca Raton, Florida, are two of the largest vendors, accounting for 76 percent of all private prison facilities. Wackenhut Corrections Corporation changed its corporate name to the GEO Group (GEO), effective November 25, 2003. GEO delivers "correctional and detention management, health and mental health, and other diversified services to federal, state, and local government agencies around the globe. . . . GEO represents government clients in the United States, Australia, South Africa, New Zealand, and Canada, servicing forty-nine facilities with a total design capacity of approximately 38,000 beds" ("Wackenhut Corrections Corporation Announces Name Change to the GEO Group, Inc." 2003).

The only institution for women in Arkansas was privately operated by Wackenhut Corrections Corporation. They also operated at least one institution each for women in Florida, Nevada, and New Mexico.

Availability of Facilities for Female Prisoners

The most recent American Correctional Association (2003) directory reveals changes in the availability of adult facilities for female prisoners. There are an estimated 108 facilities (see Table 3.1). Eleven states had only one facility that housed female prisoners, sixteen states had more than one facility, five states housed women prisoners only in co-gender institutions, and sixteen states housed women in a combination of single sex and co-gender institutions. Seventeen states contracted with private companies to provide facilities for women.

Among all the states, Texas stood out with the greatest number and variety of facilities: nine single-sex state facilities, one single-sex contract facility, three co-gender state facilities, and one co-gender contract facility. Also interesting is the fact that Mississippi, Nevada, and Utah each have just one facility, which is a co-gender facility. Finally, in addition to their secure institutions, fourteen states have single-sex community facilities, and four states have co-gender community facilities.

As indicated earlier, unlike men's prisons, which are classified as minimum, medium, or maximum security, women's prisons generally house all classifications (Bedard and Helland 2000). For example, the Maryland Correctional Institution for Women houses maximum, medium, minimum, and prerelease security classifications. Colorado does provide one of the rare exceptions. The three institutions in the state each handle a specific security classification. The Colorado Women's Correctional Facility only houses close security; the Denver Women's Correctional Facility only houses maximum security; and the Pueblo prison is a minimum security center.

Historically, a number of states sent female prisoners to other states because they did not have separate facilities in which to house women. Today, some

Table 3.1 Adult Facilities Housing Women Inmates

State	Institution	Capacity	ADP[a]	Year	Other
Alabama	Tutwiler Prison for Women	956	1,000	1942	2 community facilities
Alaska	Anvil Mountain Correctional Center	104	92	1985	All co-gender facilities
	Fairbanks Correctional Center	211	197	1965	
	Ketchikan Correctional Center	58	53	1983	
	Lemon Creek Correctional Center	164	167	1969	
	Anchorage Jail	400	400	2002	
	Hiland Mountain	311	311	1974	
	Yukon-Kuskokwim Correctional Center	88	89	1984	
Arizona	Arizona State Prison Complex, Perryville	2,302	1,881	1981	1 community facility
Arkansas	Wrightsville Unit	850	864	1981	2 privately operated co-gender facilities; 1 community co-gender facility
California	Central California Women's Facility, Chowchilla	2,004	3,109	1990	2 contract facilities
	California Institution for Women, Corona	1,026	1,553	1936	
	Valley State Prison for Women, Chowchilla	1,980	3,066	1995	
Colorado	Colorado Women's Correctional Facility, Cañon City	224	229	1968	1 co-gender facility
	Denver Women's Correctional Facility	642	770	1998	
	Pueblo Minimum Center	256	228	1994	
Connecticut	York Correctional Institution, Niantic		1,312	1918/ 1996	
Delaware	Delores J. Baylor Women's Correctional Institution, New Castle	200	370	1991	4 co-gender community facilities
District of Columbia	Central Detention Facility (co-gender)	2,498	2,159	1976	1 co-gender contract facility

continues

Table 3.1 continued

State	Institution	Capacity	ADP	Year	Other
Florida	Broward Correctional Institution, Fort Lauderdale	611	750	1977	1 contract facility;
	Dade Correctional Institution, Florida City	713	694	1999	2 community facilities
	Hermando Correctional Institution, Brooksville	459	371	1999	
	Lowell Correctional Institution	765	784	1956	
Georgia	Metro State Prison, Atlanta	905	810	1981	5 co-gender community facilities
	Pulaski State Prison, Hawkinsville	1,048	1,000	1994	
	Washington State Prison, Davisboro	1,200	1,184	1991	
Hawaii	Women's Community Correctional Center, Kailua	260	279	1983	4 co-gender community facilities
Idaho	Pocatello Women's Correctional Center	269	263	1994	
	South Boise Correctional Center	120		2002	
Illinois	Dwight Correctional Center	858	1,039	1930	1 community facility; 3 contract facilities
	Decatur Correctional Center	500	517	2000	
	Lincoln Correctional Center	500	885	1984	
Indiana	Indiana Women's Prison, Indianapolis	322	321	1873	
	Atterbury Correctional Facility, Edinburgh	90	86	1982	
	Rockville Correctional Facility, Rockville	624	1,138	1970	
Iowa	Iowa Correctional Institution for Women, Mitchellville	443	597	1982	2 community facilities
Kansas	Topeka Correctional Facility	610	488	1962	2 co-gender contract facilities
Kentucky	Kentucky Correctional Institution for Women, Pee Wee Valley	740	714	1938	1 contract facility
Louisiana	Louisiana Correctional Institute for Women, St. Gabriel	900	951	1973	
Maine	Maine Correctional Center, Windham	472	607	1919	
Maryland	Maryland Correctional Institution for Women, Jessup	856	848	1939	1 co-gender facility

continues

Table 3.1 continued

State	Institution	Capacity	ADP	Year	Other
Massachusetts	Massachusetts Correctional Institution, Framingham	452	530	1877	2 contract facilities; 1 co-gender facility
Michigan	Robert Scott Correctional Facility, Plymouth	846	807	1986	1 co-gender facility
Minnesota	Minnesota Correctional Facility, Shakopee	407	402	1986	1 community facility
Mississippi	Central Mississippi Correctional Facility, Pearl (co-gender)	3,233	3,020	1985	
Missouri	Chillicothe Correctional Center	525	520	1981	1 co-gender contract facility; 3 community facilities
	Women's Eastern Reception, Diagnostic and Correctional Center, Vandalia	1,776	2,076	1998	
Montana	Montana Women's Prison, Billings	140	150	1982	3 contract facilities
Nebraska	Nebraska Correctional Center for Women, York	139	2,543	1920	3 community facilities
Nevada	Northern Nevada Correctional Center, Carson City (co-gender)	1,267	1,220	1965	2 community facilities; 1 contract facility
New Hampshire	New Hampshire State Prison for Women, Goffstown	105	106	1989	3 co-gender facilities
New Jersey	Edna Mahan Correctional Facility for Women, Clinton	1,164	1,112	1913	6 community facilities; 1 contract facility
	New Jersey State Prison, Trenton (co-gender)	2,101	1,955	1836	
New Mexico		611	599	1989	1 contract facility; 1 co-gender contract facility
New York	Albion Correctional Facility	1,206	1,216	1977	2 co-gender contract facilities
	Bayview Correctional Facility, New York City	323	392	1974	
	Beacon Correctional Facility, Beacon	257	242	1982	
	Bedford Hills Correctional Facility	972	837	1933	
	Taconic Correctional Facility, Bedford Hills	502	433	1933	

continues

Table 3.1 continued

State	Institution	Capacity	ADP	Year	Other
North Carolina	Correctional Center for Women, Black Mountain	80	60	1986	
	Fountain Correctional Center for Women, Rocky Mount	500	520	1984	
	North Carolina Correctional Institution for Women, Raleigh	920	1,050	1934	
	North Piedmont Correctional Institution for Women	144	138	1997	
	Correctional Center for Women, Raleigh	104	140	1988	
	Residence Facility for Women, Wilmington	38	36	1986	
North Dakota					All facilities are co-gender
Ohio	Ohio Reformatory for Women, Marysville	1,246	1,854	1916	1 co-gender facility
Oklahoma	Mabel Bassett Correctional Center, Oklahoma City*	502	1,002	1974	1 community facility; 2 contract facilities; 2 co-gender contract facilities
	Warrior Correctional Center, Taft	682	652	1989	
Oregon	Coffee Creek Correctional Facility, Wilsonville	186	178	1989	2 co-gender facilities
Pennsylvania	State Correctional Institution, Cambridge Springs	901	860	1992	1 contract facility
	State Correctional Institution, Muncy	843	870	1920	
Rhode Island	Dorothea Dix Women's Facility, Cranston	195	89	1990	
	Gloria McDonald Women's Facility, Cranston	192	127	1984	
South Carolina	Leath Correctional Institution, Greenwood	384	546	1991	
	Goodman Correctional Institution, Columbia	447	414	1970	
	Camille Graham Correctional Institution, Columbia	617	568	1973	
South Dakota	South Dakota Women's Prison, Pierre		216	1997	1 co-gender contract facility

continues

Table 3.1 continued

State	Institution	Capacity	ADP	Year	Other
Tennessee	Tennessee Prison for Women, Nashville	744	723	1898	2 contract facilities
	Luttrell Correctional Center	436	407	1976	
Texas	Gatesville Unit, Gatesville	2,115	1,817	1980	3 co-gender facilities; 1 contract facility; 1 co-gender contract facility
	Halbert Unit, Burnet	504	491	1995	
	Henley Unit, Dayton	504	417	1995	
	Hilltop Unit, Gatesville	677	564	1981	
	Hobby Unit, Marlin	1,342	1,160	1989	
	Mountain View Unit, Gatesville	645	560	1975	
	Murray Unit, Gatesville	1,313	1,217	1995	
	Plane Unit, Dayton	2,144	2,008	1995	
	Woodman Unit, Gatesville	900	872	1997	
Utah	Utah State Prison (co-gender)	3,545	3,087	1951	2 co-gender community facilities
Vermont	Chittenden Regional Correctional Facility, South Burlington	195	135	1969	1 co-gender facility
Virginia	Brunswick Work Center, Lawrenceville		194	1995	2 community facilities
	Fluvanna Correctional Center for Women, Troy		899	1998	
	Pocahontas Correctional Unit, Chesterfield		231	1972	
	Virginia Correctional Center for Women, Goochland		469	1932	
Washington	Washington Correctional Center for Women, Gig Harbor	686	884	1971	2 co-gender facilities; 3 co-gender community facilities; 4 contract facilities
West Virginia	Lakin Correctional Center for Women	240		2003	2 co-gender facilities; 3 co-gender community facilities

continues

Table 3.1 continued

State	Institution	Capacity	ADP	Year	Other
Wisconsin	Taycheedah Correctional Institution, Fond du Lac	464	600	1921	1 co-gender facility; 1 community facility
Wyoming	Wyoming Women's Center, Lusk	84	104	1977	
US Bureau of Prisons	Federal Prison Camp, Alderson, WV		882	1988	20 co-gender facilities
	Federal Prison Camp, Bryan TX		861	1988	
	Federal Medical Center-Carswell, Forth Worth, TX		1,129	1994	
	Federal Correctional Institution, Danbury CT		1,336	1940	
New York City	Rose M. Singer Center, East Elmhurst	1,819	1,192	1988	
	Elmhurst Hospital Prison Ward	14	16	1957	
Cook County, Chicago	Division 4	644		1975	2 co-gender facilities
Bureau of Indian Affairs					11 co-gender adult and juvenile jails
Puerto Rico	Fajardo Detention Center	23	22	1981	
	Industrial School for Women	315	298	1954	
	Ponce Institution for Women	112	93	1991	
US Virgin Islands					1 co-gender facility

Source: American Correctional Association. 2003. *Directory of Adult and Juvenile Correctional Departments, Institutions, Agencies, and Probation and Parole Authorities.* Lanham, MD: American Correctional Association and the Corrections Connection. http://www.corrections.com/links/viewlinks.asp.
Note: a. Average daily population (ADP).

states still send female prisoners to others states for confinement, but they do so because they have no more beds available in their own prisons. For example, Wisconsin just announced the return of all inmates housed in out-of-state facilities (Wisconsin 2005).

A comparison of the institutional capacity and the average daily population (ADP) figures indicate that a number of institutions are overcrowded. All the institutions in California, Florida, and Illinois were over capacity in 2003. The single state facilities located in Alabama, Delaware, Hawaii, Iowa, Louisiana, Maine, Montana, Nebraska, New Hampshire, Ohio, and Washington were all over capacity. For example, the Tutwiler Prison for Women in Alabama had a reported capacity of 421 but an ADP of 1,000 (American Correctional Association 2003).

Over the years these institutions increased in size to accommodate the increasing female inmate population. Recall that the Indiana State Reformatory, the first separate institution for women, opened with a total capacity of between forty and sixty in 1873. Today, that institution has an ADP of 317. Two institutions in California have the largest female prison population in the country. The Central California Women's Facility at Chowchilla has an ADP of 3,109, and the Valley State Prison for Women at Chowchilla has an ADP of 3,570. Add to these numbers the ADP of 1,553 female inmates housed at the California Institution for Women at Corona and you have over 8,000 women incarcerated in these three facilities. Keep in mind that this number does not include those women housed in the two contract facilities.

The Federal Bureau of Prisons houses women offenders who have violated federal laws in four all-female facilities and twenty institutions that are either co-gender or adjacent to male facilities. The four single-sex facilities are located in Texas, West Virginia, and Connecticut; the other facilities are located throughout the country. All the single-sex federal institutions for females are over capacity.

The picture presented above of prisons for women is rather bleak. Many institutions are overcrowded. The mixing of security levels in the institutions limits the kind of programming available to the inmates. Transferring an inmate to a facility that would accommodate her needs for treatment and services is difficult, if not impossible, when the number of institutions is limited and those available are overcrowded. Furthermore, the increase in the number of co-gender facilities calls into question the struggle made by earlier reformers to provide separate facilities to address the different needs of female inmates. It is déjà vu all over again.

An Uncertain Future

A number of jurisdictions have noted a declining number of offenders. Others have suggested that they are confronted with an increasing number of ex-offenders who have been returned to their institutions, not because they have committed new offenses, but because they have violated the conditions of their release (see Chapter 8). Add to this those who are serving longer sentences and as a result need more specialized care from correctional staff, and the future of corrections becomes very difficult to assess.

Much will depend on the political climate of the early twenty-first century. One state, Kansas, has introduced a new law that would require that some low-level drug offenders be sentenced to drug treatment programs rather than to prisons. A number of jurisdictions have introduced restorative justice programs, which also provide alternatives to incarceration. The restorative justice movement views crime as an injury to the victim and the community and seeks to repair the harm caused by the specific offense through victim-offender mediation, restitution, family group conferencing, and sentencing circles. If these policies and practices, which rely less on incarceration as the form of punishment, are adopted, the future of corrections may be very different indeed.

Some jurisdictions, however, are requesting funds for the construction of additional facilities. The law and order sound bite is still used to win voters over, and there is always an upcoming election. In addition, correctional institutions have provided a boom to the economy of some small rural communities, and it will be very hard to close these facilities. The adage "if you build them, they will come," seems very appropriate to the growth and development of correctional institutions in certain communities. The future of prisons in the United States will depend on which paths we choose to travel as a society.

■ Prisoners: Yesterday, Today, and Tomorrow

> The most obvious characteristic distinguishing women and girls who have been incarcerated from those who have not is race. . . . Even prior to 1865, African-American women were disproportionately incarcerated, and after the Civil War the rate of imprisoned African-American women swelled even more. (Belknap 2001, 168–169).

Who They Were

As noted above, 1787 marked the birth of the penitentiary in the United States. There has been little detailed information provided on how many female offenders were incarcerated, who these early female offenders were, and why they were incarcerated.

Vernetta Young (2001) examined the Maryland State Penitentiary Records from 1811 to 1869. In 1812, thirty-two women entered the Maryland Penitentiary, comprising 34 percent of the total prison population. One year later, women accounted for 58 percent of the total prison population; 1813 was the only year in which female inmates outnumbered males (1.4 to 1). By

January 1825, women accounted for 20 percent of the total prison population, and almost all these female prisoners were black.

Black women accounted for a majority (72 percent) of the total female prison population from 1812 to 1869. White females made up the remaining 28 percent of the total. In addition, the white women who were incarcerated were likely to have been born outside the state of Maryland, with a large number coming from Ireland and Germany. The women serving time in the penitentiary were young, ages eighteen to twenty-four, with black inmates tending to be younger than white inmates. However, the foreign-born white females were on average older, at a mean age of thirty-three, than their US-born counterparts, who had a mean age of twenty-five (Young 2001, 75). The female prisoners in Young's study were from the city of Baltimore and were convicted in the courts of that city. Furthermore, most of the female inmates, regardless of race, reportedly worked as housemaids prior to incarceration. Still, white inmates were more likely than black inmates to have been engaged in skilled occupations, especially as seamstresses and spinners.

Not only were black women disproportionately held in the Maryland Penitentiary prior to the Civil War, but also they made up a majority of the Maryland prison population from 1866 to 1869, after the Civil War (Young 2001). This was also the case in the prisons of the Northeast, the Midwest, and the West during the post–Civil War period (Rafter 1985; Butler 1989, 1997). Anne Butler (1989) reported that according to prison registries from 1865 to 1910 in Louisiana, Texas, Kansas, Nebraska, and Montana, not only did black women make up the majority of the prison population, but also the inmates were also most commonly young and uneducated. The South was the only region in which few blacks, male or female, were held in state prisons before the Civil War. However, once the war concluded, that situation changed.

This profile of the female inmate that seems to stand throughout Reconstruction and into the turn of the twentieth century is almost two centuries old. How has the demographic profile changed since the introduction of the penitentiary? The composition of the female prison remained predominantly black as the United States moved out of slavery and Reconstruction. Then another source of social control, the Jim Crow laws, were introduced in the 1880s. These laws legalized the segregation of blacks and whites in public schools, parks, buses, railroads, restaurants, pool and billiard rooms, bathrooms, and just about any other place blacks and whites frequented for work or play. Jim Crow laws forbade intermarriage, and they disenfranchised black men. With these laws in place to control the black population, the need for institutional control, through the prison, was less necessary. Once these restrictions on blacks were institutionalized, the "color" of the female prisons changed from black to white.

In the 1950s the struggle for civil rights for blacks intensified. The increased attribution of these rights to blacks and other minorities from 1950 to the present day seems to correspond with the change in the racial and ethnic composition of the female prison. The prisons went from predominantly white in the 1950s to predominantly nonwhite. Once again, institutions have a disproportionately black female population, in addition to housing an increasing number of Hispanic female inmates. We discuss this issue further below.

Race and ethnicity account for only part of the description of the female prisoner. Young (2001) and Butler (1997) found that these female prisoners were young, from urban areas, and employed in low-paying jobs. The historical research is somewhat limited in the range of demographic variables that are included. However, Laura Bresler and Diane Lewis (1984) presented two profiles of the typical female prisoner, based on a 1979 study of black women and white women sentenced to the San Francisco County Jail.

> The typical white prisoner was in her late twenties, a high school graduate, and had been convicted of prostitution, for which she was serving a sentence of 45 days. She was separated or divorced. . . . Her children were not living with her prior to her incarceration and were in the care or often custody of either her parents or ex-husband. [She was] . . . unemployed [and] . . . usually held jobs in the past. The typical black woman was in her early twenties and had left school in the eleventh grade. She was serving a sentence of between three and six months for either a property crime or prostitution. She was a single mother and likely to have had her children with her before she was arrested. Her mother or other relative was caring for her children during her incarceration. She was less likely to have ever had a job than her white counterpart and was typically a welfare recipient.

These profiles seem relevant to the larger female prison population.

What They Did

Young (2001) found that most of the women (67 percent) in the Maryland Penitentiary from 1811 to 1869 were incarcerated for larceny-theft, more so for black females (73 percent) than for white females (52 percent). One-third of the white females were incarcerated for vagrancy, which Rafter (1985) suggested was a euphemism for sexual promiscuity. Young (2001) concluded that in addition to black and foreign-born females outnumbering white females during the antebellum period, they also received longer sentences and served more time than their white counterparts. Other research on the crimes of early female prisoners (Rafter 1985; Butler 1997) seems to support this pattern.

Philip D. Holley and Dennis Brewster (1997–1998) examined the records of women in the Oklahoma correctional system at the turn of the twentieth century, from 1900 to 1909. The seventeen cases included two sentenced for murder, three for manslaughter, one for robbery, one for burglary, two for forgery, two for larceny, and six for adultery. The largest proportion of the women in the Oklahoma institution were also incarcerated for theft (five) and moral offenses (six).

Numbers of Women Prisoners Today

Since the 1980s, the correctional population in the United States has increased tremendously. In 1980 there were 503,586 people in federal and state custody. Ten years later, the number of inmates in federal and state prisons and local jails had increased by 128 percent (to 1,148,792). The next ten years saw an even larger proportionate increase in the correctional population. By 2000, there were 1,933,503 people in custody, a 284 percent increase over the 1980 numbers (Beck and Harrison 2001). At the end of 2003, there were over 2 million people (2,212,475) in custody in the United States (Harrison and Beck 2004).

Even though males continue to account for the largest proportion of the prison population, just over 93 percent of the total (1,311,195), the proportion of females has increased over time. In 1985 females accounted for just over 4 percent of the total. By 1990 they accounted for 5 percent of the total prison population. The female inmate population as a proportion of the total prison population has continued this steady increase. Females counted for almost 6 percent of the total prison population in 1995 and almost 7 percent (101,179) at the end of 2003 (Harrison and Beck 2004). So even though there continue to be more males in prison than females, the proportionate increases for females have been greater.

Since 1990 there has been an 80 percent increase in the total number of male prisoners in federal and state prisons and a 114 percent increase in the total number of female prisoners (Beck, Karberg, and Harrison 2002). Over one-third of these female inmates are held in Texas, the federal system, and California (Harrison and Beck 2004). Moreover, Oklahoma, Mississippi, Louisiana, and Texas have consistently evidenced the highest reported female incarceration rates since the 1990s.

Characteristics of Female Prisoners Today

At midyear 2001 blacks accounted for almost 45 percent of the total federal and state prison and local jail populations (872,900). Whites added an additional 38 percent (752,500) and Hispanics accounted for 15 percent (302,900). Interestingly, when we look at gender and race, the proportions for males by race mirror the total. However, black (43 percent) and white (42 percent) females account for nearly equal proportions of the total female population, with Hispanic females accounting for 12 percent. There was a 49 percent increase in the black female correctional population from 1990 to 1997. This was much larger than the 39 percent increase in the black male correctional population in the same years (Beck, Karberg, and Harrison 2002; BJS 2000).

At midyear 2002 there were 96,099 women in state or federal prisons (Harrison and Karberg 2003). An additional 69,000 women were in local jails.

Again, there were almost equal numbers of white (68,800) and black (65,600) women in state or federal prisons and local jails. Hispanic women accounted for an additional 15 percent of the total female prison population. Even more telling is the change in the racial composition of the female prison population since the 1980s.

When we look at the incarceration rates by race, we see that black females were incarcerated at a rate of 349 per 100,000, compared to 137 per 100,000 for Hispanic females and 68 per 100,000 for white females (Harrison and Karberg 2003). These numbers show that black females were almost five and one-half times as likely as white females to be in prison, and Hispanic females were over twice as likely as white females to be in prison. The racial disparity is obvious. Moreover, this same pattern of racial disparity in incarceration has been evident at least since 1980.

Almost 60 percent of the women were between twenty-five and thirty-nine years of age. Females between thirty and thirty-four were incarcerated at a rate of 348 per 100,000; followed by those between thirty-five and thirty-nine, who were incarcerated at a rate of 297 per 100,000; and those between twenty-five and twenty-nine, who were imprisoned at a rate of 282 per 100,000.

Close to one-quarter of all female prisoners were held in just two jurisdictions, Texas and California. An additional 12 percent were held in the federal system. Although these three jurisdictions held the largest number of sentenced female inmates, the rates of female incarceration were highest in Oklahoma (130 per 100,000 female state residents), Mississippi (113), Louisiana (99), and Texas (96) (Harrison and Beck 2002). Texas has both a high number of female offenders and a high incarceration rate.

The Bureau of Justice Statistics (BJS) surveys state and federal prisons periodically. These surveys provide information on demographics, offense, and criminal history. Tracy Snell (1994) reported on the 1991 survey of state prison inmates. The female inmates largely resembled male inmates in terms of race, ethnic background, and age. They were most likely to be African Americans (46 percent); aged twenty-five to thirty-four (50 percent); unemployed at the time of arrest (53 percent); high school graduates, holders of a general equivalency diploma (GED), or present or former college students (58 percent); and never married (45 percent). Women were substantially more likely than men, however, to be serving time for a drug offense and less likely to have been sentenced for a violent crime. Nearly two-thirds of the women in prison for a violent offense had victimized a relative, intimate, or someone else they knew. Nearly six in ten female inmates grew up in a household with at least one parent absent, and approximately half reported that an immediate family member had been imprisoned. More than four in ten reported prior physical or sexual abuse. Overall, female inmates had shorter maximum sentences than men did. Half of the women had a maximum sentence of sixty months or less, and half of the men had a sentence of 120 months or less. An estimated 7 percent of the women and 9 percent of the men received sentences of life in prison or death. More than three-quarters of all women in prison had children, and two-thirds of the women had children at the time of the survey.

Richard Stana (2000), in a report to Congressman Charles B. Rangel, compared the profiles of inmate characteristics in the 1991 and 1997 BJS surveys of state and federal prisoners. Female state prison inmates in 1997 were 48 percent black, 33 percent white, 15 percent Hispanic, and 4 percent other. Over four out of ten (43 percent) were between ages twenty-five and thirty-four, and an additional 34 percent were between thirty-five and forty-four. Almost one-half (47 percent) had never been married, and 36 percent were separated, widowed, or divorced. Just over four out of ten (41 percent) had less than a high school education; with one-quarter having gained a GED. The female inmates were as likely to be employed (50 percent) as unemployed (48 percent).

There were nearly equal proportions of black (35 percent), Hispanic (32 percent), and white (29 percent) female inmates in federal prisons. This distribution differs significantly from the racial profile of female state prison inmates. Blacks and Hispanics account for almost twice as much of the federal female prison population as they do of the state female prison population.

Federal and state female prison inmates also differed with respect to age. Although those aged twenty-five to thirty-four (35 percent) and thirty-five to forty-four (32 percent) still accounted for the largest proportion of the total female population in federal prisons, the forty-five and over group accounted for almost one-quarter, over twice their contribution to the state female prison population. These two groups also differed by marital status. The largest proportion (37 percent) were either divorced or widowed, probably as a result of their older ages, with a third never married and almost three out of ten married. Among the female federal prison population, there was a nearly equal distribution with respect to education. The largest proportion of female inmates (29 percent) had more than a high school education, one-quarter had attained a GED, one-quarter had less than a high school education, and 21 percent were high school graduates. Finally, almost 63 percent were employed in the month before their arrest.

The 1997 BJS Survey of Inmates in State and Federal Correctional Facilities also allows us to compare the female prisoners by race and ethnicity. A total of 3,796 women responded to the survey. Mexican Americans accounted for the largest proportion (33 percent) of Hispanics, followed by Puerto Ricans (20 percent), Mexicans (15 percent), Central or South Americans (11 percent), and Chicanos (10 percent). The differences among these groups are significant, and knowledge of these differences would help in planning programming for incarcerated females.

The largest proportion of the female inmates were never married (43 percent) with nearly equal proportions divorced (21 percent) or married (20 percent). There were major differences in marital status by race and ethnicity.

When we examine the data across racial and ethnic groups, some differences emerge. A much larger percentage of black (59 percent) and Hispanic (46 percent) inmates were never married than white inmates (28 percent), who were more likely to be divorced (32 percent) than to have any other marital status.

Race and ethnicity also mattered with respect to whether the prisoners had children and how many children they had. Among the female inmates who reported having children, 25 percent were white, 24 percent were black, 17 percent were Hispanic, and 29 percent were of other races. However, white women and women of other races reported having more children than either black or Hispanic women. When we add this to the information about marital status, the importance of examining multiple factors as contributors to the plight of the children of incarcerated women becomes even more obvious.

The majority of the inmates reported having a job or business (51 percent), with white inmates (57 percent) more likely than black or Hispanic inmates (48 percent for both) to report having a job. Of those indicating a specific occupation, the following were most frequently listed: cashier (9 percent); nurse's aide/orderly (7 percent); waitress (6 percent); paid housekeeper (5 percent); and cook, salesperson, manager/administrator, assembler/line worker, and secretary (all about 4 percent each). Note that many of them are low-paying jobs without benefits whose availability depends on the economy.

The federal and state prisoners have been incarcerated for longer periods of time than prisoners sentenced before the introduction of mandatory minimum sentences and three-strikes-and-you're-out laws. If we add to this profile the fact that fewer of these offenders have participated in education, job training, or drug treatment programs while in the institution, the problems inherent in reentry seem almost insurmountable (see Chapter 8).

What They Did

Criminal records for women inmates at the state level indicate that one-third were incarcerated for drug offenses, 28 percent for violent and 26 percent for property. The drug of choice in almost one-half of the cases was crack cocaine, followed by powder cocaine (26 percent) and heroin (15 percent). Almost one-half (46 percent) of the women inmates had no involvement with the criminal justice system at the time of arrest, but one-third were on probation. They were as likely to report no prior sentence (34 percent) as to report having one to two (32 percent) or three or more (31 percent) prior sentences. A considerable proportion of the female incarcerated population used drugs in the month before arrest. The drugs used included crack cocaine (31 percent), marijuana (26 percent), powder cocaine (21 percent), and heroin (16 percent). Inmates were also asked if they were under the influence of drugs at the time of the offense. The drug reported most often was alcohol (29 percent), followed by crack cocaine (19 percent).

Most of the federal female inmates were incarcerated for drug offenses (71 percent), followed distantly by those incarcerated for property offenses (12 percent). A closer look at the drug offenses indicted that the larger proportion of inmates were incarcerated for powder cocaine (37 percent), followed by crack cocaine (25 percent). At the federal level, the majority of the female prisoners had no involvement with the criminal justice system at the time of arrest (85 percent). Clearly, female state prisoners looked very different from female federal prisoners.

Stana (2000) compared the 1991 and 1997 BJS surveys and noted that the number of female inmates reportedly under the influence of drugs at the time of committing the offenses increased from 1991 (10 percent) to 1997 (19 percent). The lack of access to drug treatment programs prior to, during, and after incarceration and the continued emphasis on punishing not only those who sell drugs but also those who use drugs offers little solace to those concerned about incarcerated women.

This situation is compounded by the fact that a study by the Criminal Justice Institute found that one-quarter of the prison population was idle, not participating in meaningful work or education programs (Austin 2001). In addition, participation in programs has decreased while the number of prisons has expanded since the 1970s, so we have a larger number of released prisoners who must return to their communities without having participated in educational, vocational, or prerelease programs.

Uncertain Prospects

The outlook for tomorrow is uncertain. Virginia and Tennessee are among a number of jurisdictions that have allocated funds for the construction of new prisons. The private prison industry continues to grow. The old adage, "Build it and they will come," does not bode well for a change in the direction of the incarceration explosion.

Even more confusing are some of the changes in drug laws. On the one hand, New York State recently passed legislation that would ease its infamous Rockefeller drug laws by doubling the weight of drugs an offender must be convicted of possessing to trigger certain harsh prison sentences (Benjamin 2004). On the other hand, the US Congress voted to add possession of methamphetamine to the list of offenses that would invoke a mandatory minimum sentence but excluded ecstasy, which is a methamphetamine-based drug (Huffington 2000). Representative Jesse Jackson Jr. likened this to the crack cocaine–powder cocaine disparity, in which possession of one drug, methamphetamine, that is associated primarily with minority users, results in much harsher penalties than another very similar drug, ecstasy, which is associated primarily with nonminority users. At this time, it is difficult to gauge the future course of the war on drugs.

The outcome of this battle over sentencing has become even more complicated following the recent Supreme Court decisions in *United States v. Booker* (2004) and *United States v. Fanfan* (2005). The Court ruled that the federal sentencing guidelines that required judges to make factual decisions on sentencing using factors that had not been evaluated by a jury violated the defendant's Sixth Amendment right to a jury trial. Under the ruling, the guidelines are no longer mandatory but advisory, and the Supreme Court ordered federal courts to reconsider the sentences of hundreds of defendants sentenced under the federal guidelines. This edict could have far-reaching consequences for defendants across the country.

It is unclear what will be done in terms of programmatic changes in drug laws and sentencing guidelines that would lead to a decrease in the prison population. As noted earlier, there is some indication that although the number of commitments to prisons has decreased, there has been an increase in the number of repeat offenders who have violated the conditions of their release. If, as suspected, these violations relate to the consequences of the lack of drug, vocational, and education programs, then change does not seem likely.

There has not been a groundswell of support for increasing the number of drug treatment programs in US prisons. However, the drug court movement, which began in the 1980s, has received some support. The Miami drug court is a model that has been adopted by a number of jurisdictions. In this model, "the judge works with the prosecutor, defender, and drug treatment specialists as a team to select the appropriate treatment approach, monitor progress in the courtroom, and help overcome problems (for example, housing and employment) that may hinder treatment progress" (Travis 1995, 1). Drug courts were implemented in over twenty jurisdictions from 1991 to 1993. The General Accounting Office (GAO) reported that as of March 31, 1997, there were 161 drug court programs, and the number continues to grow. Reports are that New Jersey is now moving to expand its use of the state drug court (Hester 2005).

Obviously, as a society we are somewhat ambivalent about how we should proceed. Finding a happy medium between appropriately punishing those who need punishment without "throwing the baby out with the bath water" will determine the future outlook for crime and punishment in the United States.

■ Conclusion

Since 1873, there have been marked increases in the number of female prisoners and the number of correctional facilities. However, the number of facilities has not kept pace with the number of prisoners. Rather the building of prisons and reformatories for women has been a reaction to pressure from reformers, to the need to separate male and female prisoners, and to the influx of females into institutions primarily as a result of the war on drugs and other issue-specific legislation.

Although the number of female prisoners has increased dramatically over the years, the profile of these prisoners has remained pretty much the same. Those who are incarcerated are primarily racial and ethnic minorities. They are members of the lower class. They are violators of minor property and drug offenses.

The future of our prisoners and our prisons will depend on the degree to which we adopt alternatives to incarceration and fund community drug treatment programs. The outlook will also be determined by the allocation of funds for the building of new institutions and the nationwide approach to sentencing policies and practices.

PART 2

Women Prisoners: Special Issues

Drugs: Use, Abuse, and Treatment

During the late twentieth and early twenty-first centuries, most women entered the penal system because of drugs. The skyrocketing rates of female imprisonment have largely resulted from increasing drug involvement among women, coupled with harsh sentences for even nonviolent drug crimes. Women are much more likely than men to be serving time for a drug violation, with low-income and minority women particularly likely to be incarcerated as a result of involvement with drugs. There is evidence that women inmates used illegal drugs and legal drugs illegally more frequently, used harder drugs, and used drugs for different reasons than men (Langan and Pelissier 2001). Drug abuse is now the primary reason women enter prison and the primary health problem of women who are in prison (Henderson 1998).

The number of women incarcerated in state prisons for drug offenses rose by 888 percent from 1986 to 1996, in contrast to a rise of 129 percent for nondrug offenses (Mauer, Potler, and Wolf 1999), and the increase continues, though at a slower rate. From 1995 to 2001, drug offenses accounted for 12.8 percent of the total prison growth among female inmates.

These offenses are expensive in financial as well as human terms. It is estimated that drug abuse cost the United States over $160 billion dollars in 2000. These costs are calculated by adding direct costs such as drug abuse services, health care, and dealing with crime and indirect costs such as lost earnings through illness, death, or incarceration (Swan 1998). There was a 22 percent increase in women's visits to emergency departments between 1995 and 2002, and of the 21,683 persons who died of drug-induced causes in 2001, 7,439 (34 percent) were female (SAMHSA 2004).[1] Crime associated with or attributed to alcohol use is estimated to cost the country $19.7 billion a year, and crime associated with drug abuse, $59.1 billion (Craig 2004).

Illicit involvement with drugs is both the cause and the effect of many problems that women in prison face.[2] For a great number of these women, drugs are simply the result of lives littered with social problems, particularly physical and sexual abuse. In this chapter we concentrate on women's drug use, the special problems that women face, the war on drugs, and drug treatment. We see that women begin using drugs for different reasons than men, that their patterns of and paths to drug use are different, that gender-based violence and HIV/AIDS are particular risks for drug-abusing women, and that women have different treatment needs. We also know that the war on drugs has been especially harmful for women.

■ Women's Drug Use

Women in prison are not the only women involved with drugs; women in the community also use and abuse the same drugs. Different studies reveal slightly different prevalence rates for drug use depending on the population sampled, but probably over 1.5 million community-dwelling American women have serious problems with drugs, about one-third of the total substance-using population. Many others use drugs at some time in their lives. For example, according to the 2003 National Survey on Drug Use and Health (formerly the National Household Survey on Drug Abuse) approximately 51 million females twelve years and older (about 42 percent of that age group) reported using a drug illicitly at some point in their lives. Over 12 percent of women reported using an illegal drug in the year before the survey, and about 6.5 percent had used illegal drugs in the previous month. Marijuana was the most frequently used drug, and nearly 20 percent of the sample had used a prescription drug (such as pain relievers, tranquilizers, stimulants, or sedatives) for nonmedical reasons. Nearly 2 million had used cocaine, and more than 6 million had smoked marijuana (SAMHSA 2004).

White women are more likely than black women, who are more likely than Hispanic women, to have tried illegal drugs; white women are particularly more likely to have used marijuana (Young and Harrison 2001). Furthermore, there are race and age differences in the progression of drug use: white and Hispanic females tend to smoke marijuana earlier than black females; they are also more likely to try cocaine than black females; and black females who used cocaine were more likely to use crack cocaine than white or Hispanic cocaine users (Young and Harrison 2001).

Historically, women have had a lower prevalence of illegal drug use than men. For example, in 2003, lifetime, past year, and past month drug use rates were all lower for women than for men. According to the National Institute for Drug Abuse (Zickler 2000), these gender differences in illegal involvement with drugs are largely a result of opportunity: men have more opportunities to encounter and use drugs. However, given equal opportunities, women are as likely to try them and to become addicted. For many women, opportunity only opens the door to problems with drugs. The path to substance abuse and incarceration is often one of escape from lives of poverty and pain.

Paths to Illegal Involvement with Drugs

Women, much more than men, use drugs illegally as a coping mechanism, and gender differences in the link between drugs and mental health show up early. A three-year study of 1,200 women and young girls (ages eight to twenty-two) from the National Center on Addiction and Substance Abuse at Columbia University (CASA 2003) revealed that girls and young women use substances for different reasons than boys and young men. More than one-third of high school girls reported feeling hopeless or sad, and those feelings were related to drugs and alcohol use much more strongly than for boys. In addition, drug use was more than twice as common among those girls who had been physically or sexually abused, compared to those who had not.

As we might expect from their mental health profiles, women are more likely to become dependent on sedatives or drugs that reduce anxiety or sleeplessness and are less likely to abuse alcohol and marijuana. For women, illegal drugs are often a form of self-medication; because poor women are less likely to have access to legal psychotropic drugs or mental health treatment, they may turn to street substances to cope with depression, eating disorders, domestic violence, past abuse, or low self-esteem. Women are also likely to be introduced to drug use by the significant men in their lives but unlikely to receive support for recovery from these men (Kerr 1998).

Patterns of Use at Time of Offense and Arrest

Although different numbers from different sources give slightly different pictures, it is clear that women who are arrested and eventually incarcerated are often entangled in a world of drugs. According to the Arrestee Drug Abuse Monitoring Program (ADAM), nearly two-thirds of adult females who were arrested in 2000 tested positive for cocaine, marijuana, methamphetamine, opiates, or phencyclidine (PCP), and approximately 21 percent were positive for more than one of these drugs. (The ADAM numbers, however, are based on fairly small numbers of women from thirty-eight sites where urine samples and survey data were collected on the use of ten different drugs.) For those women who went on to state prison, about half were using alcohol, drugs, or both at the time of the offense for which they had been incarcerated, and nearly 33 percent of those committed their crime to obtain money to buy drugs (BJS 2000).

Involvement with drugs that leads to arrest and imprisonment can start at a young age. Arrests of juvenile females for drug abuse violations increased 201 percent (compared to 110 percent for male juveniles) between 1992 and 2001 (Snyder 2003). And rates of drug offenses among juvenile girls increased from 13 percent of the total cases in juvenile court in 1990 to 14 percent in 1995 and to 16 percent in 1999 (Stahl 2003). These youth largely avoid prison at this age, but without treatment and available alternatives, they are likely to continue on the drug route to incarceration.

Drug Offenders in Prison

Approximately 82 percent of the women convicted of felony drug offenses in 2001 were sentenced to prison. Women made up roughly 13 percent of the total population and 8.2 percent of the federal prison population serving time for drug offenses in the mid-1990s (Mauer, Potler, and Wolf 1999). In 2001, there were 76,200 female prisoners under state jurisdiction; approximately 23,000 of them were incarcerated for drug offenses. The most serious offense for 71.7 percent of women in federal prisons and 32.3 percent of women in state prisons was violation of drug laws (Harrison and Beck 2002). The number of incarcerated women who reported drug use has also gone up over time (Acoca 1998) as Table 4.1 illustrates.

Table 4.2 presents drug charges for offenders in federal prisons according to gender, and Table 4.3 presents a similar breakdown according to race. Because statistics are not broken down by race and then by gender within races, we cannot tell how many black women were incarcerated on marijuana charges, for example.

Table 4.1   Percentage of Female Inmates Reporting Prior Drug Use, 1991 and 1997

	Federal Female Inmates		State Female Inmates	
	1991	1997	1991	1997
Ever used drugs before incarceration (%)	34.7	47.2	65.3	73.6
Used drugs in month before current offense (%)	27.6	36.7	53.9	62.4
Under influence of drugs at the time of current offense (%)	16.3	19.3	36.3	40.2
Committed offense to get money to buy drugs (%)	10.3	12.3	23.9	29.0
Number of female prisoners	4,208	6,368	38,743	65,338

Source: Adapted from GAO (General Accounting Office). 1999. *Women in Prison: Issues and Challenges Confronting US Correctional Systems.* Washington, DC: GAO (GAO/GGD-00-22).

Table 4.2   Federal Drug Offenders by Gender and Drug Type, 2001

	Percentage Incarcerated on Charges	
Drug	Female	Male
Total	13.6	86.4
Marijuana	13.7	86.3
Heroin	16.8	83.2
Powder cocaine	14.7	85.3
Crack cocaine	9.4	90.6
Methamphetamine	15.7	84.3
Other	16.3	83.7

Source: US Sentencing Commission. 2001. *Sourcebook of Federal Sentencing Statistics.* 6th ed. Washington, DC: US Sentencing Commission (USSCFY01), Table 35.

Table 4.3   Federal Drug Offenders by Race and Drug Type, 2001

	Percentage Incarcerated on Charges		
Drug	White	Black	Hispanic
Total	26.0	29.1	43.1
Marijuana	28.0	9.2	61.3
Heroin	14.0	23.0	61.3
Powder cocaine	18.1	30.5	50.2
Crack cocaine	7.0	82.8	9.3
Methamphetamine	59.0	1.6	35.2
Other	66.7	13.1	17.5

Source: US Sentencing Commission. 2001. *Sourcebook of Federal Sentencing Statistics.* Washington, DC: US Sentencing Commission (USSCFY01).

■ Special Problems for Drug-Abusing Women

Women, Drugs, and Violence

"I wore a black eye like it was part of my make-up."

Whether it is a violent relationship or the violence of the drug trade generally (Murphy and Arroyo 2000), women involved with drugs often experience violence. The terms "violence against women" and "gender-based violence" refer to many types of harmful behavior directed at women and girls because of their sex. Although all women are at risk, women who abuse drugs experience particularly high rates of such violence; it has been suggested that roughly 70–80 percent of incarcerated women and women with substance abuse problems have been victims at some point in their lives (Singer et al. 1995; Women in Prison Project 2002). Alcoholic women are two times as likely to have been beaten or sexually assaulted than men or nonalcoholic women (US Department of Health and Human Services 1999). Being physically or sexually abused can be devastating to a woman's physical and mental health for the rest of her life. In addition to the original injury, violence increases women's long-term risks for a number of other health problems, including chronic pain, physical disability, and importantly for this chapter, drug and alcohol abuse.

Violence against women and girls can take many forms, including physical violence, rape, psychological and emotional abuse, coerced isolation, and destruction of property and pets. Often a woman is subject to a combination of these tactics. Rates of violence against women in the United States are high. For example, it is estimated that a woman is battered by an intimate partner every fifteen seconds in this country (Freedman 2002). Abuse of an intimate partner (also known as domestic violence, wife beating, and battering) is almost always accompanied by psychological abuse and often by rape. The majority of women who are abused by their partners are abused many times. In fact, an atmosphere of terror often permeates abusive relationships. It is no wonder that these women resort to drugs to ease the pain, fear, and humiliation of present and past violence.

Rape is sadly common among this population for several reasons. Women using illegal drugs are even more vulnerable than women in the community. They may be trading sex for drugs or money and have no control over what occurs during the transaction, and they are often on the street where they have little protection. Rape is one of the most underreported of all serious crimes, even among law-abiding community-dwelling women; drug-abusing women are even less likely to report rape.

Many of these women have been victims of violence all their lives. At least 14–25 percent of incarcerated women were abused before age eighteen (see Table 4.4). Most sexual abuse is perpetrated by a family member, family friend or acquaintance, relative, or neighbor; in other words, young girls are most likely to be sexually abused by someone they know and should be able to trust (Lundberg-Love 1999). Victims of childhood sexual abuse are more likely than nonvictims to have certain mental health problems such as depression, panic attacks, obsessive-compulsive symptoms, and drug and alcohol abuse (Koss 1990).

Some of these abused women are likely to go on to commit violent crimes themselves. The majority of women who kill their partners were in abusive relationships. Although there is no excuse for violence, women who have been abused have seen aggressive behavior modeled, often as a successful technique for controlling other people's behavior. They may see no other option to protect their children or to escape the situation alive.

Table 4.4   Percentage of Men and Women Abused Before Sentencing

	Ever		Before Age 18	
	Male (%)	Female (%)	Male (%)	Female (%)
Abused before incarceration				
State prisoners	16.1	57.2	14.4	36.7
Federal prisoners	7.2	39.9	5.8	23.0
Physically abused				
State prisoners	13.4	46.5	11.9	25.4
Federal prisoners	6.0	32.3	5.0	14.7
Sexually abused				
State prisoners	5.8	39.0	5.0	25.5
Federal prisoners	2.2	22.8	1.9	14.5

Source: Modified from Caroline Wolf Harlow. 1999. *Prior Abuses Reported by Inmates and Probationers.* Washington, DC: Bureau of Justice Statistics (NCJ 172879).

In the absence of alternative behaviors and in the presence of stressful situations, these women may return to the community with their pain, fear, and anger intact. Incarcerated women with histories of physical and sexual violence need opportunities for counseling to deal with their pasts; drug treatment programs that overlook this crucial component of women's history are unlikely to "cure" a woman's need for relief. Men are much less likely to have the same psychological profile as a result of past violence; again, treating women with the same techniques used for men insures only that another opportunity is lost to restore or even develop women's healthy sense of self and purpose.

"Condoms?": Drugs and HIV/AIDS

Although different studies report slightly different rates of infection, one fact is clear—drug abuse contributes to a greater percentage of human immunodeficiency virus/acquired immune deficiency syndrome (HIV/AIDS) diagnoses among women than men. In all, drug abuse is nearly twice as likely to be directly or indirectly associated with AIDS in women (estimates vary from 66 to 70 percent) than in men (34 percent) (NIDA Notes 2000). Whether because of the effects of the drugs or to raise money to buy more, these women are also likely to be involved in other risky behaviors. The most obvious is unprotected sex. Addicted women, as well as women who smoke crack or inject drugs, are more likely to use condoms inconsistently despite multiple partners, to exchange sex for money, to contract repeated sexually transmitted diseases, and to have sex with someone who injects drugs. Drug-abusing women may turn to prostitution and have little control over condom use. These behaviors all put these women at high potential risk for HIV/AIDS infection (Guyon et al. 1999; Cotten-Oldenburg et al. 1999).

Another major risk factor for HIV/AIDS is injection drug use (IDU), and infection rates vary by gender and race (National Coalition of Hispanic Health and Human Services Organizations 1998; Day 2003). About 30 percent of new AIDS cases among women result from injection drug use, compared to about 20 percent for men; among those who do inject drugs illicitly, about 25 percent of white, 66 percent of black, and 7 percent of Hispanic women are infected (US Department of Health and Human Services, 2005). These statistics make sense because women are more likely than men to report injecting illegal drugs (33 percent and 25 percent, respectively) and sharing a needle (18 percent and 12 percent, respectively). In these cases we see the impact of poverty and its accompanying poor access to medical care and poor overall health increasing a woman's vulnerability to this disease.

These statistics on the relationship between injection drug use and HIV/AIDS infection are especially compelling within the policy context. In 1989, the federal government began prohibiting the use of any funds for programs that distributed sterile needles. Paradoxically this followed the 1988 introduction of policies that set funding aside to emphasize the importance of injection drug use in educational prevention programs. HIV/AIDS is discussed further in Chapters 5 and 8.

◼ Women and the War on Drugs

The enormous increase in the number of women in prison can be traced largely to a series of presidential policies that came to be called the war on drugs. In 1972, President Richard Nixon stated that drugs were "public enemy number one" and set the wheels in motion for a major shift in dealing with illegal drugs. During his administration, he signed the Comprehensive Drug Abuse Prevention and Control Act of 1970, which established the "schedules" of substances according to their legal acceptability (see Table 4.5 for examples) and reorganized federal agencies to create the Drug Enforcement Administration in 1973. There were few big legal guns in Nixon's arsenal, however, and during the next several years drug use and acceptance were high (McBride, Terry, and Inciardi 1991).

The battle lines were clearly in place, however, with the creation of the Rockefeller drug laws in New York State in 1973. At the time the toughest in the nation, these laws were intended to deter drug use and sales and to isolate or severely punish those not deterred. Mandatory prison sentences for the unlawful possession and sale of controlled substances were keyed to the weight of the drug involved. Generally, possessing 4 ounces or more or trafficking 2 ounces or more of a narcotic (typically heroin or cocaine) resulted in a mandatory fifteen years to life sentence. (Although marijuana was originally in-

Table 4.5   Examples of Drug Classifications and Schedules

Classification	Examples	Justification
Schedule I	Marijuana LSD MDMA Heroin	High potential for abuse No currently accepted medical use No accepted safe use
Schedule II	Cocaine Opium Morphine Amphetamine	High potential for abuse Currently accepted medical use or accepted medical use with restrictions Potential for severe psychological or physical dependence
Schedule III	Anabolic steroids (Dronabinol, Marinol)	Potential for abuse but less than I and II Currently accepted medical use Potential for moderate psychological or physical dependence
Schedule IV	Diazepam (Valium) Alprazolam (Xanax) Chlordiazapox (Librium)	Low potential for abuse compared to III Accepted medical use Potential for limited psychological and physical dependence
Schedule V	Prescription drugs containing low levels of codeine or opium	Low potential for abuse compared to IV Accepted medical use Potential for limited psychological or physical dependence

Source: Adapted from DEA (US Drug Enforcement Administration). 2004. *Drug Scheduling.* www.usdoj.gov/dea/pubs/scheduling.html.

cluded in the list of substances covered by the Rockefeller laws, it was removed from the list in 1977. By 1979, in response to extensive criticism, the legislature had amended the laws somewhat to increase the amount of drugs needed to trigger the fifteen-year-to-life sentence for both sale and possession.) Michigan soon followed with the 650 Lifer Law, which mandated life without parole for anyone convicted of distribution or conspiracy to distribute 650 grams (less than a pound and a half) or more of heroin or cocaine. These laws basically prohibited judges from using any discretion in sentencing and gave power to the prosecutors making the charge.

During the conservative 1980s, President Ronald Reagan called drug abuse "one of the gravest problems facing us as a nation," and his wife Nancy enjoined the nation to "just say no." More importantly, the Sentencing Reform Act (SRA) of 1984 and the Anti–Drug Abuse Act (ADAA) of 1986 began to substantially redefine federal punishment standards. The SRA, which took almost eight years to be fully implemented, had four goals for sentencing reform: (1) elimination of unwarranted disparity; (2) transparency, certainty, and fairness; (3) proportionate punishment; and (4) crime control through deterrence, incapacitation, and the rehabilitation of offenders (US Sentencing Commission 2004, iv).

These goals were seen as a way to overcome two basic problems of the old sentencing system: (1) that judges had the discretion to choose the punishment they thought most appropriate, without explanation and largely without opportunity for appeal; and (2) that the time of actual incarceration was set by the Parole Commission, and offenders served only about 58 percent of their actual sentences. The new guidelines set forth in the SRA gave a sense of transparency, consistency, and fairness (US Sentencing Commission 2004). This "truth-in-sentencing" denied the judge the opportunity to take into account the circumstances of the crime or the life circumstances of the accused—factors especially important for women. Furthermore, it led to more certain imprisonment (because of a decline in simple probation) and longer punishment (because of changes in the parole system); between 1987 and 1992, the average prison time served by federal felons more than doubled (US Sentencing Commission 2004). The effects of SRA were most obvious in sentencing trends for drug offenders (who have made up the bulk of the federal criminal docket since the 1970s), more than doubling their time served (US Sentencing Commission 2004).

These sentencing guidelines were influenced by the passage of the ADAA in 1986. This act was prompted by the death of a well-known athlete, Len Bias, who had been celebrating his draft into professional basketball when he overdosed on cocaine. His death frightened and outraged the public and mobilized a Congress eager to get tough on drugs. The omnibus bill appropriated $1.7 billion to fight drugs, $97 million to build new prisons, $200 million for drug education, and $97 million for treatment. More importantly, it also established mandatory minimum penalties based on the weight of various drugs. (The difficulties in establishing appropriate punishment for different drugs by weight are apparent in the 100-to-1 discrepancy in sentencing between powder cocaine and crack cocaine.) This combination—money for the fight against drugs, mandatory minimums, sentencing guidelines, and "truth-in-sentencing"—began to fill prisons beyond capacity.

In 1988 the crime of conspiracy was defined to ensure that mandatory sentences were applied to *all* members of a drug-trafficking organization. The result was that everyone connected to a crack house, for example, whether it was the woman answering the phone or the man importing large quantities of the drug, was liable for all the crack ever sold by the organization. Within six years, the number of federal prisoners accused of drug crimes increased 300 percent (Frontline 2005). That same year the weight threshold for crack cocaine was lowered to increase arrests and prosecutions of individuals possessing small amounts of the drug, even though the racial ramifications of the enormous sentencing discrepancy between powder cocaine and crack cocaine (100 to 1) was recognized very quickly.

In 1989 President George H. W. Bush funded the National Drug Control Policy, with William Bennett as director. He became known as the "drug czar" as he led a campaign for "denormalization" in the hopes of making illegal drug use socially unacceptable. Bush gave the term "war on drugs" real meaning when he proposed a 50 percent increase in military spending for use in the fight (Frontline 2005).

Although these laws were intended to punish and deter drug kingpins, most federal drug defendants were low-level offenders; only 11 percent were classified as high-level dealers (US Sentencing Commission 1995). High-level drug dealers are rarely caught with large amounts of drugs because they are able to pay others to take that risk. Poor women or women afraid to refuse abusive men may take that risk—often with serious consequences.

The Rockefeller drug laws, federal sentencing guidelines, and mandatory minimums have remained essentially unchanged since then and have been joined by "three strikes and you're out" laws in many states (Mauer 2001). However, laws regarding sentencing are constantly being scrutinized and revamped because they have become more and more unpopular and expensive. (Michigan has eased its sentencing policies somewhat.) The policies have met with significant criticism for their imposition of mandatory minimum sentences. Many members of the public and some members of the judiciary and criminal justice communities feel that the guidelines are too confining and do not allow for the appropriate consideration of mitigating factors and the appropriate imposition of penalties. Even the US Sentencing Commission urged their reversal, but Congress continues to support them (Frontline 2005).

Drug Schedules

The possession, distribution, and manufacture of illegal drugs are prohibited by federal law, as is participation in a plan to violate the law. Strict penalties are provided for drug convictions, and all penalties are doubled for subsequent drug convictions. Penalties are based on the federal government's decision regarding if and how a drug should be classified (see Table 4.5). Psychoactive (mind-altering) chemicals are categorized by the Controlled Substances Act (CSA), Title II of the Comprehensive Drug Abuse Prevention and Control Act of 1970. The CSA places all substances that are regulated under existing federal law into one of five schedules based upon the substance's medicinal value, harmfulness, and potential for physical or psychological dependence. Schedule I is reserved for the most dangerous drugs that have no recognized medical use, whereas Schedule V is the classification used for the least dangerous drugs. This schedule also designates if the drug can be prescribed by a physician and under what conditions. Different penalties apply to drugs of different classifications. What is considered incriminating evidence of involvement in the drug trade is presented in Table 4.6.

Table 4.6   Drugs and Incriminating Evidence

Drug Offenses	Evidence
Simple possession	Small amount of a controlled substance
Possession of a controlled substance for sale	Larger quantity of the drug, and other evidence such as large amounts of cash, weapons, or drug paraphernalia (such as pipes or syringes)
Distribution of a controlled substance	Proven transfer of drugs for wealth
Manufacture of a controlled substance	Creating, refining, and processing illegal drugs
Conspiracy	Knowing participation in a scheme to violate the law (in this case, the suspect need not have direct involvement in manufacture or distribution of the illegal drug)

Source: US DEA (US Drug Enforcement Administration). 2004. *Drug Scheduling.* www.usdoj.gov/dea/pubs/scheduling.html.

Implications for Women

These laws mean that a woman with no prior offenses can, in an extreme case, be given a sentence of life in prison; one estimate suggested that 95 percent of women convicted in New York of drug offenses had no prior convictions. Some considered these "gender-neutral" laws progressive, but this neutrality has worked against women. Mitigating circumstances largely unique to women were no longer admissible; relevant facts such as a relatively minor role in the drug operation, an abusive and coercive relationship with the dealer, single motherhood, or women's lower recidivism rates were not allowed before the judge (see Box 4.1 for the example of Kemba Smith.)

The restrictions on presenting the details of the crime and of their lives hinder the defense of many women. For example, many women are arrested bringing drugs into the country or delivering them from place to place within the country. These "drug mules" are sometimes unaware of what they are carrying or are tricked into the transport by men who are active dealers. A study by the Department of Justice found that women are typically low-level, non-violent drug dealers, with minimal or no prior history of crime, but that they receive similar sentences to men with much higher levels of involvement in the drug trade. Furthermore, because of conspiracy charges, a woman can be sentenced for simply telling an undercover officer where to buy drugs.

Women often receive the same, if not higher, sentences than men in a drug case because they are unable or unwilling to offer substantial assistance toward the prosecution of someone else. For example, in New York a drug crime with a minimum penalty of three years to life could be reduced to lifetime parole if the suspect provided "material assistance" leading to the arrest

Box 4.1   Kemba Smith

The tragedy of drug sentencing came alive for many people with the case of Kemba Smith. Smith was the only child of professional parents from the suburbs of Virginia. She went away to college at Hampton University. She was having trouble adjusting to college and dealing with low self-esteem when she met Peter Hall. Peter was not a student but seemed to have it all—money, style, charm. They began a relationship, but after a few months she found out that he was dealing drugs, and he became controlling and abusive. Kemba never actually carried or sold drugs, but she did travel with large sums of money strapped to her waist.

When Peter went on the run, she went with him until she became pregnant and returned home. She was afraid for her own and her family's safety; her boyfriend had allegedly killed his best friend for cooperating with the authorities. Finally she turned herself in to the police.

She was charged with conspiracy to distribute crack cocaine, money laundering, and making false statements. At twenty-three years of age with no prior convictions, she was sentenced to twenty-four and a half years in prison. She delivered her baby in jail and had one foot shackled to the bed immediately after giving birth. She kept him for two days before her parents took him home.

Kemba was released after six years in prison when President William J. Clinton commuted her sentence.

of a drug dealer. The case of Monica Boguille, reported in the *Minneapolis Star* (Rigert, 1997), is illustrative. When she was twenty years old, Monica was given a ten-year sentence for handling the money in a drug deal. It was the same sentence given to the two actual suppliers, one of whom was known to be violent. Despite her low level of involvement, she was sentenced as a result of mandatory minimum sentencing requirements. The best explanation for this disparate punishment: they cooperated with the government to implicate others; she did not. Tracy Huling (in Amnesty International 1999) noted that women rarely are able to offer assistance because they are so marginally involved with the drug operation. Additionally, women are much less likely to give information on a boyfriend or husband than men. In other words, it is much more likely that men will turn in their women for reduced sentences; women are much less likely to turn in their men.

This is not to say that women are not active dealers in the drug trade themselves. Surely they are, and they are gaining equality of opportunity in this, as in other lines of work. But women still usually function at the bottom of the drug distribution hierarchy; they typically work for male dealers making street-level sales or, less frequently, run homes where they sell drugs (Johnson, Dunlap, and Tourigny 2000). Once a woman is addicted, she may be eager to sell drugs (or sex) in exchange for drugs.

Women have been hit hard by the war on drugs. From the time that truth-in-sentencing and mandatory minimum sentencing were introduced in 1986 until 1996, the number of women sentenced to state prison for drug crimes increased tenfold from 2,370 to 23,700. During that same ten-year period, the number of male drug arrests increased by 55.1 percent (Amnesty International 1999). Between 1990 and 1996, the number of women convicted of drug felonies increased by 37 percent (from 43,000 in 1990 to 59,536 in 1996). The number of convictions for simple possession was up 41 percent over that period, from 18,438 in 1990 to 26,022 in 1996 (Greenfeld and Snell 1999). Women of color have been particularly hard hit; black women were more than eight times and Hispanic women were almost three times as likely to be in prison as white women (BJS 2000).

■ Drug Treatment

As we have seen, women have unique experiences with drugs and gender-specific needs for and from treatment—their bodies are different, the reasons they use drugs are different, and the context of their problems are different than those of men. Clearly, although most women who use illegal drugs or who use drugs illegally do not encounter the criminal justice system, they do not get necessary substance abuse treatment either. The federal government keeps track of the admissions to treatment programs that receive state or federal funding. According to their data (SAMHSA 2004), women made up only 30 percent of admissions; it was only when tranquilizers or sedatives were the primary substance of abuse at admission did women's admission rates approximate men's, even though alcohol use accounted for more women in treatment. And although it is well accepted that the more time an individual spends in treatment, the better the outcome, women spend less time in treatment than men. Even in the community, women have difficulty receiving help for drug problems, despite their vulnerability.

The study by the National Center on Addiction and Substance Abuse at Columbia University (CASA 2003) found that girls and young women are more easily addicted: they get hooked faster and suffer the consequences sooner than boys and young men. This is in part due to differences in biology: women weigh less and have more body fat and less water per pound. These physiological differences mean that women's bodies react differently to the same amount of drugs and alcohol and experience different long-term effects. For example, when same-sized women and men use equivalent amounts of cocaine, women ended up with higher drug levels in their bloodstream (Anderson, Rosay, and Saum 2002) and a stronger cardiovascular response (though females may be protected from some of the deleterious effects on the brain such as impairments in concentration and memory) (NIDA Notes 2000). Although women generally drink less than men, women who are heavy drinkers are more likely to have serious health consequences as a result of their alcohol consumption (Craig 2004). The same pattern of increased morbidity and mortality from consumption is true of African Americans (Craig 2004) who, again, are disproportionately represented among women in prison. Although it is possible for women to use drugs sporadically without developing serious problems with abuse, women who use drugs become addicted more quickly than men. These findings again point to the fact that approaches to treatment need to be designed to meet women's physical as well as emotional needs.

The benefits of treatment for substance abuse are impressive; effective treatment saves taxpayer money, reduces criminal behavior, and, most important, relieves associated human suffering. Although there are few controlled studies (Hall et al. 2004), those that exist suggest that women who complete drug programs feel more positive toward the staff and themselves (Strauss and Falkin 2000) and that appropriate treatment reduces recidivism and relapse (Butzin, Martin, and Inciardi, 2002; Peugh and Belenko 1999). For women in prison with drug problems, it would seem that treatment would be a high priority. However, the reality is that most women do not receive the drug abuse services they need while they are in prison or the follow-up services they need when they return to the community. Considering the large numbers of women who are in prison for drug-related crimes and who were regular drug users before entering prison, as well as the known benefits of drug treatment, there is a surprising lack of effective substance abuse treatment designed for women in prison.

"The failure to rehabilitate substance-abusing inmates may be the greatest missed opportunity in the war on crime" (Amnesty International 1999, 32).

In fact, despite increases in the numbers of incarcerated women with substance abuse problems in the 1990s, participation in drug treatment programs dropped during that time, with the result that fewer than half of all inmates who needed treatment participated in any professional program in 1997 (Mears et al. 2003). The Bureau of Justice Statistics (1997) estimated that only 20 percent of women in state and 13 percent of women in federal prisons were treated for substance abuse since their admission. The trend seems to be away from treatment run by trained clinicians and to self-help, faith-based, and peer groups (Mears et al. 2003); it is also true for community substance abuse treatment (SAMHSA 2003). One survey (Young and Reviere 2001) found that Alcoholics Anonymous and Narcotics Anonymous were the most frequently offered programs in federal and state prisons for women that reported offering onsite drug counseling. At the same time, when prison health care providers were asked about the problems facing their facilities, the need for substance abuse treatment came up repeatedly. Clearly, self-help programs have their place, but most incarcerated women need more than confession and discussion to change their lives.

The discrepancy between treatment need and availability is a result of both a lack of knowledge and the complexity of women's troubles. The recognition that women have serious issues with drugs is relatively recent. Until the 1980s, women were largely absent from the data on drug use; one study (Kerr 1998) found that of the thousands of research articles published on substance abuse between 1929 and 1970, only 28 were about women. When it was "discovered" that women were abusing drugs in significant numbers, they were subjected to the same treatment regimes as men.

Further substance abuse rarely is the lone problem for these women and cannot be treated in isolation. Women who use drugs illegally have more interwoven issues that require treatment than men or non-substance-abusing women. These women have histories of previous physical and sexual abuse, relationship difficulties, little or no job training and limited education, and physical and mental illness (Peters et al. 1997; Kerr 1998). These co-occurring problems and disorders make drug treatment a complicated issue that requires a coordinated and comprehensive approach for reducing dependence on drugs while improving the overall "health" of the user.

Even with new knowledge about gender differences, most prison drug treatment programs are still based on a male model and modified only slightly for women (Langan and Pelissier 2001). Yet if a drug treatment program is not specifically designed for women, by default it is a program designed for men. Many of these programs use more confrontational tactics and ignore the relationship aspects of women's drug use. Group therapy sessions in which prisoners are barraged with accusations to break down defenses (Peugh and Belenko 1999) are inappropriate for women who already have low self-esteem and feel helpless because they have been accused, abused, and yelled at all their lives. Further, women's drug use is intertwined with the men in their lives; many of them were introduced to drugs by the men in their lives and use drugs to combat depression related to earlier abusive relationships.

Treatment modalities are beginning to change both inside and outside prisons (Peugh and Belenko 1999; Gillece and Russell 2001; Hall et al. 2004), as researchers and practitioners realize the extent of the damage these women have to heal and the inefficiency of "gender-neutral" approaches. Counseling that addresses self-image and teaches relationship skills is more useful in helping women deal with life outside prison than confrontation and shame. Therapy must also be coupled with educational, occupational, health training, and opportunities for success in these areas. An ex-convict with good self-esteem but health problems and no job may feel better about herself, but her ability to support her family will still be limited. Payment for services must also be available, both in and out of prison. Successful programs teach generalizable skills, provide contacts and supports for a successful return to community and family, and recognize and treat co-occurring disorders. Box 4.2 provides guidelines for treating women who have both mental health and substance abuse problems.

Box 4.2 Principles for Treating Co-occurring Disorders

- An extensive baseline assessment is made as soon as possible after a prisoner is incarcerated; ongoing assessment is provided.
- Each problem (such as past trauma, depression, and substance abuse) is considered equally and equally important.
- Problems are prioritized; those causing the most immediate difficulty are treated first so the inmate can begin to cope and deal with the others.
- As much as possible, co-occurring problems are treated simultaneously rather than sequentially.
- Staff receives training on the co-occurring problems and their interactions.
- Relevant and appropriate community and follow-up treatment is provided upon release.

Source: Adapted from Roger H. Peters, Anne L. Strozier, Mary R. Murrin, and William D. Kearns. 1997. "Treatment of Substance Abusing Jail Inmates: Examination of Gender Differences." *Journal of Substance Abuse Treatment* 14 (4): 346.

■ **Conclusion**

Despite the human and financial costs of drug abuse, most of what we know about illegal drug use, its effects, the addictive properties of drugs, and treatment still comes from studies and observations on men. Even now we know relatively little about women and drugs, despite women's substantial rates of drug use. We do know that the biggest increase in women's incarceration rates is due to illegal involvement with drugs. This involvement, however, is generally low-level and nonviolent. These women are not innocent but are often guilty more of poor choices and lack of options than of crime.

Because of a myriad of other untreated problems, women become entangled in the drug world. Most women have not received any drug or alcohol treatment before their arrest (SAMHSA 2003) and will not receive sufficient help in prison. They will return to their families and their communities having made little progress in their own private war on drugs. As a society, we lose the opportunity to intervene in these women's lives while they are literally a captive audience; for many of these women there is no other time and place, and their individual costs become society's costs as well.

■ Notes

1. Drug-induced deaths include poisoning deaths from either legal or illegal drugs but not indirect causes such as accidents, homicides, and newborn deaths due to mother's drug use.

2. The National Survey on Drug Use and Health (NSDUH) collects information on nine different categories of illegal drug use (CASA 2003): marijuana/hashish, cocaine (powder and crack), heroin, hallucinogens (including LSD, PCP, peyote, mescaline, mushrooms, and Ecstasy/MDMA), inhalants (including amyl nitrate, cleaning fluids, gasoline, paint, glue), nonmedical use of stimulants (including methamphetamine), nonmedical use of tranquilizers, nonmedical use of sedatives, and nonmedical use of pain relievers. These drugs are the focus of this chapter.

Physical and
Mental Health Care

Health is defined in the constitution of the World Health Organization (WHO) as "a state of complete physical, mental and social well-being and not merely the absence of disease or infirmity" (1948).[1] When we apply that definition to women in prison, we see a population that embodies the complete antithesis of what many consider "health." Most women in prison have at least one physical or mental health problem (Acoca 1998); given these conditions, the health burden of race, the stress of incarceration, and histories of victimization and poor medical treatment, it is no wonder that health care for women in prison is considered a top priority. In this chapter, however, as we explore the problems of mental and physical health and the available solutions, we find that although health is emphasized, the prison system may not actually meet the needs of these women, despite legal mandates. The unique combination of background factors and the abundance of health problems that women bring to prison require more and different options for women's health care, but prisons largely rely on a male or emergency-ward model for delivery of health services.

We know relatively little about the actual health of incarcerated women. Valid, reliable, representative, up-to-date, and disaggregated information on the health of state and federal prison inmates is not readily available. Many prisons do not collect comprehensive and accessible data on the health status of their inmates; these data are usually self-reported by inmates themselves or estimated from surveys of the health status of the noninstitutionalized civilian population (Maruschak and Beck 2001). Because of inconsistent measurement, estimates of conditions and treatments vary from study to study. True rates of illness and disability in prison are hard to determine, not only because of measurement problems but also because women may report symptoms out of boredom or a need for attention. Despite this variability, we know enough to surmise that as the number of women in prison increases, the need for quality health care will continue to be a major concern for correctional institutions in the coming years.

■ Contributing Factors to Poor Health

Women do not enter prison in the best of health. The specific reasons and problems vary for each individual, but these women share characteristics that predispose them to poor health. Many have spent their lives receiving minimal health care, following poor health habits (Brewer and Baldwin 2000), abusing drugs and alcohol, and suffering various forms of violence. Furthermore, the unique and cumulative effects of gender, race, and poverty predispose these women to an abundance of health problems.

Gender

Women in general have poorer health than men, regardless of how health is measured.[2] According to a classic review by Lois Verbrugge (1985), explanations for this gender differential fall into five categories that are as relevant for incarcerated women as they are for women in the community: (1) women have *different biological risks*, such as increased rates of heart disease after menopause and higher susceptibility to some sexually transmitted diseases; (2) women have *different acquired risks*, such as prior exposure to violence and drugs; (3) women in general are more likely to *evaluate symptoms differently* and in terms of needing care; (4) women *report more problems* to health professionals; and (5) these women have not had *access to quality health care*.

The gender differences in health found in the community transfer to prison, where women report more illnesses and more visits to health care providers than men (Acoca 1998; Lindquist and Lindquist 1999). From the point of entry into the criminal justice system, roughly 30 percent of women entering a federal facility reported at least one physical impairment or mental condition, compared to 23 percent of men reporting such a condition, and the percentage of female prisoners whose health problems require special twenty-four-hour medical care housing is nearly four times that of male prisoners (Maruschak and Beck 2001). In addition, long-term substance abuse is more strongly associated with liver disease and higher rates of physical health problems for women than for men.

Race

Roughly two-thirds of women in prison are women of color, and they tend to have poorer health in general and heightened risk for certain health conditions. African American women are at particular risk for hypertension, asthma, sickle cell anemia, and breast and cervical cancer. The prevalence of diabetes, hypertension, tuberculosis, sexually transmitted diseases, alcoholism, cirrhosis of the liver, homicide, and HIV/AIDS is higher among Hispanics than non-Hispanic whites. More than 75 percent of women with HIV/AIDS belong to racial or ethnic minorities, and more than 50 percent of new infections are among African American women. Minority women in prison have the highest rates of HIV and associated tuberculosis (Harrison Ross and Lawrence 1998). These differences can be explained in part through lack of access to health care; minority women are less likely to have private insurance than white women (Office of Research on Women's Health 1998) and have less access to medical care despite higher needs (Williams 2003). Racism cannot be ignored as an explanatory factor in these health discrepancies. Most immediately, the relationship of race to poverty explains much of the poorer health of black women in particular. Race is strongly related to poverty, as Table 5.1 illustrates.

Poverty

The inverse relationship between socioeconomic status (SES is one's social class, in other words) and health is one of the oldest and most universal of all the documented relationships between social indicators and health status. Poverty and lower-class status affect health directly through such things as poorer diet, inferior housing in more dangerous neighborhoods, and higher levels of stress and indirectly through the availability of and access to good health care.

Poor people have more acute and chronic diseases, poorer self-reported health, more disabilities, and higher mortality rates. There is also a powerful association between social class and mental health; poorer individuals have more and more visible mental health problems. Most women who enter prison come from difficult economic circumstances. Nearly 20 percent of mothers reported that they were homeless in the year before they were incarcerated, and 42 percent of women in prison did not have a job prior to incarceration (Greenfeld and Snell 1999). Low-income women are twice as likely as those with higher incomes to report fair or poor health (Salganicoff et al. 2003). Medical problems and physical impairments or mental conditions are higher among inmates who were homeless or unemployed before incarceration (Maruschak and Beck 2001). And as Table 5.2 indicates, women are poorer than men.

Table 5.1   Poverty Rates by Race and Ethnicity

Race/Ethnicity	Percentage of Population	Percentage Below the Poverty Line
Non-Hispanic white	77.1	8.0
Hispanic (all races)	12.5	21.8
African American	12.9	24.0

Source: US Census Bureau. 2002. *2002 Poverty Highlights.* Washington, DC: US Census Bureau.

Table 5.2   Economic Indicators for State Prisoners

	Women (%)	Men (%)
Full-time work prior to arrest	40	60
Incomes less than $600 a month		
prior to arrest (1999 dollars)	37	28
Receiving public assistance before arrest	30	8

Source: Adapted from Lawrence A. Greenfeld and Tracy L. Snell. 1999. *Women Offenders.* Washington, DC: Bureau of Justice Statistics (NIJ 175688).

■ Physical Health Problems

Incarcerated women present a variety of medical issues. Catherine Ingram-Fogel (1991) interviewed and followed up on women in a North Carolina prison. Those inmates reported high levels of physical and mental health problems, such as headaches, back problems, fatigue, drug and alcohol abuse, and past sexually transmitted diseases. Over half were obese, and many had gained weight while in prison. Over three-fourths reported abnormal pap smears, and 100 percent reported health problems when they were interviewed a second time. (This figure is in stark contrast to the 25 percent of female inmates estimated by Maruschak and Beck [2001] to report a medical problem since admission.) However, only about 28 percent actually reported going for treatment or consultation; most suggested that the health care system in the prison was so unresponsive that it would not do much good to go. In addition, more than half of women in prison report their physical health as being fair or poor (Brewer et al. 1998), compared to about 10 percent in the nonelderly community population (Salganicoff et al. 2003). Below we discuss specific health problems.

Accidents

Men in federal prisons are more likely to be injured or killed in an accident or a fight than women (28.7 percent and 20.5 percent, respectively) although rates go up for both as length of imprisonment increases (Maruschak and Beck 2001). The Bureau of Justice Statistics does not release information on the type of unintentional injury, but more occur during recreation than work or other times.

Reproductive Issues

Pregnancy and its difficulties are among the most problematic aspects of health for incarcerated women, and women of color are at particular risk. Women in prison report higher than expected numbers of reproductive problems, such as menstrual difficulties and unintended, interrupted, or lost pregnancies (Ingram-Fogel 1991; Harrison Ross and Lawrence, 1998). Studies suggest that roughly 6–7 percent of all women admitted to prisons are pregnant (American Correctional Association 1998; Snell 1994). Being pregnant in prison carries more risk, both physical and psychological, than being pregnant outside prison (Acoca 1998). Many women present several characteristics that put their pregnancies at risk: poverty, minority status, previous histories of substance abuse, victimization, smoking, multiple abortions or miscarriages, and/or sexually transmitted diseases or pelvic inflammatory disease. These factors, combined with minimal social supports during pregnancy and delivery, put these women and their newborns at risk for increased perinatal and postnatal (before and after birth) morbidity and mortality.

Despite their high-risk profiles, pregnant women who are incarcerated are not guaranteed quality care. Women report that they do not receive regular pelvic exams or sonograms, that they receive little to no education about prenatal care and nutrition, and that they are unable to maintain an appropriate diet to suit their changing caloric needs (one woman reported that the only change to her diet with her pregnancy was an extra ration of crackers every afternoon). Most demeaning and dangerous is the practice of shackling women's hands and feet during transportation and sometimes chaining her during delivery. In one case reported to Amnesty International (1999), the woman was in the delivery room, ready to give birth, but the attendants did not have the key to remove her chains. (They did find them in time to deliver the baby.) Lawsuits are challenging this practice.

Furthermore, in many prisons women are not permitted to breastfeed after delivery and are only allotted between twenty-four and seventy-two hours with their baby before the infant is turned over to a family member for guardianship or enters the state's foster care system. Fortunately, model programs do exist where pregnant, incarcerated women learn about appropriate prenatal care and parenting skills. In these programs, the mother may be allowed to keep her child during her prison sentence or at least for weekend visits; unfortunately, these programs are few and far between and do not reach many of the pregnant women or new mothers in US prisons. The topic of women and their children is discussed more fully in Chapter 6.

One obvious requirement for good health care for women in prison is the availability of quality gynecological services. Young to middle-aged women in the general population are encouraged to have annual pelvic examinations and pap smears and information on birth control. Prisons, however, do not always perform baseline gynecological examinations on intake, keep an annual examination schedule for prisoners, or provide specialized obstetric-gynecological services. Delays in diagnosis and absence of service can mean the difference between life and death for a woman with breast cancer, ovarian cancer, or abnormal pap smears.

Sexually Transmitted Diseases

Sexually transmitted diseases (STDs) are among the most common infectious diseases in the United States today and are significant health problems for African American women (NIAID 1999). More than twenty STDs have been identified, including genital herpes, genital warts, gonorrhea, syphilis, chlamydia, and HIV/AIDS, and the incidence is rising as young people have sex earlier and more individuals have multiple sexual partners. For women, an STD may not cause obvious symptoms, but the associated health problems tend to be more severe and frequent for women than for men, largely because its asymptomatic nature may allow a disease to progress to dangerous levels before it is noticed. For example, untreated STDs in women may cause pelvic inflammatory disease, leading to infertility or ectopic pregnancy (a sometimes fatal condition in which the fertilized egg attaches to an area outside the uterus), may be associated with cervical cancer, or may be passed on from the mother, resulting in pneumonia, eye infections, and permanent neurological damage to the baby (NIAID 1999).

According to the Centers for Disease Control and Prevention (CDC 1999), the prevalence of certain sexually transmitted diseases is higher among incarcerated women than among women in the community. For example, estimates vary, but in one study approximately 35 percent of incoming women were positive for syphilis, 20 percent for chlamydia, and 8 percent for gonorrhea ("STDs in Incarcerated Women" 2000). In addition, incarcerated women have high rates of human papillomavirus (HPV) infection, herpes simplex II, and chronic pelvic inflammatory disease (Harrison Ross and Lawrence 1998). One California study found that roughly 48 percent of the women entering the state prison system were infected with hepatitis B and 54.5 percent with hepatitis C (Marble 1996). There are several possible causes of hepatitis infection among inmates; women may share contaminated needles, receive body piercings and tattoos, and have a history of unprotected sex with multiple partners. Hepatitis C is also likely to occur among patients who are HIV-positive.

HIV/AIDS

Human immunodeficiency virus (HIV) is the virus that causes AIDS. This virus may be passed from one person to another when infected blood, semen, or vaginal secretions come in contact with an uninfected person's broken skin or mucous membranes. In addition, infected pregnant women can pass HIV to their babies during pregnancy or delivery, as well as through breastfeeding. AIDS is now the leading cause of death for black women ages twenty-five to thirty-four. The rate of HIV/AIDS infection is higher among female inmates (3.0 percent) than male inmates (1.9 percent) and than among community-dwelling women, although it has decreased since 1995 (Maruschak 2002,

2004). The rate of HIV infection among white female inmates (1.6 percent) is nearly half that of black female inmates (3.0 percent) and Hispanic female inmates (2.9 percent) (Maruschak 2004). This disease is among the most serious for women in prison: with proper treatment, it becomes a chronic disease; without treatment, it causes death.

Testing in prison. HIV testing is not mandated for those entering prison; it is not required in the noninstitutionalized population, and as a result, compulsory prison testing could be construed as discriminatory and unethical (Behrendt et al. 1994). Each facility must then make its own policy. Voluntary testing works to some extent, but stigma, denial, and concerns about confidentiality keep many women, even high-risk women, from being tested. Worries about the health of their own or future children and about other sexually transmitted diseases motivate many women to undergo voluntary testing (DeGroot 2001), but if they test positive, confidential, reliable, quality treatment may not be readily available.

HIV/AIDS education. Many prisons have prevention programs in place, and most studies suggest that brief intervention does change behavior (St. Lawrence et al. 1997). Whether this is a residual of the program or true change is unclear at this point because there is little follow-up research. Importantly, however, women who have gone through educational programs may not have immediate opportunities to practice their new skills (such as putting a condom on a partner) in real-life situations (St. Lawrence et al. 1997).

Care. Providing medical care for HIV-infected individuals is problematic. HIV/AIDS patients in prison are expensive; drugs are increasingly costly. The recommended highly active antiretroviral therapy (HAART) may cost more than $1,000 a month, and additional treatment is often needed for opportunistic infections, side effects, and other problems (Institute of Medicine 2004). Complete compliance is rare (this is also true in the community); most treatment requires several daily doses and dietary modifications. Historically, HIV/AIDS services have had to compete with other demands on correctional budgets for funding and personnel time, even though the correctional health care unit is a unique and highly cost-effective access point for providing HIV/AIDS prevention and care for high-risk populations of women.

Coalition building between correctional staff, medical staff, and, in some cases, departments of public health has established some outstanding programs for HIV/AIDS-infected women. By diagnosing and reporting HIV/AIDS and instituting plans for treatment, education, and prevention, correctional facilities can play a critically important role in the reduction of morbidity and mortality among HIV-infected women in prison and after their release (DeGroot 2001). One example was the Brown University AIDS Program, a collaboration between the Rhode Island Departments of Health and Corrections (Flanigan et al. 1996). This follow-up program was designed so that HIV/AIDS-infected women could meet with a coordinator (up to five times, depending on need) prior to release to discuss their plans for housing, substance abuse treatment, family support, and medical care. The goal was to help provide initial linkages with community services. Program officials followed the women three to six months after release and estimated that 68 percent followed through with drug rehabilitation, and more than half of these were enrolled in outpatient methadone maintenance programs. Importantly, 83 percent successfully followed up with medical services for their HIV/AIDS infection. In addition, recidivism rates for these HIV-positive women were significantly lower than those who were not affiliated with the program. Programs like this one, however, are expensive, labor-intensive, and, therefore, rare.

Because the public and policymakers are rarely enthusiastic about quality health care for prisoners, HIV/AIDS care, as well as prison health care in general, is variable. The rationale for good HIV/AIDS care among inmates usually focuses on their eventual return to the community and the possibility that they may spread their infection. This scenario, prisoner as dangerous vector of a deadly disease, further reinforces the notion that prisoners are outside the purview of community charity and allows a serious disease to be dismissed. HIV/AIDS is also discussed in Chapters 4 and 7.

Tuberculosis

Rates of tuberculosis (TB) are falling for men but increasing for women in prison (American Correctional Association 1998). This bacterial infection (usually of the lungs) is emerging not only as a frightening by-product of HIV/AIDS but also a serious life-threatening disease in its own right. This infectious airborne disease is becoming increasingly problematic because of the emergence of multidrug-resistant TB (a form of tuberculosis that is resistant to two or more of the primary drugs used for the treatment of tuberculosis). Further, to be effective, the full dose of prescribed medication must be completed, or the disease becomes more serious and remains infectious. Prison conditions are ripe for its spread: overcrowding, poor ventilation systems, unhealthy inmates, and lack of medical follow-up. More than 90 percent of prisons screen for TB (Young and Reviere 2001), and most report that inmates with suspected or confirmed TB are isolated in negative pressure rooms. These rooms must be tested to ensure that the air exchange is working properly, and if it is not, the use of the rooms must be terminated. There is little evidence that these precautions are always in place, however (National Commission on Correctional Health Care 2002). Early detection and proper management are crucial to preventing TB's spread to other prisoners and to the community if the infected prisoner is released.

Dental Health

Dental problems, like other health problems, are increasing for women in prison. A lifetime of poverty and poor dental hygiene predisposes these women to trouble with their teeth; they may have had their teeth knocked out as a result of domestic or other violence. The dental disaster that results from methamphetamine use has become so common it is known as "meth mouth" ("Methamphetamine Use" 2004). Most prisons have dental health care available, although maximum security prisoners may be handcuffed to the dental chair and guards posted at the doorway during exams.

■ "I Just Want to Hold My Grandbabies": A Look at Older Inmates

As the US population has grown older, so has the prison population. This, in combination with "three-strikes" crime laws, mandatory minimums, and truth-in-sentencing, has operated to keep prisoners incarcerated for longer periods (Schiraldi 1995). Still relatively young by community standards, the average age of women in prison has increased from twenty-nine years in 1986 to thirty-one years in 1991 to thirty-three in 1997 (GAO 1999). Because their preprison lives were often lacking in access to quality health care and in good health habits, women in prison may experience health problems more characteristic of "older" women in the community. These deficiencies, coupled with the stress of prison life, add years to a prisoner's chronological age; most studies consider women in prison to be old at age fifty (Corwin 2001; Reviere and Young 2004) instead of age sixty-five for those in the community. These older women require special consideration for both health and nonmedical reasons (Cavan 1987).

Health Problems of Older Inmates

As individuals age, physiological changes occur in every part of their bodies. The senses dull, and information is processed more slowly and less accurately. Muscle mass and strength decline. All bodily systems, from respiratory to renal, become less efficient. Because of these changes, older individuals need different environments, diets, and routines, even when they are relatively healthy. In addition, older women report more chronic diseases than younger ones. Chronic conditions can range from relatively mild, such as partial hearing loss, to disruptive and disabling, such as arthritis and asthma; to severe and life-threatening, such as cancer and diabetes. One of the most unpleasant aspects of many chronic diseases is pain, and pain is one of the most common complaints of older adults (Cavanaugh and Blanchard-Fields 2002). All these problems are compounded for women in prison, where they may not have the resources or education to cope with their problems.

Older women in prison report high rates of chronic diseases such as hypertension, heart disease, diabetes, cancer, emphysema, arthritis, asthma, ulcers, and stroke. In addition, many report high rates of comorbidity; in other words, they report more than one condition at a time (Aday 1994). The typical older inmate has an average of three chronic conditions and twenty-four medical encounters a year (Corwin 2001). Further, because diseases such as HIV and hepatitis C are often underdiagnosed and incompletely or inappropriately treated, prisoners may be faced with the possibility of premature death from complications of diseases that could be successfully managed in the community with proper resources.

Older women also face other unique physical problems. Some women will become menopausal in prison. Although menopause is certainly not a health problem in most cases, there are times when treatment or advice is needed. Incontinence (the inability to control elimination of urine) troubles some older women; the embarrassing condition can often be alleviated with proper diet, certain exercises, and medication. Protective pads are available to absorb leaks. However, prisoners may not have access to treatment, protection, or education; at the minimum this condition should be considered, and allowances made in transportation, schedules, and facilities (Morton 1992).

Nonmedical Needs of Older Inmates

The WHO definition of health implies that nonmedical conditions are relevant to well-being. Although some prisons in the United States have been designated for elderly inmates or for the chronically ill, many elderly and sick inmates remain in prisons that cannot address their unique situations, either medically and socially. They have different needs for leisure activities, social support, and housing than younger inmates. There are few programs designed for this population since the usual sports and training programs may be inappropriate (Rosefield 1993), and older inmates may be unwilling to participate in the activity programs that are offered (Kratcoski and Babb 1990). Some prisons do provide day rooms with games, crafts, and reading nooks for their geriatric inmates, however (Neeley, Addison, and Craig-Moreland 1997).

Without special treatment protocols and programs, sick, frail inmates are left to their own resources to receive daily care, including eating, grooming, socializing, finding spiritual outlets, and getting physician attention. Feelings of isolation are particularly acute. Another inmate may care for a friend, but often older inmates complain of being left alone in a cell. In addition, older women in prison are likely to be unmarried and far from home; as a result, they have few visitors (Kratcoski and Babb 1990).

There are unique housing considerations for elderly inmates. They have higher needs for privacy, safety, and emotional connections but fewer needs for social stimulation, activity, and freedom of movement than younger inmates (Walsh 1992). In addition accessibility becomes more important as they become more disabled; ramps, hand rails, and levers instead of knobs are simple examples of the needs of older prisoners. As many of 70 percent of prisons report having disabled inmates, and these provide a variety of services including handicapped rooms and showers, wheelchairs, and walkers. Most prisons do not yet fully comply with the requirements of the 1990 Americans with Disabilities Act, however (Young and Reviere 2001).[3]

Costs of Caring for Older Inmates

Older inmates require more physical and mental health services, such as prescription drugs and medical visits, than comparable women in the community, which make their care more expensive. The confinement of inmates over fifty-five costs state and federal facilities well over $2 billion annually. With the average cost of confining an elderly prisoner about $69,000 a year, the National Criminal Justice Commission (Corwin 2001) estimates that elderly prisoners cost three times more than the average for confining a younger inmate and much more than the average cost for maintaining an individual in a nursing home (roughly $42,500, according to National Center for Health Statistics [1999]). Health care costs are increasingly burdensome for prisons, just as they are for communities. It would seem reasonable to expand early release programs for elderly or terminally ill individuals, if not for reasons of compassion, then for reasons of money. It is estimated that even a conservative release policy for nonviolent offenders over the age of fifty-five who had served at least one-third of their sentences could save more than $900 million a year (Center for Juvenile and Criminal Justice 2001). Chapter 7 gives a further discussion of early release programs for terminally ill inmates.

Despite quite a bit of press and media attention, the aging of the prison population is still largely ignored by the prisons themselves. There is as yet little obvious advance planning for the increasing numbers of older inmates with serious and costly mental and physical health problems (Reviere and Young 2004).

■ "There's No One to Run To": Health Care for Women in Prison

Prisons are faced with a population of women with tremendous needs for good health care. All prisons are mandated to provide health care to meet basic medical needs, but although adaptations are evident, most still use the typical prisoner, a young, healthy male, as their standard for care. Most prisons do conduct intake examinations (although of varying comprehensiveness) and schedule fairly regular physical examinations, particularly for inmates who are older or have chronic conditions. But the more pervasive lack of fit between health care needs and health care services has implications for women's health, not only when they are in prison but also when they leave to return to their families and communities. Furthermore, prisons face the same constraints, such as lack of qualified personnel, facilities, and changes in the delivery of care, that hamper accessible and appropriate health care in the outside world.

Health care providers trained for and sensitive to women's unique problems are the front lines of medicine, but most sources agree that staffing for prison medical facilities has not kept pace with the burgeoning prison population. Although the majority of prisons have both physicians and registered nurses in the facility at least part of the time (Young and Reviere 2001), both the physician-to-inmate ratio and nurse-to-inmate ratio greatly exceed recommendations in many facilities (National Commission on Correctional Health Care 2002). Furthermore, there are many reports of unlicensed physicians and nurses serving in correctional facilities. Specialists such as obstetricians, gynecologists, and dieticians are more likely to be offsite; appointment timing, escorts, and transportation then become problematic. It is not always easy to hire qualified health practitioners, however; low pay and potential danger deter some good physicians and nurses ("Virginia Corrections Chairman" 1998). In addition, there is a need for Spanish-speaking health care providers or translators. Staffing shortages can result in delayed diagnosis and treatment. Delays in interrupted drug regimes, for example, can exacerbate chronic physical and mental health problems.

Many prisons have tried to fill the gap by using nonmedical staff (Amnesty International 1999; Marble 1995) as gatekeepers. In these instances, inmates must obtain permission from medical technical assistants (MTAs) before they can see a physician. MTAs may have little or no medical training or experience and often do not have to follow written protocols ("Suit Challenges Women's Health Care in Prisons" 1995). Their decisions can determine if and when prisoners receive health care.

Some prisons are designated medical facilities with specialized medical and mental health services. The Federal Medical Center (FMC) Carswell, in Fort Worth, Texas, is the only medical referral center that houses federal female offenders. The Paris Lamb Treatment Center is the only licensed skilled nursing facility for the more than 11,000 women incarcerated in California; because it is small, there is regularly a waiting list (Chandler 2003).

Prison health care has evolved over the period of increased incarceration, medical advances, and managed care. Changes are apparent, but their implications are not always clear. For example, the increasing use of telemedicine, providing medical consultation via telephone or computer, may or may not be more useful for women who are less computer-savvy and enjoy human contact. Another emerging trend in prison health care is the system of co-payments. As they are in the community, co-pays in prison are relatively low (usually between \$2 and \$5), but even a small sum can be enough to prevent a poorer inmate from seeking help in a timely fashion. Although the co-pay does not usually apply to emergencies, it may become substantial for inmates with chronic conditions such as sickle cell anemia who need frequent medical visits ("Suit Challenges Women's Health Care in Prisons" 1995). These trends have yet to be evaluated for their impact on women.

Some critics argue that prisoners already have better health care than uninsured individuals in the community and that criminals should suffer retribution for their crimes and lose their rights to care. Although few would argue that prisoners should be medically neglected, prison health care is easy to ignore, and there have been few public outcries about the conditions of prison health care. Despite this relative lack of interest, some prisons have come under fire for failure to refer seriously ill inmates for treatment, delays in treatment, lack of qualified personnel and resources, use of nonmedical staff to provide health care, and lack of health care resources (Amnesty International 1999). For some prisoners, the prescription for good health care has been a good attorney.

Litigation on Prison Health Care

Since there is little public or political support for quality mental or physical health care for inmates, prisoners have turned to the courts for protection of their rights to treatment (Center for Public Representation 1999). Class action suits have resulted in more oversight and a broader awareness of the need for better access to health care, regular medical screenings, a system of reporting and follow-up on lab work, and adequate and systematic medical records.

The case that set the constitutional benchmark for prisoners' claims to health services, however, was *Estelle v. Gamble* (429 US 97). W. J. Estelle Jr. was the director of the Texas Department of Corrections in the 1970s when J. W. Gamble injured his back during a work assignment; Gamble claimed that he was not given adequate treatment. In a decision written by Justice Thurgood Marshall, the Supreme Court held that the Eighth Amendment's prohibition against cruel and unusual punishment endowed all inmates with a right to medical care. Specifically, the court ruled that prison officials must not exhibit "deliberate indifference to the serious medical needs" of inmates.

These standards can be subjective and confusing, however. In the case of "deliberate indifference," prison officials must do more than show poor judgment, negligence, or even gross negligence. The inmate must prove that the official was reckless in the criminal sense; in other words, the inmate must show that the official had actual knowledge of the condition or of the known risk but did not act appropriately. For example, an official who knowingly denied an asthmatic inmate her inhaler during an attack could be accused of deliberate indifference.

But in recent decisions on HIV cases, circuit courts (the regional federal appellate courts directly below the Supreme Court) with similar cases of a combination drug treatment for HIV/AIDS have come up with drastically different results. In one case, the court held that by denying the full combination of HIV drugs, the jail was guilty of deliberate indifference to the inmate's medical needs. By contrast, when another inmate challenged his HIV treatment that consisted of only two of the three recommended drugs, the court held that denial of one component of combination therapy was simply a "disagreement" about appropriate treatment.

The cases that have tested the standards of "serious medical need" have also yielded inconsistent results. Generally, prisoners have a right to treatment if a physician or other health care provider "concludes with reasonable medical certainty" (1) that the prisoner's symptoms evidence a serious disease or injury, (2) that such disease or injury is curable or may be substantially alleviated, and (3) that the potential for harm to the prisoner by reason of delay or the denial of care would be substantial. Serious medical needs that must be addressed do not have to be life-threatening and may even be elective, but length of sentence is considered in the decision to provide care. Clearly, both "deliberate indifference" and "serious medical need" are difficult requirements to operationalize.

Three basic rights have emerged from litigation, however (Anno 2001). The *right to access to care* includes routine and emergency care and specialty care, when warranted. The *right to the care that is ordered* requires prisons to provide the physician-requested treatment within the specified amount of time. Finally, the *right to a professional medical judgment* ensures that medical personnel make medical decisions based on medical reasons, in appropriate locations, and with proper equipment. In addition to basic rights, requirements for a quality and constitutional prison health care system have also been elaborated; Box 5.1 has details.

Filing a lawsuit for any reason, however, has become significantly more difficult since President William J. Clinton signed the Prison Litigation Reform Act in 1996. The act increased filing fees, limited the ability to file multiple suits, and narrowed the definition of "prospective relief" (remedies designed to rectify unconstitutional conditions). The end result will limit an individual prisoner's ability to litigate many issues, including those concerning health care, although it will eliminate, at least in theory, trivial and unnecessary lawsuits.

Despite the best intentions, prison health care is still largely uncoordinated and underfunded, with relatively little accountability. This is remarkable considering the fact that most women will leave prison and return to their homes and families. Without medical care and health education provided in prison, they may return in worse physical health than when they left. This is also true of mental health and mental health care.

Box 5.1   Components of a Constitutional Prison Health Care System

1. A communications and sick call system: depending on the facility, prisoners should have an opportunity to communicate their health care needs to trained professionals in a timely manner.
2. A priority system: if a prison cannot meet all of a patient's demands for health care, relieving pain and restoring functioning should become priorities.
3. Personnel: prisons should provide adequate trained staff to meet the needs of the prison population.
4. Contracting out: a prison is responsible for ensuring that those components of its health care system that are contracted out to private companies meet the Eighth Amendment standard.
5. Medical records: there should be a separate medical record for each inmate.
6. "Outside care": care that is not available onsite must be found if it is required for a patient. Medical determinations override cost and transportation concerns.
7. Facilities and resources: space and supplies should be adequate to meet the health care needs of the population.
8. Quality assurance, accreditation, and compliance with standards: prisons should undergo both internal and external reviews to ensure that the health care delivery system follows standards set by national organizations.

Source: Anno, B. J. 2001. *Correctional Health Care. Guidelines for the Management of an Adequate Delivery System.* Washington, DC: National Commission on Correctional Health Care and the US Department of Justice, National Institute of Corrections.

■ Mental Health

In the words of the Harvard Medical School psychiatrist and expert witness Stuart Grassian (Center for Public Representation 1999, 1), "I've seen people who are horribly ill, eating their own feces, eating parts of their body, howling day and night and it's ignored, like 'who cares?' You think it belongs to some other century, but you go into the prison and you think you're back in some medieval torture chamber. The prison has become this place that's hidden and secret and it's really awful."

Although the above quote may or may not overstate conditions in women's prisons, there is no question that prisons have become the repository for the nation's mentally ill. It is estimated that prisoners have mental health problems at five times the rate of the general population (Kupers 1999) and that female inmates have more symptoms than males (National Commission on Correctional Health Care 2002).

One difficulty in dealing with mental health issues is the fact mental illnesses are less easily recognized and defined than physical disorders (Mechanic 1999), which usually have an obvious symptom such as a fever or a broken bone. Despite the existence of the *Diagnostic and Statistical Manual of Mental Disorders*, which presents diagnostic criteria for mental illnesses, there are still many contrasting and conflicting views of mental disorders.[4] These inconsistencies partially explain the difficulty in recognizing and treating mental illness in the community and, more importantly here, in prison.

In general, a mental illness is recognized as behavior that is bizarre, irrational, or unusually distressful; the behavior makes no sense to an observer (Mechanic 1999). According to the *DSM-IV*, the definition of a mental disorder is

> a clinically significant behavioral or psychological syndrome or pattern that occurs in an individual and that is associated with present distress (a painful symptom) or disability (impairment in one or more important areas of functioning) or with a significantly increased risk of suffering, death, pain or disability. In addition, this syndrome or pattern must not be merely an expectable and culturally sanctioned response to a particular event, e.g., the death of a loved one. Whatever its original causes, it must currently be considered a manifestation of a behavioral, psychological or biological dysfunction in the individual. Neither deviant behavior, e.g., political, religious, or sexual, nor conflicts that are primarily between the individual and society are mental disorders unless the deviance or conflict is a symptom of a dysfunction in the individual, as described above. (American Psychiatric Association 1994)

Because mental illness is recognized by evaluating behavior, cultural differences become apparent; for example, minority groups and women manifest different types of mental disorders than do whites and men. Looking at the high rates of mental illness, the common disorders, and available treatment for women in prison reveals a striking picture of problems unaddressed by communities and unsolved by prisons.

Rates of Mental Illness for Women in Prison

Estimates of the rates of mental illness among the female prison population vary, largely due to differences in definitions of mental illness, sampling strategies, and measurement. Box 5.2 includes survey items used to measure mental illness. These questions rely exclusively on inmate self-report and prior contact with a mental health professional. Therefore, we do not have in-

---

Box 5.2   Survey Items Used to Measure Mental Illness

Do you have a mental or emotional condition? *(prison and jail inmates only)*

Have you ever been told by a mental health professional such as a psychiatrist, psychologist, social worker, or psychiatric nurse, that you had a mental or emotional disorder? *(probationers only)*

Because of an emotional or mental problem, have you ever—
  Taken a medication prescribed by a psychiatrist or other doctor?
  Been admitted to a mental hospital, unit or treatment program where you stayed overnight?
  Received counseling or therapy from a trained professional?
  Received any other mental health services?

Source: Paula M. Ditton. 1999. *Mental Health and Treatment of Inmates and Probationers.* Washington, DC: Bureau of Justice Statistics (NCJ 174463).

---

formation from professionals trained in recognizing and diagnosing problems of this population of women.

One study reported that 40 percent of incarcerated women in California had a diagnosable disorder (American Correctional Association 1998). According to another study, 64 percent of women in jail who responded to a symptom inventory were in the clinical range for mental health problems (Singer et al. 1995); another suggested that as many as two-thirds of women in prison required mental health services after their incarceration (James et al. 1985).

Despite variations in estimates of actual mental health conditions, most studies agree that women in prison have much higher rates of certain mental health problems, more co-occurring disorders (the co-occurrence of a psychiatric disorder and a substance abuse problem), and more substance abuse problems than men in prison (Anderson, Rosay, and Saum, 2002; Kerr 1998). For example, nearly 24 percent of female state prison and local jail inmates were identified as mentally ill, compared to 16 percent of a comparable male population. In addition, women's mental health problems and treatment are complicated by their histories of physical and sexual abuse.

Common Disorders Among Female Prisoners

Depression, more common in women than men generally, is among the most common disorders for incarcerated women. In one study (Martin and Cotton 1995) of inmates in the North Carolina Correctional Institution for Women, researchers found that 70 percent of the women surveyed had enough symptoms on the widely used Center for Epidemiologic Studies Depression Scale (CES-D) to be diagnosed as clinically depressed. This percentage contrasts starkly with the 20–30 percent of adult women found clinically depressed with this instrument in community samples. The relationship between antisocial behavior and depression may show up early; Dawn Obeidallah and Felton Earls (1999) reported that depressed girls were more likely to engage in antisocial behavior (behavior that is contrary to the normative standards of society, such as breaking laws, lying, being impulsive, lacking remorse, ignoring safety) than girls who were not depressed.

Another disorder found more often in women in prison than in women in the community is post-traumatic stress disorder (Kupers 1999). This disorder is most common among people who experience or witness a traumatic event; symptoms may include recurring thoughts of the event; drug and/or alcohol abuse; family problems; and feelings of worthlessness, uneasiness, frustration, anger, guilt, shame, anxiety, and/or depression. Physical and sexual abuse during one's early years is probably the most common trigger for this disorder, as roughly 80 percent of female inmates with mental health problems reported physical or sexual abuse (Ditton 1999). Untreated trauma can have severe long-term psychological and behavioral repercussions, including a return to previous abusive relationships after release. There is too little time and there are too few professionals, however, to allow an abused woman to deal with her traumatic memories in a therapeutic setting (Kupers 1999).

Explanations for the High Rates of Mental Illness in Prison

There are several reasons that mental health problems and mental illnesses are so common in prison, especially among women. Some are present upon entry. The most common mental health problems for women in prison are also the most common disorders for women in the community. For many women, these mental health problems are both caused and exaggerated by substance abuse and prior exposure to violence, poverty, racism, and sexism. For some women, behaviors resulting from their mental illness were responsible for the incarceration.

Worsening mental health problems may be a response to imprisonment itself. Existing problems continue and may become complicated by confinement, separation from family and support systems, overcrowding, fear of victimization, boredom, and lack of access to mental health services (AACP 1999). Those women who might have managed to cope with life's circumstances in the community, supported by friends and family, may fall apart under the stress of prison life. An additional problem of prison life for women is sexual harassment and sometimes outright abuse by guards; women are touched inappropriately during searches, watched while they shower, and, in some cases, raped (Amnesty International 1999). This is hard to bear for anyone, but a woman who endured earlier abuse and resulting emotional problems may find the combination of past and present hardships impossible to shoulder.

According to the Sentencing Project (2002), much of the increase in mental illness in prison can be traced to governmental policy. In the early part of the twentieth century, mentally ill individuals were institutionalized in large mental hospitals. As new treatments were discovered, the views of mental illness reconceptualized, and hospitals criticized as "warehouses," the deinstitutionalization movement began, and large numbers of the hospitalized mentally ill returned to the community. The intentions behind deinstitutionalization were noble; many people had been locked up for years with little hope of release or quality treatment. Policymakers assumed that improved psychotropic medications and available community mental health center support would allow released patients to live independently. However, inadequate funding for treatment facilities, neighborhood reluctance to establish group homes for those who needed transitional support (the "not in my backyard syndrome," or NIMBY), and the greater than anticipated needs of ex-patients resulted in the transfer of many who were unprepared for life in the community. At the same time that community needs for mental health care increased, government spending to meet those needs slowed (Sentencing Project 2002; US DHHS 1999).

Spending for mental health services accounted for only about 7.6 percent of total health care expenditures in 2001 and has been declining as a proportion of overall health spending (SAMHSA 2005). Funding affects treatment, and without proper treatment, people with mental illness may exhibit behaviors ranging from disorderly conduct to prostitution to assault that can bring them to the attention of the criminal justice system. As spending for community mental health systems eroded, the number of mentally ill in the judicial system increased (American Psychiatric Association 2004), and deinstitutionalization became "transinstitutionalization" for many patients who left mental hospitals to eventually enter prisons.

The case of Felicia Jennings, thirty-five, exemplifies the dilemma. Felicia, who had been diagnosed with schizophrenia and borderline personality and committed twice for mental health care, was charged with two counts each of involuntary manslaughter, child endangering, and abuse of a corpse for disposing of her newborn twin sons in the trash. She pleaded innocent by reason of insanity (see Box 5.3), but her mental evaluation showed she was fit enough to assist her lawyers. Jennings told police that the boys died in her bed four days after she delivered them at home, three months premature, and that she packed their corpses in a plastic bag for trash pickup. She was apparently not taking her medication at the time she gave birth to the twins.

Box 5.3   "Insanity" Is a Legal Term

"Insanity" is a legal term, not a psychiatric term. Although the definition of insanity varies from state to state, the essence of an insanity defense is similar: when an individual committed the crime, she could not tell right from wrong or could not control her behavior because of severe mental defect or illness. This person would not be held legally responsible for her behavior.

The insanity plea is rarely used; a 1991 study by the National Institute of Mental Health reported that it was employed in less than 1 percent of cases before the sampled states' courts. Of those pleas, only 26 percent were successfully argued (American Psychiatric Association 2003).

One famous case illustrating this concept is Andrea Yates, a thirty-seven-year old Texas woman. After drowning her five young children in the bathtub, she called 911. When authorities came to the crime scene, they found four children on the bed; one was still in the tub. She explained to the authorities that she wanted to save them from eternal damnation and that she believed she was not a good mother. She pleaded not guilty by reason of insanity. Despite a previous diagnosis of postpartum depression, psychiatric hospitalizations, and two previous suicide attempts, the jury found her guilty and rejected her claim of insanity. She was sentenced to life in prison, but in 2005 her sentence was overturned because of erroneous testimony during the trial. She is unlikely to be released from psychiatric custody.

Source: American Psychiatric Association. 2003. *Public Information: The Insanity Defense.* Washington, DC: American Psychiatric Association.

■ "Let 'em Eat Skittles": Mental Health Treatment

We know much less about mental health treatment in prisons than about physical health treatment. According to the Department of Justice (Beck and Maruschak 2001), as of June 2000, nearly 70 percent of state prisons reported mental health screening for all inmates at intake, 65 percent conducted psychiatric assessments, 51 percent provided twenty-four-hour mental health care, 71 percent provided counseling by trained professionals, 73 percent provided psychotropic medications (drugs for mental illness) to their inmates, and 66 percent helped released inmates obtain community mental health services. Despite these relatively impressive assessment and treatment rates, mental health needs still go largely unmet in correctional facilities. Women are more likely to receive therapy or counseling (27 percent for females, 12 percent for males) but equally likely to be in twenty-four-hour mental health care (the rate for both females and males is about 1.5 percent) than men (Beck and Maruschak 2001).

Mental health interventions in prisons are only truly successful if a woman can function in the community when she is released. This usually requires follow-up treatments after a prisoner returns home. Health gains can be maintained only with continued services, a supportive environment, and a woman highly motivated to adhere to treatment. Social support is required both before and after women leave prison (Jacoby and Kozie-Peak 1997). These prerequisites require a tremendous coordination of communication and services between the prison and the community and are rarely available.

Payment for services is also a problem. Poor inmates must reapply for Medicaid after leaving prison before they can receive services. Most mental health funding is currently provided at the state and local levels, with Medicaid, the state-run health insurance program for the poor and disabled, accounting for 50 percent of that funding (Buck 2001). Without Medicaid or some source of payment for treatment, most prisoners released into the community are unlikely to access the services that do exist.

Psychotropic Medication as Treatment for Mental Illness

Drug treatment is the most prevalent form of therapy for women with mental health problems. Drugs are relatively easy-to-use and cheap forms of treatment for mental illness, making them more attractive than individual treatment. Many consider the use of psychotropic medication (known as "skittles" to the prisoners themselves) the key to efficient and cost-effective mental health treatment (Baillargeon and Contreras 2001); others see the widespread use of drugs as a simple way to control the prison population.

The biggest female-male treatment gap (22 percent for women, 9 percent for men) is in the use of psychotropic medications, drugs such as antidepressants, stimulants, sedatives, and tranquilizers. It is estimated that in some prisons 80 percent of women receive drugs on a daily basis to make them more manageable (Burkhart 1973). Women who have been convicted of a violent crime (controlling for institutional infractions and prior psychiatric history) are twice as likely to receive psychotropic medications as men (Auerhahn and Leonard 2000; Baskin et al. 1989), and a sentence for a violent crime is a better predictor of receiving mental health services for women than their levels of depression (Steadman, Holohean, and Dvoskin 1991). Some theorize that women's higher medication rates can be explained by the tendency to "psychiatrize" women's role-incongruent behaviors (Auerhahn and Leonard

2000). In other words, women are not expected to be violent, so when they are, they contradict the norms of society and are consequently "controlled" with psychiatric medication. If criminality in women is not normal, then it must be a mental health problem.

Amnesty International (1999) expressed concerns about the overuse of psychotropic medications for women in prison. Its report concluded that women were given these drugs because other mental health treatments were unavailable or because the women needed help coping with the stress of imprisonment. One woman shook so badly after heavy doses of medication that she could hardly speak to the attorney during her interview.

Mental Health Guidelines for Prisons

Some prisons specialize in psychiatric confinement (BJS 2000), but most mental health care is provided by personnel available on or off site (Young and Reviere 2001). Prisons have guidelines for mental health screening and assessment upon intake, but that does not mean that the complete needs of an individual inmate with a serious mental illness will be met. Psychiatrists are often responsible for too many patients with too little funding (AACP 1999), and prisons without a mental health focus usually cannot provide specialized housing for prisoners with stable mental illness (National Commission on Correctional Health Care 2002).

The courts have established a clear set of minimum requirements for the provision of mental health care for all prisons. The guidelines require that prisons provide (1) screening and evaluation, (2) a range of meaningful treatment modalities, (3) qualified mental health staff, (4) special needs units and inpatient hospitalization, (5) accurate mental health records, (6) discharge planning, and (7) quality assurance. These are broad mandates and are only as effective as their implementation for and application to individual prisoners.

■ Conclusion

Quality physical and mental health care and appropriate health education can save lives and dollars, both in and out of prison. For example, testing and treatment for common sexually transmitted diseases is a simple and reasonable safeguard; this is especially true for HIV-infected women. Health promotion and health education should be the cornerstone of every prison medical program.

The need for trained staff, with expertise in women's problems, is vital. There are many issues—the prisoner's cultural background, race, and age and the effects of sexual and physical violence—that staff should consider. The importance of mutual trust, understanding, and clear communication cannot be overstated in health encounters.

Notes

1. The World Health Organization is the agency for health of the United Nations.

2. Health can be measured many ways: number of chronic conditions, number of acute conditions, number of disabilities, information from medical records, visits to medical facilities during a particular time period, or self-rated health, which is how an individual rates her own health (usually excellent, very good, good, fair, poor).

3. The Americans with Disabilities Act (ADA) is a federal civil rights law that gives protection to persons with disabilities similar to those provided to individuals on the basis of race, color, sex, national origin, age, and religion. In prisons, for example, this act requires that 5 percent of cells in new prisons be accessible for persons with mobility restrictions.

4. *The Diagnostic and Statistical Manual of Mental Disorders (Fourth Edition)*, *DSM-IV*, was published by the American Psychiatric Association in 1994. It is accepted as the common language of mental health clinicians and researchers in the United States. Psychiatrists are physicians who treat mental illness; therefore, the *DSM* is primarily important to diagnosis. Proper diagnosis leads, logically, to proper treatment. There is a risk, however, in using this diagnostic information to make legal judgments because of the imperfect fit between questions relevant to the law and the information contained in a clinical diagnosis (American Psychiatric Association 1994).

Women and
Children First

6

The life circumstances and needs of families affected by maternal incarceration cannot be adequately understood without attending to the impact of race, class, and gender oppression. (Young and Smith 2000, 132)

The impact of the increase in the number of inmates in prison extends far beyond the correctional institution and its population because incarceration affects not only those who are incarcerated but also their children; other members of their families, especially caregivers; and the community. Paula Dressel, Jeff Porterfield, and Sandra Barnhill (1998, 90) stressed that the hidden costs of incarceration reach across generations, beyond the courts and the correctional system to a number of other social institutions.

The majority of the female prisoners are also mothers. Because mothers are far more likely to be the primary caregivers of children than fathers, the devastating impact of the increase in the number of women who are incarcerated is far-reaching. According to Roberta Richmond, warden at the Rhode Island Women's Prison, "When you lock a man up, the family unit usually stays intact. When you lock a woman up, you're destroying families (Gaouette 1997, 5)."

Estimates are that anywhere from two-thirds to four-fifths of the women behind bars are mothers and that most of these women have children under age eighteen (Women's Prison Association [WPA] 1995; Greene, Haney, and Hurtado 2000; Kauffman 2001). Allen Beck (2000) added that most of the children of incarcerated women were under age ten, with an average age of eight. Additionally, the reports indicate that the women generally had an average of two to three children each. In 1995, the WPA (1995) estimated that incarcerated women were mothers responsible for an estimated 165,000 children, usually between seven and twelve years of age.

Since 1998, the female prison population has increased, and with the increase in the number of female prisoners, we also have an increase in the number of children whose parents are incarcerated. At end of 2003, there were 101,179 women in state and federal prisons (Harrison and Beck 2004). We estimate that there are now more than 300,000 minor children with mothers in prison or jail. This pattern is expected to continue unless and until we alter our approach to incarceration. The Women's Prison Association (2003) projects that if current rates persist, by 2013 there will be over 850,000 children with mothers (350,000) returning from prison.

Tracy Snell (1994) reported that according to a 1991 survey of state prisons, 6 percent of women entering state prisons were pregnant. More recent reports estimated that one in twelve female inmates, or approximately 8 percent of all female inmates were pregnant at the time of admission (Kauffman 2001). It is expected that as the number of female inmates increases, the number of pregnant inmates will also increase. C. Ingram-Fogel (1991) presented an even more telling picture, noting that 25 percent of women admitted to prison were pregnant or had recently delivered a child. This percentage adds to the number of children of concern and changes the nature of the programs required to provide support for incarcerated mothers and their children.

As noted in Chapter 3, the number and characteristics of women in prison have changed dramatically. Prisoners are older, more likely to be substance abusers, and more likely to be a member of a minority. The number of Hispanic women prisoners has increased significantly. They are also poor, unemployed at the time of arrest, and undereducated, with many (more than 40 percent) having less than a high school diploma (Wright and Seymour 2000). There are also differences between black and white women prisoners with respect to family relationships, education, and employment. Black women prisoners were more likely to come from female-headed households, have lower educational achievements, and have lower-paying jobs than white women prisoners (Bresler and Lewis 1984). Data from the 1997 survey of prisons indicate that these differences have been consistent over time (see Chapter 3).

Moreover, the children of incarcerated women reflect the differential demographic profiles of their parents. Black children were nine times more likely to have an incarcerated parent than white children (Krisberg and Temin 2001). Black children represented 43 percent of children of incarcerated mothers in 1992, 52 percent of whom were female children (Bloom and Steinhart 1993).

In 1995 the WPA found that prior to their incarceration, many women were supporting their families on less than $500 a month. Four years later, the Bureau of Justice Statistics survey (1999b) of women under correctional supervision indicated that less than 40 percent of women in state prisons had been employed full-time and that about 35 percent were living on less than $600 per month. Since 1999 the cost of living has increased, but it is doubtful, given the recent educational and employment profile of female prisoners, that there have been comparable increases in their average family income level. In fact, according to Aid to Inmate Mothers (AIM), 80 percent of incarcerated women reported that they made less than $2,000 in the year prior to their arrest.

The number of women in prison has risen sharply. Accordingly, the number of children, in particular underage children who are without their mothers as a result of incarceration, has also increased. These families were disadvantaged before incarceration and move further into the margin upon reentry. In this chapter we discuss the Adoption and Safe Families Act of 1997 and the impact of the incarceration of women with children on the mother, the children, and the caregivers.

■ The Adoption and Safe Families Act of 1997

In 1997 Congress passed the Adoption and Safe Families Act (ASFA). In a review of child welfare policy, Peter Schneider (2002) noted that ASFA was a departure from the 1980 Adoption Assistance and Child Welfare Act (AACWA). The earlier legislation aimed to discourage states from removing children from their homes unnecessarily and required states to make reasonable efforts to reunify children with their families. According to Schneider (2002, 59) the ASFA was a shift

> away from family preservation and reunification. ASFA made children's safety the paramount consideration in determining whether or not removal is necessary. ASFA set forth a list of circumstances in which states need not work toward reunification. Even more significantly, ASFA placed strict time frames on reunification efforts and encouraged states to terminate parental rights in most cases where reunification efforts are not successful with the specified time frames.

Philip Gentry (1995) reported that more than twenty-five states had termination of parental rights statutes or adoption statutes that were specific to incarcerated parents. For example, by statute, the Alabama court was allowed to consider the termination of parental rights for parents who were convicted of and imprisoned for a felony and who were convicted of the murder or voluntary manslaughter of another child of that parent (Alabama Code, Section 26-18-7). The court could also consider the conviction of the parent for felony assault or abuse resulting in serious bodily injury of the surviving child or another child of that parent as grounds for the termination of parental rights.

At the federal level, ASFA makes it increasingly likely that women will lose their parental rights entirely as a consequence of serving long prison terms (Acoca and Raeder 1999). ASFA places limits on the length of time that children can be in foster care before a parental petition is filed. The legislation requires that a plan for permanency be initiated within twelve months of placement in foster care. Reports indicate that over 10 percent of all children in the United States are placed in foster care. Children are placed in or remain longer in foster care because their mothers cannot afford housing.

Under ASFA, an incarcerated parent who has not had contact with his or her child for six months can be charged with "abandonment," and steps to terminate parental rights can be taken. The act further requires states to initiate or join termination of parental rights proceedings for children who have been in foster care for fifteen of the most recent twenty-two months.[1] In certain cases, states were required to initiate such proceedings "upon placement" (i.e., when the parent committed murder, involuntary manslaughter, or felony assault resulting in serious bodily injury of a sibling). Exceptions to this requirement include (1) that at the option of the state, a relative cares for the child, (2) the state agency has documented that there is a compelling reason that filing a termination petition is not in the best interest of the child, and (3) the state has not delivered services it deems necessary for the child's safe return in cases where reunification efforts are required. The legislation also allows the state to identify, recruit, process, and approve a qualified family for an adoption unless the child is being cared for by a relative (Acoca and Raeder 1999).

Federal legislation such as ASFA provides guidelines for states to follow to ensure, among other things, eligibility for federal funds and comparability with federal information systems. They should be viewed as minimum guidelines that states take under advisement. They do not prohibit states from developing their own, more jurisdiction-appropriate practices and policies. Schneider (2002) examined state policies pertaining to the use of incarceration as a ground for the termination of parental rights. For example, Ohio, Arizona, Iowa, and Michigan were included among the states in which incarceration serves as a per se ground for termination, whereas Pennsylvania and Oklahoma consider incarceration as a contributing factor to termination of parental rights. These states include as contributing factors the duration of incarceration, prior criminal history, age of the child, evidence of abuse or neglect, failure to perform parental duties, current relationship between parent and child, and the best interests of the child. Schneider (2002) also reported that Vermont and Georgia are among the states in which conviction of a serious crime is sufficient grounds for termination of parental rights.

The maintenance of the bond between the child and the incarcerated parent has become an important factor in planning and programming by state departments of corrections and other agencies responsible for addressing the needs of children. In the remainder of this chapter, we address preprison child care; the impact of incarceration on the parent, the child, and the caregiver; and the programs that have been introduced in female prisons to support the maintenance of positive parent-child relationships.

■ Preprison Child Care

The demographic profile of the female prisoner indicates that many are parents, and a smaller but significant number are single heads of households. Christopher Mumola (2000) found that prior to their incarceration, 40 percent of incarcerated mothers had relinquished responsibility for their children to others. Whether that was due to their involvement in criminal activities or other life conditions is not clear. It is important to recognize that for this group of children, child care arrangements will remain relatively stable.

Even so, studies support the view that women in prison are far more likely to have been solely responsible for the care and maintenance of their families than are men in prison. Carolyn Temin (2001) reported that 90 percent of incarcerated fathers said that children lived with their mothers, whereas only 28 percent of incarcerated mothers said fathers were the primary caregivers. Both Nancy Schafer and A. B. Dellinger (1999) and Mumola (2000) reported that children were more likely to live with their mother (60 percent) prior to incarceration than with their father (40 percent).

It is the children whose mother had sole responsibility for them prior to her incarceration that are in need of immediate alternative placements. According to the 1997 Survey of Inmates in Adult State and Federal Correctional Facilities (BJS 2000), 47 percent of incarcerated women were never married. This means that the remainder, 53 percent, were either married (17 percent) or divorced, separated, or widowed (36 percent). There are any number of questions that arise if the woman was married and living with her husband prior to her incarceration: Will the children remain with the father? Will the paternal grandmother take over child care responsibilities? Will the maternal grandmother care for the children? Will some other "woman" take over caregiver responsibilities? Each of these questions provokes very real concerns. The Center for Children of Incarcerated Parents (CCIP) suggests that a significant but unknown number of children will have both parents incarcerated, simultaneously. If this is the case, all of the other questions become more urgent. There may be a significant period of time during which the children are placed in temporary custody, until officials can investigate both the maternal and paternal family background to determine if appropriate family placement if possible.

Having some other "woman" who is not a family member (someone involved with the children's father) caring for the children may be the most problematic for the incarcerated mother. This same outcome may come into play if the woman was divorced or separated from her husband prior to her incarceration. In either case, the incarcerated mother has no control over the situation and may have little, if any, knowledge of the sensibilities and priorities of the other "woman" with respect to her children. If the woman was widowed, it is possible that another set of factors may come into play, namely conflict between the paternal and maternal families. This uncertainty and the possible responses of the specific caregivers only compound the distress that incarcerated mothers feel.

Laura Bresler and Diane Lewis (1984) reported that preprison child care differed by race, with black women more likely than white women to have had their children living with them prior to arrest. In addition, a significant proportion of black women actually lived with family members, most often their mothers, prior to their arrest. These preprison living situations tend to influence the living situations of children once their mothers are incarcerated because child welfare workers are reluctant to disrupt healthy living situations. In this case, the mother has determined by default who will look after her children, which should help to alleviate some of the anxiety resulting from her incarceration.

The preprison living situation of the children of incarcerated mothers is one in which the mother was most likely the sole caregiver. In addition, these caregivers were generally reported to be undereducated and unemployed. Estimates are that these children live in households with incomes that are at or below the poverty level (CCIP 2001), which presents a very precarious situation for their continued care. It is also probably the case that the mother's family and peers, those who would look after her children, are in a very similar living situation. They are likely to be overextended and lacking the resources necessary to care for additions to their household. This situation further limits her options in choosing a substitute caregiver. Furthermore, the unstable nature of the home life of these children entails addressing their immediate need for housing, financial support, and education maintenance.

■ Who Cares for the Children?

There are a number of factors that determine who will take care of the children of incarcerated mothers (Kiser 1991). They include the age of the children, the number of children in the family, and the willingness of potential caregivers to take on the responsibility of caring for the children. The wishes of the mother may also influence who will be given the responsibility of caring for her children. The mother's wishes are likely to be taken into account when the possible sentence is short and when a prior caretaking relationship exists between the children and other family members. Mothers are likely to consider who will nurture and care for their children, who will allow them to maintain contact with their children during their incarceration, and who is more likely to support the return of their children upon their release (Kiser 1991). In addition, consideration will also be given to who shares their values and parenting styles. However, even before these factors are taken into account, the parental rights of the birth father(s) will have to be considered. If their parental rights have not been terminated, they can ask for their children. The possibility of placing the child(ren) with the birth father has to be assessed in light of all the factors introduced above.

As indicated earlier, mothers are more likely than fathers to have custody of their children prior to incarceration (Temin 2001). When fathers are incarcerated, their children are likely to be cared for by their biological mothers over 80 percent of the time (Phillips and Harm 1997). When mothers are incarcerated, however, fathers are much less likely to care for minor children. Rather, minor children are most likely to be cared for by maternal grandparents (Belknap 2000; Bloom and Steinhart 1993; Schafer and Dellinger 1999). Minor children were also cared for by older siblings, other relatives, neighbors, the church family, and the foster care system. Barry Krisberg and Carolyn Temin (2001) noted that the children of incarcerated women are five times more likely to be placed in the foster care system than children of incarcerated fathers. A consequence of foster-care placement in some states is that after one year, the state is authorized to initiate the termination of parental rights (Moses 1995).

The literature suggests that the maternal grandparent is the most likely caregiver (Phillips and Harm 1997; Bloom and Steinhart 1993). In a survey of 439 mothers in jails and prisons in eight states and the District of Columbia, Barbara Bloom and D. Steinhart (1993) found that the minor children of incarcerated women were most likely to live with grandparents (46.6 percent), followed by other relatives (18.5 percent) and fathers (17.4 percent). Similarly, according to the 1991 national survey of state prison inmates, 50.6 percent of children of incarcerated mothers lived with grandparents, 25.4 percent with their fathers, and 20.3 percent with other relatives (Snell 1994). Sandra Barnhill (1996) reported that grandmothers are the most likely of the grandparents to act as parents and that upward of 75,000 grandmothers would be caring for the children of imprisoned mothers by the turn of the twenty-first century. We do not have reliable numbers available to examine the accuracy of this projection. However, the fact that the number of incarcerated women has increased and that the rate of increase has changed lends support to Barnhill's projection.

Placements of children with relatives vary by race and ethnicity. Researchers report that the children of women of color are more likely than those of white women to be placed with grandparents and other relatives (Enos 1998; Young and Smith 2000). The children of white women, however, were more likely than those of African American women to be placed in foster care and with their fathers (Enos 1998). A factor that may present some very real challenges is the finding that many fathers and mothers in prison have had children with more than one partner (Hairston 1995). There has been little research on this aspect of continuity in parenting, but in the case of incarcerated mothers, in particular white women, it may prove to be especially problematic. Recall that the research indicates that the children of white women are more likely to be placed with their fathers than the children of women of color. If this is the case and there are multiple fathers, it becomes even more difficult for mothers to maintain contact with their children and just as difficult for children to maintain contact with each other.

Denise Johnston (2001) indicated that her preliminary findings demonstrate increased parental rights terminations since the passage of the Adoption and Safe Families Act of 1997. Furthermore, C. Finney Hairston (2002) noted that few prisoners are able to meet the requirements of the law because their stay in prison exceeds the fifteen months that is the time period in which termination procedures are required to begin. Additional research is needed to determine if this legislation is promoting safe and stable families.

Although some caregivers had shared responsibility for the children prior to the incarceration of the mother, a number of new challenges face them. First, Paula Dressel, Jeff Porterfield, and Sandra Barnhill (1998) noted that family members frequently share the economic marginalization of imprisoned mothers. Additional child care responsibilities present these new caregivers with additional financial concerns. Second, family members must also oversee the medical care and treatment and the educational well-being of the children. If these caregivers are employed, these additional child care responsibilities could place their jobs in jeopardy. If they are unemployed, these additional child care responsibilities require resources that may be in short supply. Third, D. D. Petras (1999) and C. Finney Hairston (2002) noted that many of the grandparent caregivers are elderly and have health problems. These existing conditions make it more difficult for them to tend to new child care responsibilities.

Recent studies have examined the impact of child care on these "unlikely" parent figures. Barnhill (1996) reported that according to Aid to Children of Imprisoned Mothers (AIM),[2] grandmother caregivers needed access to the means-tested social welfare system for public assistance and emergency aid, help with understanding the legal system holding their daughters, and help in interacting with the educational system that engaged their grandchildren. Even though more children of incarcerated parents are cared for by grandparents than by other relatives, in a number of states foster parents are paid higher public assistance benefits than relatives of the children (Dressel, Porterfield, Barnhill 1998). Furthermore, Bloom and Steinhart (1993) reported that laws in some states prohibited foster care payments to the relatives of incarcerated parents. Hairston (2002) added that even if grandparents are eligible for welfare assistance, benefits generally do not cover the full cost of providing care for the children.

A review of kinship care practices and policies in thirteen counties in four states—Alabama, California, Connecticut, and Indiana—revealed that foster parents received a monthly foster care payment, as well as "health insurance for the children they care for; payment of health-related services not covered under insurance; vouchers for clothing, for school supplies, or other specific needs; and children care and respite care assistance" (Geen 2003, 3). Unfortunately, kin who were not licensed foster parents were often ineligible for the foster care payments; many were not eligible for welfare payments that were significantly less than the foster care payments (Geen 2003). This state of affairs has caused some to forgo involvement with state welfare systems, whereas others have fought to change the situation.

Recently, the US Court of Appeals for the Ninth Circuit ruled in *Rosales v. Thompson* that children in kinship foster care, like foster children placed with strangers, could receive benefits from the federally funded Title IV-E, Aid to Families with Dependent Children Foster Care Program (Ancar 2003). This court decision, though only binding on states in the Ninth Circuit (Alaska, Arizona, California, Hawaii, Idaho, Montana, Nevada, Oregon, and Washington) could have nationwide application because it addresses a federal program. Regrettably, the US Department of Health and Human Services, which administers this program, has requested that Congress overturn this ruling (Ancar 2004). The requisite changes were included in the 2005 federal budget.

Another factor that affects child care arrangements is the long-term nature of care. Because of the increase in sentence length, children stay with their caregivers for much longer periods of time, forcing caretakers to make long-range educational, medical, and maintenance plans. Dorothy Ruiz (2002) added that for some grandmothers, caregiving is permanent because many of the incarcerated mothers suffer from chronic problems such as HIV/AIDS, drug addiction, and depression. These problems will necessitate long-term care and treatment, which will make it difficult for mothers to reunite with children.

Incarceration separates the incarcerated person from family and friends, which negatively affects the lives and well-being of all involved: the incarcerated parent, the children, and the caregivers. This separation leads to behavioral problems, emotional problems and stress for both mother and child, and financial, emotional, and lifestyle problems for caregivers. Each of these issues will be addressed below.

■ The Impact of Separation on the Mother

There has been considerable research on the "pains of imprisonment" and the application of the deprivation model to incarceration (Sykes 1958; Thomas and Petersen 1977). Gresham Sykes (1958) argued that prison deprives prisoners of basic needs. These deprivations include lack of autonomy, lack of heterosexual activity, lack of privacy, loss of responsibility, lack of security, and lack of emotional support (Toch 1977). The responses to deprivation include anger, frustration, despair, pressure, and strain, all of which make adjusting to the institution very difficult.

Researchers report that these deprivations differ for male and female prisoners, and that for female prisoners, the most difficult consequence of imprisonment is their separation from their children (Ward and Kassebaum 1965; Harris 1993; Jones 1993). In addition to concerns about the general well-being of their children, incarcerated mothers also risk losing custody of their children as a result of their incarceration.

The separation from their children leads to numerous problems that may affect the inmates' adjustment to the institution. Velma LaPoint (1980) reported that like other mothers who are separated from their children, incarcerated mothers also suffer from "filial deprivation," which is characterized by remoteness, emptiness, helplessness, anger, guilt, fears of loss of attachment, and rejection. These deprivations may lead to the violation of institutional rules and an increased dependence upon the provision of medical and psychological services (see Chapter 5). AIM noted that prior to incarceration, their children are the only important asset that many women have. In addition, some of the women feel that they have failed as a mother and fear reunion with their children.

One very specific concern reported by Ingram-Fogel (1991) relates to the fear of women inmates that their younger children will not know them. Recall that some women in prison have very young children. As a result of their incarceration, some mothers are away from their children at a critical stage in the child's development, leaving to others the role of nurturer. This can lead to high levels of depression, guilt, grief, and distress.

A number of studies have addressed the role that inmates' family relationships play in improving their potential for rehabilitation, in improving the mental health of inmates, in increasing the probability that families will reunite after release, and in decreasing recidivism rates (Fuller 1993; Kiser 1991, Feinman 1983). The overriding conclusion is that the separation of parent and child as a result of incarceration should be handled as carefully as possible to ensure the peaceful adjustment of the inmate to the institution, to help children adjust to the absence of their parents, and to aid in the postincarceration reunion of the inmate and her family.

■ The Impact on the Children

The mother's arrest and subsequent incarceration may lead to a series of traumatic episodes that are visited upon her children. In some instances, children are present when their mother is arrested. The Child Welfare League of America (1996–2005) reported that one in five children of incarcerated mothers witnessed their mother's arrest. They may not understand what is happening or why it is happening, but they are aware that something "terrible" has changed in their lives. If those present, including the police, neighbors, other family members, and the mother, are not sensitive to the children's need for information and support, then they aggravate an already tenuous situation.

Some children may not know of the incarceration of their mothers. If children were not present when their mother was taken into custody, other family members may be unwilling to tell young children just what has occurred. Still other children may not fully understand why their mother is absent. The age of the child and the nature of the explanation provided for the mother's absence may contribute to this lack of clarity or understanding. Nevertheless, all these children are affected by their mother's absence.

Some researchers report that the mother's incarceration has more negative effects on children than that of the father because it leads to more upheaval and change (Devine 1997; Woodrow 1992). Because the mother is likely to be the primary caretaker, her incarceration usually means that children will be placed with other relatives and possibly separated from each other. It may also mean a change of schools for many children and a loss of peer support.

It is important to keep in mind that most of these children are under age eighteen and that many are actually preteens. A number of researchers suggest that the consequences of separation differ by age, with separation likely to be more harmful for younger children (McGowan and Blumenthal 1978; Johnston 1992; Henriques 1996). Denise Johnston (1992) reported that the youngest children experience disorganized feelings and behaviors; that those who are slightly older experience maladaptive behaviors; and that older children engage in sexual misconduct, truancy, delinquency, substance abuse, and gang activity. Furthermore, Zelma Henriques (1996) noted that younger children "may not readily retain the memory of their mothers and are likely to bond with whomever is providing the child-care function." Finally, Johnston (1995) reported that parental incarceration had a different effect on children's development, depending on the age of the child. For infants, parent-child bonding was impaired, whereas for older children, reactive behaviors and acute traumatic stress resulted. All these effects may affect future reunification.

The effect of parental incarceration on a child varies according to many factors, including the length of the separation, the strength of the parent-child relationship, the length of the parent's sentence, the number and result of previous separation experiences, the circumstances of the arrest, the children's knowledge about the incarceration, the frequency of both telephone and written communication, and the number and quality of visits to the institution (Seymour 1998; Reilly and Martin 1998).

Research suggests that children of incarcerated mothers suffer emotional, psychological, physical, and behavioral problems (Krisberg and Temin 2001). Some argue that children who experience parental incarceration often experience separation trauma, trouble eating and sleeping, anxiety, guilt, anger, sadness, loneliness, shame, and fear (Moses 1995). It is important to keep in mind that many of these children have lost their support system and must adjust to a new support system, which may not always be prepared to handle their needs. In addition, many times the stigma attached to having an incarcerated parent is visited upon the child by family and friends, adults and peers. Children are often teased at school and in the neighborhood about their parent's incarceration. Other family members, in moments of stress, may declare to the child that "you are just like your mother." The child or children remain as the closest reminder of or connection to that incarcerated family member. How caregivers, family, and friends handle the reminder or connection affects the child or children left behind.

Children may suffer a decline in school performance, truancy, use of drugs or alcohol, and an increase in aggressive and antisocial acting out (Gabel 1992; Fuller 1993; Krisberg and Temin 2001; Simmons 2000). There is also the social aspect of school. Jose-Kampfner (1995) reported that children are teased at school and suffer post-traumatic stress disorder symptoms, including withdrawal, hyper-alertness, sleep disturbances, guilt, and impaired memory and concentration. They also suffer stress; withdrawal; low self-esteem; depression; feelings of sadness, abandonment, and shame; thoughts of suicide; and worry about parents (Simmons 2000; Bloom and Steinhart 1993; Dressel, Porterfield, and Barnhill 1998).

Having incarcerated parents has a number of long-term and generational consequences for children. Marilyn Moses (1995) reported that these children are more likely to become pregnant in their teens. These young mothers are unlikely to have completed high school, will have difficulty getting a job to support themselves and their child, and will be disadvantaged economically and socially.

Children whose parents are incarcerated, as compared to children whose parents are not, are also more likely to become embroiled in the criminal justice process (Gabel and Johnston 1995; Temin 2001; Bloom and Steinhart 1993; Jose-Kampfner 1991). The Center for Children of Incarcerated Parents (2001) estimated that the lifetime risk of incarceration for children whose parents are incarcerated is two to three times the average risk. Johnston (1995) suggests that the cumulative effects of behavioral problems in school, low-level school performance, depression, and withdrawal experienced by these children increase the risk of illegal activity on their part. According to Justice-Works, children whose parents are incarcerated are five times more likely to be imprisoned than other children. Others (Bloom and Steinhart 1993; Jose-Kampfner 1991) report a strong correlation between maternal incarceration and future criminal behavior and imprisonment.

A number of children of incarcerated parents are shifted among multiple caregivers (WPA 1995; Krisberg and Temin 2001). Johnston (1992) estimated that just 11 percent of the children of incarcerated parents would have at least two different caregivers while their mothers were in prison, whereas the WPA (1995, 6) reported that most children of an incarcerated mother would have at least two different caregivers.

In addition, most of the children of imprisoned mothers have siblings, and often as a result of child care arrangements, a majority of these children will live apart from their siblings (WPA 1995; Dressel, Porterfield, and Barnhill 1998). This additional separation compounds the problems of stability, bonding, and the establishment of close relationships.

Children of incarcerated mothers suffer far-reaching consequences. This separation affects behavior at home as well as at school. It affects relationships with family members and friends. It affects physical and emotional well-being. It shapes all aspects of their daily lives. Moreover, the future well-being of the child is largely determined by how this separation is handled.

The Impact on Caregivers

When the primary caregiver is incarcerated, others must make up for a serious loss of income and oversight. For many alternate caregivers, this additional responsibility poses financial, employment, and health concerns. Many grandparents live on fixed incomes or marginal employment (Young and Smith 2000). According to Ruiz (2002), many of these grandparents are also handling other child care or kinship care responsibilities. With the added responsibilities and demands of new family members, some caregivers may have trouble maintaining employment (Dressel, Porterfield, and Barnhill 1998). The caregiver must provide basic material needs that include food, clothing, and any special supplies needed immediately and regularly. Providing for these needs poses added financial burdens and demands on the employment status of the caregiver.

A number of caregivers, especially family members, have unresolved issues of shame, disappointment, and anger toward the incarcerated mother (Hungerford 1996). In addition, Gregory Hungerford (1996) indicated that in interviews, many caregivers resented having to alter their lifestyles to care for the inmate's children. It was estimated that most caregivers were between fifty and sixty years of age. How these issues are addressed changes the relationship between the caregiver and the child or children of the incarcerated parent. Hungerford (1996) reported that most caregivers were unprepared for the initial tasks of caregiving, which included dealing with the emotional and psychological reactions of a child traumatized by the incarceration of their parent. Moreover, as indicated above, the majority of the children of incarcerated mothers are in their preteen years. Caring for children that age requires a level of daily social activity that proves difficult for many caregivers.

Meredith Minkler and Kathleen Roe (1993) looked specifically at the consequences of caregiving for African American grandmothers. They reported that depression, insomnia, hypertension, back pain, and stomach pain were all health problems attributed to the demands of child care. Other common problems included an increase in cigarette smoking, alcohol consumption, and fatigue (Burton 1992; Minkler and Roe 1996).

The caregiver is faced with a monumental task. She must subvert her own interests to deal with an unexpected intrusion. For the benefit of the children, she must allay her feelings of resentment and betrayal and try to put the best interest of the children in the forefront. If she has children of her own, she must perform a delicate balancing act. If she is an older woman, a grandmother, then depending on her age and living circumstances, she may be stretched to her physical, emotional, and financial limits. Unfortunately, few resources exist to address these very important needs of the caregivers.

■ Programs for Families: Nurseries

Kelsey Kauffman (2001, 62) posed the following question: What do the prison systems of Liberia and Suriname have in common with most prison systems in the United States? The response, derived from a survey of seventy nations, was that these two countries and the United States are the only ones that routinely separate young children from their incarcerated mothers. The practice of separating the incarcerated mother from her child is a relatively recent phenomenon.

Joann Morton and Deborah Williams (1998) reported that young children were incarcerated with their mothers during colonial times. This practice continued with the establishment of separate institutions for women. According to Cynthia Blinn (1997), when the Massachusetts Reformatory for Women opened at Framingham in 1877, 241 women lived there with thirty-five children. Children were allowed to stay in the institution for up to four years. Katherine Davis, superintendent at Bedford Hills in New York, established nurseries for the children of inmates in 1901. These facilities were common in women's prisons throughout the 1950s (Kauffman 2001). The time infants were allowed to stay in the prison varied from institution to institution and ranged from several weeks to two years (Kauffman 2001; Boudouris 1996). By the late 1960s, New York's Bedford Hills was alone in providing nurseries for mothers with children. Tammerlin Drummond (2000) reported that "only 10% of women who successfully completed the program returned to prison, in contrast to 52% of inmates overall." This change in prison policy was the result of budgetary concerns, as well as a reassessment, by some, of the impact of institutional living on the children of incarcerated women (Boudouris 1996; Hawkes 1994).

The 1990s saw a reintroduction of the prison nursery in the Nebraska Correctional Center for Women. Infants up to a year old can live with their mothers in private rooms with cribs. The Rose Singer Center in New York City also allows mothers to keep their babies with them while they are incarcerated (US DOJ 1998). According to the GAO (2000), the Federal Bureau of

Prisons and only eleven states (California, Connecticut, Illinois, Iowa, Massachusetts, Minnesota, Nebraska, New York, North Carolina, South Dakota, and Wisconsin) provide residential programs for inmate mothers and their infants and/or children.

Mothers and Infants Together, established in 1988 in Forth Worth, Texas, was the pilot program introduced by the Federal Bureau of Prisons. Programs are now located in Ventura, California; Hartford, Connecticut; Tallahassee, Florida; Springfield, Illinois; Raleigh, North Carolina; Sioux Falls, South Dakota; and Hillsboro, West Virginia. These community-based facilities receive qualified low-risk inmates two months before delivery, and these women stay for three months after delivery. They receive prenatal and postnatal instruction (GAO 2000). The mother is then returned to an institution to complete her sentence. If she is eligible for prerelease services, she may remain at that facility only if she is going to be supervised in that judicial district. In all fairness, there has been an attempt by some to respond to the special needs of incarcerated women. But the introduction of programs for inmate mothers and their infants and/or children by the Federal Bureau of Prisons and a limited number of states does not address the magnitude of the need.

The child care programs in Nebraska, New York, and South Dakota are housed within the prison. The other residential programs are in separate, community-based contract facilities (GAO 2000). What's more, the prison nurseries generally restrict the use of the facilities to younger children, infants or toddlers. It has been more difficult to get institutions to provide for older children.

The Federal Bureau of Prisons now offers Mothers and Infants Nurturing Together, a component of the Mothers and Infants in Transition (MINT) program, which promotes bonding and parenting skills for low-risk female inmates who are pregnant. Mothers and Infants Nurturing Together uses the same acronym and is a community residential program. Female inmates are eligible to enter the program at the Community Corrections Center (CCC). The program is available to inmates in their last three months of pregnancy, as well as those who have less than five months to serve on their sentence and those who are eligible for furlough.

■ Maintaining Contact

Visits

Face-to-face contact through visits to the prison provides the most direct way for inmates to maintain contact with family and friends. Less than one-quarter of the female inmate parents reported contact with their children via an on-site visit (Mumola 2000). It is important to keep in mind that some incarcerated parents have misgivings about children's visits. They may think such visits are too emotionally painful for the children, that custodial parents may not want them to maintain contact with their children, or they may not want their children to see them in the institution because they are ashamed (Hairston 2002). Visits also provide an opportunity, however, for the inmate to keep open the lines of communication with other family members. If family members become new kinship caregivers, then visits may give the parent, the child, and the caregiver an opportunity to bridge the gap and clarify expectations. For husbands and wives, visits may serve a very important role in helping them to heal and build their relationship. Unfortunately, some may choose not to visit or may not be able to visit because of personal, financial, or situational factors.

Nevertheless, all institutions provide an opportunity for such visits. However, these visits are governed by institutional restrictions on time and schedule. Some institutions limit visitation to the weekends. Others offer very limited visitation hours. For example, the visiting hours at the Chowchilla Women's Prison in California are only on Saturday and Sunday and on major holidays (New Year's Day, Independence Day, Labor Day, Thanksgiving, and Christmas) from 9 a.m. to 3 p.m. The Maryland Correctional Institution for Women, however, allow visits for the general population on Monday and Thursday from 5 to 8 p.m. and on Saturday and Sunday from 8 a.m. to 2 p.m. and again from 5 to 8 p.m. According to the rules for the general population, visits are for one hour, an inmate may receive no more than two visits per week, and an inmate may receive up to eight visits per month. Inmates can have a maximum of four visitors at one time, and at least one must be an adult. Other restrictions may include requiring custodial parents (those who have the legal right to the physical custody of the children) to accompany children on visits and the presentation of a birth certificate. Conflict between the inmate and the custodial parent may make it difficult for the incarcerated parent to receive visits from their children.

Many institutions also use visits as a behavioral control mechanism. Inmates at the Maryland Correctional Institution for Women who are in disciplinary segregation, administrative segregation, or maximum security may not be allowed visitation. If they are allowed visits, then the days for visits are limited, the time schedule for visits is shorter, the length of the visits is shorter, and the inmate is allowed fewer visits.

In addition, the number and frequency of visits by children most often depend on who cares for the children while the mother is incarcerated, their attitudes toward her incarceration, and the resources available to them. Some institutions also place age restrictions on which children can visit and when they can visit. According to Krisberg and Temin (2001), most parents are confined more than 100 miles from their last place of residence. For example, Nicole Gaouette (1997) reported that the California Institution for Women is five hours away from Los Angeles, the closest city, whereas Rini Bartlett (2000) reported that in Florida, driving to the facilities holding incarcerated female offenders took from six to ten hours and required overnight motel stays. California includes visitation and transportation services among its provisions for preserving the relationship between incarcerated parents and their children (Schneider 2002; California Welfare and Institutional Code Section 361(e)(1)).

In addition, CCIP (2001) reported that over half of all children of incarcerated parents never visit and that incarcerated women are less likely to receive visits than incarcerated men. Perhaps women receive fewer visits because most states provide only one institution for women, usually located in a remote, rural area, which makes visitation difficult and costly. Hairston (2002) noted that, in addition to transportation, the costs of prison visits include overnight lodging and meals and vending machine snacks during visits.

In the case of federal female offenders, the situation is even more dramatic because these institutions are even more remote. Furthermore, women are generally shipped out of state, and therefore distances to the institutions are even greater for visitors. For example, a female offender from Washington, D.C., convicted of a federal offense could be housed as near as Alderson, West Virginia (285 miles and almost six hours by car) or as far away as Dublin, California (2,829 miles and close to forty-four hours by car). J. C. Coughenour (1995) reported that because there were fewer federal prisons for women than for men, women inmates were on average more than 160 miles farther from family than male inmates. These distances make regular visits next to impossible and make the maintenance of family relationships very difficult.

A number of issues determine the ability of children to visit their mothers in prison. Transportation is the primary concern (see Box 6.1). Those under eighteen are dependent upon others, namely caregivers, to bring them to the institutions. Caretakers must have personal transportation or be able to secure hired transportation. There are organizations and programs that provide transportation for family members. In Saint Louis, Missouri, the Mothers and Children Together program provides free bus transportation to the prison four times a year for families that need it. In all cases, underage children must be supervised by adults. Our Place in Washington, D.C., operates a family transportation program that provides monthly transportation and lodging for families and friends to visit women incarcerated in the federal prison in Danbury, Connecticut.

Scheduling visits poses a problem for many caregivers. Visitation hours are set by the institution. In some cases, family members can visit any day of the week, but only every other weekend (WPA 1995). Unfortunately, for some family members these weekday visits conflict with work schedules and present added hardships. If sufficient leave from work with pay is not available, then unpaid absences incur additional financial expenses. In other cases, visits are allowed only on weekends and holidays. These options require careful time management on the part of caregivers.

Box 6.1   "Taking the Kids to Visit Their Mother"

Georgia Howard lives in Washington, D.C. Her daughter is currently serving a five-year sentence at the Danbury Federal Correctional Center in Danbury, Connecticut. Georgia is the caregiver for her daughter's two children, ages five and eight. She had promised the children that she would take them to visit their mother last week, but at the last minute her boss asked her to work overtime on Saturday. As a result, she was unable to take advantage of the monthly trip sponsored by Our Place. The children were really looking forward to visiting their mother, and Georgia did not want to make them wait another three weeks. She has learned that the facility is 297 miles from the District. This is a 594-mile round trip.

Georgia has learned that visiting hours at the facility are Thursday and Friday from 12:30 p.m. to 8:00 p.m. and Saturday and Sunday from 8:30 to 3:00 p.m. Visits cannot exceed two hours. Georgia works Monday through Friday from 7 a.m. to 3:30 p.m. She cannot take off from work, so she will have to leave after work on Friday. Georgia has four options: car, bus, train, airplane. She has calculated the cost of the trip for herself and her two granddaughters.

Option 1: Car
Estimated time: 5 hours and 19 minutes one way
　　　　　10 hours and 38 minutes round trip
Car expenses
　　　　　Oil change and road check: $45
　　　　　Gas: $44.00
　　　　　Tolls: $20.00
Meals (McDonald's): lunch ($15), dinner ($30), breakfast ($15),
　　　　　lunch ($15) = $75
Hotel (Super 8): $66.00 per night
　　　　　　　　　　　Total = $250

Option 2: Bus (Greyhound)
Depart 10 p.m. Friday. Arrive 6:05 a.m. Saturday.
　　　　　8 hours and 5 minutes
Depart 3:25 p.m. Sunday. Arrive 10:30 p.m.
　　　　　7 hours and 5 minutes
Cost for 1 adult and 2 children: $282
Meals (McDonald's): $75
Hotel (Super 8): $66
Taxi (A Cab Company): estimate $30 round trip
　　　　　　　　　　　Total = $453

continues

Box 6.1   continued

Option 3: Train (Amtrak)/Bus[a]
Train: Depart 5:25 a.m. Saturday. Arrive Bridgeport, Conn., at 10:12 a.m.:
        $160 round trip
Bus: Depart 12:05 p.m. Saturday. Arrive Danbury 5:30 p.m.: $118 round trip
        10 hours and 12 minutes
Bus: Depart 11:25 a.m. Sunday. Arrive Bridgeport 4:05 p.m.
Train: Depart 4:31 p.m. arrive Washington, D.C., at 9:40 p.m.
        8 hours and 49 minutes
Meals (train and McDonald's): $75
Hotel (Super 8): $66
Taxi (A Cab Company): estimate $30 round trip
        Total = $449

Option 4: Airplane[b]
Airplane: Depart 6 a.m. for Philadelphia. Depart for New Haven at 10:05 a.m.
        Arrive 11:15 a.m.: $165 X 3 = $495 round trip
Bus: Depart New Haven 2:20 p.m. Arrive Danbury 5:25 p.m.: $128 round trip
        8 Hours and 10 minutes
Bus: Depart Danbury 11:25 a.m. Arrive New Haven 4:20 p.m.
Airplane: Depart New Haven 7:55 p.m. for Philadelphia. Depart Philadelphia
        10:30 p.m. Arrive Washington, D.C., 11:25 p.m.
        8 hours 15 minutes
Meals (McDonald's): $75
Hotel (Super 8): $66
Taxi (A Cab Company): estimate $30 round trip
        Total = $794

Georgia has decided that she will drive her 1999 Chevrolet to Danbury. It will be the least expensive way to travel, and it will probably make it easier for her to manage the two young children. In addition, Georgia has learned that visitors are not allowed to bring food into the facility, but that they can purchase snacks from the vending machines. Snacks for Georgia, her two granddaughters, and her daughter should add about $10.00 to the cost of the trip and allow the family members to interact in a leisurely manner.

Source: http://www.greyhound.com/; http://www.orbitz.com/; http://tickets.amtrak.com/itd/amtrak; http://maps.yahoo.com/.

Notes: a. Amtrak does not go to Danbury, so Georgia has to take the bus to Danbury.
        b. There were no flights going directly into Danbury, so Georgia has to take the bus to Danbury.

Another issue arises from the legally mandated requirement that child welfare workers facilitate parent-child visits when such visits are not viewed as detrimental to the child (Seymour 1998). Child welfare workers are required to make "reasonable efforts" to reunify families. Cynthia Seymour (1998) noted that as a result of *In re Sabrina N.* (1998) 60 Cal.App.4th 996 (70 Cal.Rptr.2d 603), child welfare agencies are "legally accountable for maintaining ongoing communication with parents in prison and exploring fully the extent to which services might be provided to incarcerated parents."

In addition to problems related to scheduling visits and observing visiting procedures, some additional obstacles to facilitating these parent-child visits confront child welfare workers. They include inadequate information about visiting procedures, lack of cooperation from departments of corrections, problems coordinating visits with kinship caregivers and foster parents, and difficulty maintaining contact with parents in prison.

Another issue of major concern is the nature of security in the institution. It is important to note that most of the institutions that house women are medium security. This means that, ordinarily, visitors will not be separated by a window of plate glass but rather will be allowed contact visits. Although most family members are approved for visits, these visits are still supervised and monitored.

More significantly, in many institutions visitors may be subject to searches. Krisberg and Temin (2001) also reported that the National Council on Crime and Delinquency found that infants and small children were subjected to strip searches and body cavity intrusions. Entry into most institutions requires that adults and children pass through metal detectors and submit to pat-down searches.

Dressel, Porterfield, and Barnhill (1998, 91) reported: "Most prison visits are held in large, highly public and noisy settings, such as gymnasiums, where family privacy is unavailable." Without toys, books, and other resources, these visiting areas are not "child friendly" (Covington 2002). But there have been a number of attempts to make these settings more child friendly by providing these resources. V. Taylor (1999) noted that among the problems identified in a report on prison visiting in Florida were long waits, rude treatment by staff, and changing dress codes (for an example of one system's dress code, see Box 6.2). This is of particular concern given the clash of urban youth and minority cultures with rural, older, majority cultures.

Clearly, regular visitation policies limit the number of children who can be accommodated. More specifically, there are restrictions on the age of visitors and on the number of visitors at any one time. Other programs have been introduced to help incarcerated mothers maintain contact with their children. One attempt to address this problem has been the institutionalization of overnight visits.

Box 6.2   Visitor Dress Code

Visitors shall dress appropriately for visitation. All clothing shall cover from the neck to the kneecaps.
The following types of clothing are not allowed to be worn:

- tube tops, tank tops, or halter tops
- see-through clothing
- mini-skirts, mini-dresses, shorts, skorts, or culottes (above the kneecap)
- form-fitting clothes such as leotards, spandex, and leggings
- clothes that expose a person's midriff, side, or back
- tops or dresses that have revealing necklines and/or excessive splits.

Source: The Corrections Connection, www.dpscs.state.md.us/locations/mciw.shtml.

Overnight Visits for Children

In a survey of prison programs in seventy-four state prisons and nine federal facilities, J. Boudouris (1996) reported that overnight visitation programs were allowed in thirty-one institutions in twenty-one states. However, he also noted that the use of these visits had declined. This decline has been attributed, in part, to the increased financial costs of transportation and lodging. In 1998 Joycelyn Pollock (2002) sent letters to departments of correction in all fifty states. Ten states—California, Connecticut, Illinois, Kentucky, Massachusetts, Mississippi, New York, Oklahoma, South Dakota, and Tennessee—reported that overnight visits were available.[3] The fact that only ten states had programs seems to suggest that the decline noted in the earlier study by Boudouris (1996) has continued. Even more disquieting is the caution by Pollock (2002) that availability does not always translate into utilization: one institution indicated that only five women were cleared for these visits.

It is important to note that Oklahoma, the state with the highest rate of female incarceration, and California and New York, the states with the largest numbers of incarcerated females, are included on the list of states with available overnight visits. We will examine some of these programs in greater detail.

The Mother Offspring Life Development program (MOLD) operates in Kentucky and Nebraska. This program allows overnight visits for older children. The Nebraska MOLD program was established in 1976. Boys up to age eight and girls up to age eleven are allowed to stay with their mother for up to five nights once a month. The program in Kentucky is more restrictive: children can visit their mothers, but only for the weekend; that program is housed in a separate building with a playroom filled with toys. The Illinois Dwight Correctional Center has a similar program, a Family Service Program, which includes an overnight weekend visitation program in a camp setting (US DOJ 1998).

The National Council on Crime and Delinquency started the Mothers and Their Children (MATCH) program in 1978. It has been replicated in eleven states, including Texas (Weilerstein 1995). MATCH focuses on improving visiting procedures and developing centers where mothers and their children can play and learn together (Morton and Williams 1998).

A number of other programs have been introduced across the country to address the need for contact between incarcerated mothers and their children. The Washington Correctional Center for Women (formerly the Purdy Treatment Center for Women) has a foster day care program, a day care and nursery program, and overnight stays. Michigan has developed the Children's Visitation Program (CVP); Virginia has the Mothers/Men Inside Loving Kids (MILK) program; Pennsylvania has Inside Muncy Parents and Children Together (IMPACT) program; and in a number of other institutions the Sesame Street program aids in the nurturing of parent-child relationships.

The National Institute of Justice funded the demonstration program, "Girl Scouts Behind Bars." It allowed Girl Scouts between ages five and thirteen whose mothers were incarcerated to have two meetings per month in the prison. The women spend supervised time working with their daughters on troop projects. First implemented at the Maryland Correctional Institution for Women at Jessup in 1992, the program now called "Girl Scouts Beyond Bars" has been replicated in a number of jurisdictions across the country, including Florida, Ohio, Arizona, and Missouri (Moses 1995; Morton and Williams 1998). These programs are now funded through private contributions and foundation and state grants.

Karen Casey-Acevedo and Tim Bakken (2002) reported on a summer program in a maximum security prison in the Northeast. It allows the children of inmates to stay with volunteer host families who live near the prison for one week. Children come to the prison for six hours each day to visit their mothers.

Still, visits and involvement in these programs do not occur on a regular basis, so some others have introduced alternatives that allow for indirect but more sustained "interaction" between mothers and their children. One such program is the Reading Family Ties Program, which uses high-speed videoconferencing to facilitate visits between inmate mothers and their children (Bartlett 2000). A number of facilities, including Florida's Hernando Correctional Institution, provide these virtual visits for incarcerated mothers and their children. The Motheread Program at the North Carolina Correctional Institution for Women (see Box 6.3) is a literacy program that teaches mothers how to read and develop critical thinking skills that they can share with their children by making book audio tapes that they send home to their children (Martin and Cotton 1995).

Congress passed the Family Unity Demonstration Project Act as part of the 1994 Violent Crime Control and Law Enforcement Act. This legislation was introduced to establish community correctional facilities where eligible offenders who had been primary caregivers could live with their children under age seven. These centers were to provide a safe and stable environment, pediatric and adult medical care, educational resources, parenting classes, and substance abuse treatment.

One other method that could be used to provide virtual visits is e-mail. However, the use of e-mail as a method of communication between mother and child is dependent upon both mother and child having access to a computer. Eric Newburger (2001) reported that 51 percent of households in the United States had one or more computers, with 42 percent of households having at least one member who used the Internet at home in 2000. Not surpris-

---

Box 6.3 Motheread

In January 1987 Nancye Gaj walked into the North Carolina Correctional Institution for Women to teach inmates how to read to their children and, in the process, improve their own literacy skills. The class started with the women reading Maurice Sendak's classic children's book, *Where the Wild Things Are*. The women met twice a week for four months to read classic and multicultural stories. The women also learned to tell or write their own stories that their children could take home in remembrance of their visit.

Motheread is a national, nonprofit organization that has grown to serve more than 50,000 learners in thirteen states, including Hawaii. The organization trains educators, family service agency staff, and prison staff. The organization is becoming known as Motheread/Fatheread because it is also being adopted in men's correctional institutions.

Gaj says she starts with children's literature because a parent and child can read the entire piece together in one sitting, and the books are full of tremendous lessons that help them to be better parents.

Source: Humanities News: Newsletter of the Hawai'i Council for the Humanities, www.motheread.org/pubs1.htm, and "The Storyteller: Nancye Brown Gaj, Founder of Motheread" by Robin Herbst, www.neh.fed.us/news/humanities/1998-11/medalists.html.

ingly, access to computers and the Internet was linked to income, race, and age. Based upon the profile of the incarcerated woman and her family (see Chapter 3), it is unlikely that there is access to a computer and the Internet in her household. In addition, even though computers are present in most correctional institutions, access to e-mail is often restricted because of safety concerns. Consequently, this is not a method of communication that is being used to nurture relationships between incarcerated mothers and their children.

Family Visiting Programs

Even though the majority of the visitation programs focus on maintaining and improving relationships between the incarcerated mother and her children, there are also programs that broaden their scope to the larger family. Virginia Neto and LaNelle Bainer (1983, 133) observed that the conjugal visit was "conceived as an idea by men for men." They argued that originally, these visits were introduced under the assumption that if the men had a satisfactory sex life, their work performance would increase.

Camille Camp and George Camp (1997) discovered that six states allowed conjugal visitation: California, Connecticut, Mississippi, New Mexico, New York, and Washington. Probably due to the sensitive nature of these programs, there has been little discussion of and even less empirical research on the impact of such programs on family reunification. According to an incarcerated woman in Mary Dodge and Mark Pogrebin's study (2001, 46): "My husband chose to go to another woman. He cheated on me. It's so much to go through. You lose your husband, you lose your kids, your kid's gonna always love you, but someone else takes care of your kids, another woman, it's so much to go through. It's tragic. It's a terrible thing that you wake up and say I want to go home."

Little attention has been paid to the pros and cons of conjugal visits for incarcerated women. We know that a large percentage of the women are single and that physical and sexual abuse plays a significant role in their lives. Still, for those who were involved in committed relationships prior to their incarceration, opportunities to maintain these relationships could be beneficial. They could serve to promote family cohesiveness, as well as encouraging good behavior within the institution.

Nonetheless, instead of conjugal visits, the notion of family visitation was adapted to the female institution in an effort to address both the emotional and sexual needs of female offenders. Neto and Bainer (1983) identified four prisons that had family visiting programs: Purdy Treatment Center in Washington (now Washington Correctional Center for Women), the California Institution for Women, Bedford Hills Correctional Facility in New York, and Goodman Correctional Institution in South Carolina. In Pollack's (2002) survey of thirty-nine states, nine (Arkansas, California, Connecticut, Mississippi,

Missouri, New York, Oklahoma, Washington, and West Virginia) reported that "family" visits were available. These private overnight family visiting programs include visits with immediate family members like parents, siblings, aunts, and uncles, as well as conjugal visits.

In California, inmates may apply for family visits. These visits are in apartment-type housing with approved immediate family members. In the case of conjugal visits, these programs usually restrict participants to legal or common law husbands. Visitors are permitted to stay from thirty to seventy-two hours.

It seems clear that corrections departments and researchers have recognized the importance of programs that help to maintain the relationship of parent and child through visitation programs. However, we must go one step further and acknowledge the critical need to look at incarcerated women holistically. Many of these women will be returning to their families. These are families that include not just children, but also husbands, mothers, fathers, siblings, and other relatives. Visitation programs that encourage the maintenance of healthy relationships with these family members may help in both the transition to the institution and in reunification efforts once the inmate is released.

Telephone Calls

A major source of contact for mothers and their children are telephone calls. Barbara Owen and Barbara Bloom (1995) reported that 34 percent of women in the study had telephone contact with children three to four times a week. The findings in a national survey of state corrections facilities were much more encouraging, with just over one-half of the inmate parents reporting that they had telephone contact with their children (Mumola 2002). However, imposed restrictions and the expense of toll calls sometimes make these avenues difficult. Many institutions do not allow family members and caregivers to call in, so inmates must call collect, which is one of the most expensive methods of calling.

Hairston (2002) reported that a thirty-minute call once a week could cost $125 or more. This added expense for a family that is already struggling to provide for a child may result in very infrequent telephone communication between the parents and their children. It may also become a source of conflict between caregivers and the incarcerated parents, as well as between the children of incarcerated parents and their caregivers, which adds to the difficulties of trying to maintain relationships.

There have also been complaints charging that institutions are entering into telephone contracts in exchange for commissions from telephone charges. This practice gives these telephone companies a monopoly and prevents family members from shopping around for lower rates. Inga Miller (2000) reports that in California, each phone call an inmate made costs $3, plus an additional charge for each minute, with 33 to 44 cents on every dollar going to the state. Reports indicate that in some other jurisdictions, states get as much as 60 cents on a dollar and collect millions of dollars from the contracts. The high costs of these telephone calls has led inmates in Illinois, Indiana, New Hampshire, New Mexico, New York, Ohio, and Wisconsin to file lawsuits ("Inmates Sue over High Phone Costs" 2000). Florida, Iowa, and California are among the states reevaluating their telephone policies.

Schneider (2002) described California's provisions for preserving the parent-child relationship as far-reaching. Included among the reunification services was the requirement to maintain contact between the parent and child through collect telephone calls (California Welfare and Institutional Code Section 361(e)(1)). Schneider added that New York also mandates services to incarcerated parents, though the services were not as comprehensive as those required in California. The telephone is the major means of communication for people today. It is important that corrections do what they can to make it easier and more cost-effective for incarcerated women and their children to take advantage of this method of maintaining contact.

Mail

A less direct way of maintaining contact between parents and children that seems to be easier and is cheaper than visits is mail. Each institution has its own rules, with limits on who can receive and send mail and what kind of mail (see Box 6.4). Mumola (2002) found that a majority of inmates indicate that they correspond with their children by mail weekly (see Box 6.5). The Florida Committee on Corrections (1998) examined the state policies on mail and found that inmates could send and receive mail from any person they wished and that mail was delivered to the inmate within twenty-four hours, excluding weekends and holidays. Mail declared to be obscene, mail that indicated plans for breaking the law, and mail that threatened harm to correctional personnel was not sent out or delivered. The committee also indicated that as of 1995, family members were not permitted to send packages to inmates via the mail. Consequently, personal items such as toiletries, books, and magazines had to be purchased at the canteen, probably at an increased cost. Family photos, magazines, and books were often a part of the "care packages" sent before 1995. These materials gave inmates a glimpse of what was happening on the outside and provided common ground for communication with family members.

One issue of concern relates to the literacy of respondents. Some children will need help composing their letters. For younger children, composing and reading a letter can be a valuable learning experience. Older children will be able to write their own letters. Doing so will provide them with an opportunity to "talk" one-on-one with their parent about the matters that are most impor-

Box 6.4   Written Correspondence Guidelines, Connecticut

4. *Inmate Correspondence.* Inmates may write and receive letters subject to the following provisions:

   A. *Frequency.* There shall be no limit placed on the number of letters an inmate may write or receive at personal expense, except as a disciplinary penalty in accordance with Administrative Directive 9.5, Code of Penal Discipline.

   B. *Timely Handling.* Incoming and outgoing correspondence shall be processed without unnecessary delay.

   C. *Correspondents.* An inmate may write to anyone except:

      (1) a victim of any criminal offense for which the inmate has served or is serving a sentence, or stands convicted of, or disposition is pending;

      (2) any person under the age of 18 when the person's parent or guardian objects in writing to such correspondence;

      (3) an inmate in another correctional facility, other than immediate family;

      (4) a parolee or inmate on community confinement without the express permission of the Unit Administrator and the addressee's supervisor;

      (5) any person whom the inmate is restrained from writing to by court order; or

      (6) any other person, when prohibiting such correspondence is generally necessary to further the substantial interests of security, order or rehabilitation.

   D. *Cost of Correspondence.* Each inmate shall pay personal mailing expenses, except an indigent inmate. An indigent inmate, as defined in Administrative Directive 6.10, Inmate Property, shall be permitted two (2) free social letters each week, and five (5) letters per month addressed to the court or attorneys, including any request for speedy trial under Sections 54-82c and 54-186 of the Connecticut General Statutes. Additional free correspondence to courts and attorneys may be authorized by the Unit Administrator based upon the reasonable needs of the inmate.

continues

tant to them. Children will also need postage and assistance with the actual mailing of the letter. Caregivers must decide how they will deal with this issue.

Another area of concern relates to the inmates' need for writing materials. In Florida, the Department of Corrections does not provide free stamps,

---

Box 6.4   continued

E. *Outgoing General Correspondence.*
1. *Review, Inspection and Rejection.* All outgoing general correspondence shall be subject to being read at the direction of the Unit Administrator, by person(s) designated in writing by such Administrator, for either a specific inmate(s) or on a random basis if the Commissioner or Unit Administrator has reason to believe that such reading is generally necessary to further the substantial interests of security, order or rehabilitation.
2. *Notice of Rejection.* In the event that the designee of the Unit Administrator determines that outgoing general correspondence shall not be sent as provided for above in Section 4(E)(1), the inmate sender shall be notified in writing of the correspondence rejection and the reason therefore. The inmate may seek review in writing within five (5) days thereafter from the Unit Administrator.
3. *Limitations on Restrictions.* Any restrictions imposed on outgoing general correspondence shall be unrelated to the suppression of expression and may not be restricted solely based on unwelcome or unflattering opinions or factually inaccurate statements.
4. *Procedure for Mailing.* Outgoing general correspondence shall be inserted into the envelope and sealed by the inmate but shall be subject to inspection, review and rejection subject to the provisions of Section 4(E)(1) above. All outgoing general correspondence shall include: (a) a complete legible name and address of the party the correspondence is being sent to; (b) the inmate's complete legible name, inmate number, and present unit address; and (c) the name under which the inmate was committed to the facility.

Source: Corrections Connection. www.ct.gov/doc/LIB/doc/PDF/AD/ad1007. pdf.

---

envelopes, and paper for routine mail. Inmates must purchase these materials from the canteen or ask family members to send these items by mail. The institution does allow indigent inmates to send one free letter every month.

Written correspondence gives the writer and the reader a chance to practice needed skills. This method of communication can work hand-in-hand with educational programs within the institution. It also allows incarcerated parents

---

Box 6.5   Letter to My Children

My dearest babies,

Each time you leave after visiting me, I start counting the days until you will return. I wish I could at least call you, but you know I'm not allowed to use the phone. . .

I want each of you to know how proud I am of you. In spite of the battles you face because I'm not there, you always do your best. I didn't, and now I am engulfed by one of the greatest sorrows a mother could know. . . . I can't oversee you brushing your teeth in the morning. Can't wash your clothes. I can't even bug you. But I want you to know that you are my greatest joys. . . .

Love forever, Mother Dear.

Source: Erica Sheppard, as told to Patrice Gaines. 2003. "Backtalk: A Remorseful Mother of Three Reaches Out to Her Children from Her Cell on Death Row" *Essence*, April.

---

some insight into the progress that their children are making in school. Again, the benefits for the parents, the children, and the institution are evident.

■ Conclusion

Although criminal law focuses on individual acts and aims to punish those directly responsible for their wrongdoing, it inevitably touches the lives of those who have no involvement in the wrongdoing. This fact becomes very apparent when we look at the female offender. Because most incarcerated female offenders are mothers, their children are left behind. Others must then care for children who have lost their primary caregiver. Those who provide substitute care for the children of incarcerated mothers must draw from available resources that many times may be inadequate.

The incarceration of the mother affects both the offender and those charged to provide for her while she is institutionalized. For the offender, the loss of her children results in a range of emotional as well as physical maladies. The maladies affect her adjustment to the institution and must be addressed by institutional staff.

The incarceration of the mother also has long-range effects on the children left behind. They may suffer from emotional, psychological, social, behavioral, and physical problems. Their care becomes the concern of others. They are caught between the past with their mother, the present with her substitute, and a future that is unknown. The resolution of the problems these children experience will have consequences that are likely to extend beyond the return of their mother.

Currently, institutions provide a number of programs aimed at maintaining the ties between the incarcerated mother and her children. The provision of nurseries, upgraded visiting areas, and more flexible visitation policies and practices have made things easier for both the mother and her children. Other programs aimed at improving the parenting skills of mothers and aiding in the psychological and social development of children have been introduced in a number of institutions and should be expanded.

The incarceration of the mother requires that others take over her role. Who these others are and how they handle their caregiver role has an important effect on the children and their mother. In addition, the additional responsibilities will draw upon all the resources available to these caregivers. The added financial costs, along with emotional, psychological, and social costs, may take their toll.

In most cases, the incarceration of the mother will end, and reunification will occur. However, although reunification with her family is viewed as the goal, a number of obstacles have made successful reunification more difficult. Several pieces of federal legislation prevent the returning mother from taking advantage of a number of programs that would allow her to improve her condition and be better able to care for her children (see Chapter 8). If reunification is truly a goal supported by our society, then a realistic look at who these offenders are and what they will need to become viable caretakers must guide legislation.

■ Notes

1. The Adoption and Safe Families Act of 1997 prohibited states receiving funding under Title IV-6 of the Social Security Act from denying or delaying the placement of a child for adoption when an approved family was available outside the jurisdiction with responsibility for handling the case of the child; and failing to grant an opportunity for a fair hearing to an individual who alleges that the state has denied or delayed the placement of a child under such circumstances. The penalty for failing to comply was that all funds to which the state was entitled could be withheld.

Title IV—Grants to States for Aid and Services to Needy Families with Children and for Child-Welfare Services—was a part of the original Social Security Act of 1935 (Public Law 74-271 49 Stat. 620). This act has been amended a number of times. Title IV includes sections covering block grants to states for temporary assistance to needy families, child and family services, child support and establishment of paternity, and federal payments for foster care and adoption assistance.

2. In 1994 Aid to Imprisoned Mothers changed its name to Aid to Children of Imprisoned Mothers. However, the acronym, AIM, remained unchanged.

3. There is some discrepancy in the text. Pollack (2002) stated that eleven states reported that overnight visits were available. However, there were ten listed in the table. Arizona, Delaware, Georgia, Hawaii, Louisiana, Minnesota, Nebraska, Nevada, New Jersey, New Mexico, and Utah did not participate in the survey.

Death and Dying

7

Women in prison have a great deal of time to consider death. Many of them know and have known violence and loss all their lives. And although unlikely, some women will be executed in prison. For most incarcerated women, however, their own death is not that immediate, but as that population ages and rates of chronic disease rise, they increasingly cope with the possibility of dying in prison (Aday 1994). Some prison programs exist to ease this last transition, but when incarcerated women do die, it is rarely with the "dignity" that has become the rallying cry for death in the community.

▪ The Death Penalty

The death penalty has been part of the US criminal justice system since the first known execution in 1622; the first woman executed was Jane Champion, who was hung in James City, Virginia, in 1632 (O'Shea 1999). Official records have been available since 1608, and since then only about 3 percent of executions have involved women; this makes sense, of course, because the vast majority of women's crimes are nonviolent.

Rates of executions vary over time. Of the 3,859 individuals executed between 1930 and 1967, only thirty-two were women, and there were only 564 documented cases in the United States of females sentenced to death from 1632 until 2000 (Streib 2003). After reaching an all-time high in 1935, the number of executions dropped steadily until the late 1960s, despite the fact that all but ten states had laws authorizing capital punishment. Strong forces opposed to the death penalty were able to create an unofficial moratorium on executions for several years during the 1960s and 1970s. It was a case that reached the Supreme Court that officially changed the face of capital punishment in the United States, however.

William Henry Furman was an African American man sentenced to death for the murder of a white man during an attempted robbery. His appeal reached the US Supreme Court in the case of *Furman v. Georgia* in 1972. In a 5 to 4 decision, the Court found that the death penalty as administered in Georgia violated the Eighth[1] and the Fourteenth[2] Amendments to the US Constitution. Two justices ruled for the appeal on the basis of the death penalty's inherently "cruel and unusual" nature. Three justices based their opinions on the discriminatory application of the death sentence, which was obvious since 54 percent of all executions between 1930 and 1967 were of black prisoners. Stating that present death penalty laws were "arbitrary and capricious," the Court ruled directly on the Georgia statutes under appeal and, by extension, all other death penalty statutes. More than 600 death row inmates sentenced between 1967 and 1972 had their sentences lifted as a result. Following the *Furman* case, fourteen states and the District of Columbia abolished their death penalty statutes, and thirty-five revised their laws. These revised laws were later tested by Tony Gregg, accused of murdering two men, in *Gregg v. Georgia* (1976) and found constitutional. Furthermore, the Court in *Gregg* found that the death penalty did not offend the "evolving standards of decency which mark the progress of a maturing society."

Sentencing

Two types of death penalty laws emerged as states frantically reworked their own statutes to protect society from now seemingly uninhibited murderers and to fit the Supreme Court's *Gregg v. Georgia* ruling. The first provided the mandatory death penalty for certain crimes (such as killing a police officer) and allowed for no discretion beyond determination of guilt. The second type allowed the lower courts to use guided discretion in applying the death penalty to specific crimes through a two-part trial. The first stage found the defendant's guilt or innocence; the second stage determined the sentence based on mitigating or aggravating circumstances.[3]

This second stage of the trial is particularly important for women. Aggravating factors presented by the prosecutor might include a prior criminal record or the "heinous, atrocious, or cruel" nature of a crime. These considerations show the crime more serious or the defendant more repugnant. Following *Gregg*, states cannot impose the death penalty unless the jury finds unanimously and beyond a reasonable doubt that the defendant had aggravated the circumstances of a crime. Mitigating factors presented by the defense are those reasons why an individual should *not* be sentenced to death and might include the age of the defendant or evidence of former abuse that a woman might have suffered.

At one time almost half the women on death row had a history of abuse and were there because they had murdered the spouse or lover who had been abusing them or their children (O'Shea 1993). However, because investigating abuse is time-consuming and costly for the defending attorneys, the in-depth investigation required is most often left undone. Furthermore, since over 90 percent of death row inmates are represented by overworked public defenders, they rarely receive the services they need. Similarly, many of these women have a very dim understanding of the appeal process, and their court-appointed attorneys may do little to clarify the situation. The application of the death penalty reflects class privilege; the wealthy, with the help of their private attorneys, are rarely on death row.

Removal of Death Sentences

Prisoners who are sentenced to death are not always executed; clemency is an option. There are three types of clemency relevant to capital punishment (Bohm 2003): reprieve, which postpones the execution while the prisoner completes an appeal or an official considers the case; commutation, which involves a lesser sentence, typically life with or without the opportunity for parole; and pardon, in which the prisoner is released and the crime expunged from the record. State governors, the president of the United States, and the military have the authority to commute (or reduce) the sentences for prisoners on death row. The most striking case occurred in 2003, when Governor George Ryan of Illinois commuted the sentences for 167 prisoners on death row, including four women.

Women on Death Row

The number of prisoners on death row increased steadily from 1953, until it leveled off in the early twenty-first century; the number of women sentenced to death has been increasing also, from thirty-six in 1992 to fifty-one in 2002 (Bonczar and Snell 2003). Currently, women represent less than 2 percent, or roughly one out of seventy individuals on death row, although they make up about 12.5 percent of those arrested for murder. Since 1973, the highest percentage of women receiving the death sentence occurred in 1989, when eleven of the total 261 death sentences were handed down to women (Streib 2003). Of the 139 death sentences imposed on women between 1973 and 2000, ninety-one were white, thirty-six were African American, eight were Latina, and four were Native American. Of the ten women actually executed during this period, nine were white.

Different states apply the death penalty differently. Of the 139 death sentences for women handed down since 1973, four states (North Carolina, Florida, California, and Texas) have accounted for 42 percent of the total sentences (Streib 2003). There are different methods of execution. Most states and the federal prison system authorize lethal injection; nine states use electrocution; four, lethal gas; three, hanging; and three, firing squad. Sixteen states authorize more than one method; in those states prisoners may choose their method of execution (Snell and Maruschak 2002).

Women living on death row are housed alone; they are isolated, for the most part, twenty-three out of every twenty-four hours. They have no access to other prisoners, any outside and often any inside activities, or their families. These women are on death watch before execution; this means that they are watched twenty-four hours a day to prevent suicide (an act that would rob the state of the opportunity to put the prisoner to death). In one Tennessee prison, the death chamber was next to the death cell; the prisoner could hear the tests and retests on the equipment that would eventually be used to kill her (Atwood 2000).

The first woman executed after the 1976 reinstatement of the death penalty was Margie Velma Barfield. Velma was a middle-aged North Carolina woman who was accused of poisoning her mother, her fiancée, and three elderly people for whom she had worked. She was sentenced to death, despite her drug use and alleged abuse as a child. After a last meal of Coca-Cola and Cheeze Doodles, she was executed by lethal injection in 1984. She had celebrated her fifty-second birthday four days before her death (O'Shea 1999).

The case of Karla Faye Tucker captivated the attention of the public. Tucker, a Texas woman and the second woman executed after the death penalty was reinstated, confessed that she and her boyfriend had broken into a Houston apartment and killed the two occupants with a pickax. She admitted her guilt but asked for a life sentence; the jury, after seventy minutes of deliberation, recommended the death sentence. Despite appeals from religious conservatives, Amnesty International, and the Pope, then Governor George W. Bush denied clemency. In 1998, wearing prison whites and her own shoes, Karla Faye Tucker was put to death after her last meal of a tossed salad, a banana, and a peach (Atwood 2000). The case was a lightning rod for discussion of gender and the death penalty.

The Gender Gap on Death Row

Death row may be the only place in the prison system that women have a decided advantage (see Box 7.1). Only 1.4 percent of prisoners under sentence of death were women in 2001 (Snell and Maruschak 2002). In *Furman v. Georgia*, Supreme Court Justice Thurgood Marshall specifically noted the gender gap in executions: "it is difficult to understand why women have received such favored treatment since the purposes allegedly served by capital punishment seemingly are equally applicable in both cases" (Baker 1999, 365).

According to law professor Victor Streib (2003, see Box 7.1), an expert on women and capital punishment, women are held to less rigorous sentencing at every point of the process. He stated: "Prosecutors are more reluctant to charge women with capital murder, and juries more easily believe that women are under emotional distress while committing a crime."

> **Box 7.1   Screening Female Offenders from the Death Penalty**
>
> - Women account for about one in ten murder arrests (10 percent);
> - Women account for only one in fifty-two death sentences imposed at the trial level (1.9 percent);
> - Women account for only one in sixty-nine persons presently on death row (1.5 percent); and
> - Women account for only ten of the 807 persons actually executed since 1973 (1.2 percent).
>
> *Source:* Victor Streib. 2003. "Death Penalty for Female Offenders, January 1, 1973, through June 30, 2003." http://www.law.onu.edu/faculty/streib/femdeath.htm.

There is, however, an alternative view—that women who are seen as less feminine lose the chivalrous edge in sentencing. Women who kill intimates are more likely to receive the death penalty than men who commit an equivalent crime (Baker 1999). There has also been discussion about the impact of a woman's lesbianism on her sentencing. Streib (2003) discussed the possibility that a woman's sexual orientation might be introduced as an aggravating factor, thus dehumanizing her to some juries, but there is no hard evidence to suggest that this is true.

■ "Am I Going to Die in Here?" Dying in Prison

Executions are certainly not the only way that women die in prison. But because most prison health records are incomplete, reliable data categorized by gender are largely unavailable, and private prisons do not release information about their inmates, there is no easily interpretable figure of how many terminally ill women are in prison or how many die there each year. According to the Bureau of Justice Statistics (2001), in 1998, there were 139 deaths among sentenced women under state or federal jurisdiction. Table 7.1 gives details.

According to A. Liebling and Tony Ward (1994, 1), "deaths in custody remain one of the most urgent yet poorly researched and documented issues in criminology, sociology, and the public and policy arena." The often secretive nature of prison death contrasts directly to the United Nations mandate in Principle 34 of *Deaths in Custody*, which states, "whenever a death or disappearance of a detained or imprisoned person occurs during his [*sic*] detention or imprisonment, an inquiry into the cause of death or disappearance shall be held by a judicial or other authority" (in Liebling and Ward 1994, 64). Although an inquiry may be made, little information is released to the public about the circumstances of the death. This will change with implementation

**Table 7.1   Reported Causes of Death Among State and
Federal Prisoners**

Cause of Death	Number of Female Deaths	Number of Male Deaths
Illness or natural cause	87	1,744
AIDS	14	325
Suicide	13	163
Accidents	0	41
Execution	2	66
Unspecified	23	485
Caused by another	0	55

Source: Adapted from BJS. 2001. *Correctional Population in the United States, 1998.*
Washington DC: BJS (NCJ 192929).

Note: Jurisdictions that did not break down cause of death by gender reported all deaths as
male.

of the Deaths in Custody Reporting Act of 2000; this act requires that the Bureau of Justice Statistics collect quarterly reports with information on individual deaths (Maruschak 2004).

The notoriety attached to a string of eight deaths in the Central California Women's Facility at Chowchilla during seven weeks in 2000 reveals some
of what is behind that veil of secrecy. One of the women died after surgery for
a benign brain tumor; she worried to her attorney that she would not be able
to keep her incision clean and her dressings changed. She died after an abscess
developed in the wound; but because she also had AIDS, her death was classified as expected and HIV-related (Chandler, 2003). When three other
women died within a three-day period, the media picked up the story. All three
women were chronically ill: one with hepatitis C, one with bone cancer, and
one with lung cancer. They were not allowed compassionate release (discussed below) and died in pain (Do Valle 2003).

Earlier studies of deaths in a men's prison (Novick and Remmlinger
1978) found that nonviolent deaths often resulted from deficiencies of care;
the most common was a delay in hospitalization of prisoners who needed
care. Deaths due to deficiencies of care were historically attributed to "death
by the visitation of God," although in the eighteenth century, these deaths
began to be explained as institutional inadequacies (Liebling and Ward 1994).
Because prisoners must wait to have their hospital visits approved, often by
guards or medical technical assistants, women may not receive necessary
health care in a timely manner. Deficiencies in care may be a more common
underlying cause of death than is apparent. One controversial aspect of care
for prisoners is organ transplantation; individuals that might be candidates for
new organs in the community are less likely to receive them in prison. Box
7.2 discusses this further.

Box 7.2   Organ Transplantation

The issue of organ transplants is relevant for prisoners who might like to be either donors or recipients of organs. Certainly the question of organ transplantation is not necessarily one only for the end of life, but it is most often associated with medical exigency. The question of organ transplantation among prisoners is hotly debated: in 2003 a male inmate on death row in Oregon requested a kidney and sparked a firestorm of controversy. His request was denied, but the case began a discussion about health care costs and the "worth" of prisoner's lives.

In the community a patient whose condition is deteriorating despite treatment and who is reasonably likely to recover with the procedure is the ideal candidate for transplantation (DeSpelder and Strickland 2005). One consideration in receiving a transplant is the patient's ability to care for the new organ in order to recover. It is one of the main reasons that prisoners are rarely on eligibility lists, even though the United Network for Organ Sharing states that one's institutionalization should not preclude a prisoner's receiving organs. Health care following an organ transplant is complicated and extensive. Elaborate medical regimens are necessary to prevent organ rejection; continuous monitoring is required; and healthy, infection-free environments are crucial. The uncertainty of ensuring good, reliable care makes prisoners high-risk recipients for such valuable commodities as organs; however, some have received transplants.

Community-dwelling individuals can donate their organs through the Uniform Anatomical Gift Act, which provides for the donation of the body or specific body parts upon death of the donor (DeSpelder and Strickland, 2005). In China organs are routinely harvested from executed prisoners, even without permission from the family. This practice is forbidden in the United States (Wallich and Mukerjee 1996), despite any possible wishes of the prisoners and the desperate need for usable organs.

Sources: Maurice Bernstein. 2002. "A New Liver for a Prisoner." *Hastings Center Report* 32 (4): 12–13. Lynne Ann DeSpelder and Albert Lee Strickland. 2005. *The Last Dance.* New York: McGraw-Hill. Susan Okie. 1998. "Inmates with Kidney Disease Call Transplant Policy Cruel." *Washington Post*, October 12, A6. P. Wallich and M. Mukerjee. 1996. "Regulating the Body Business." *Scientific American* 274 (3): 12–13.

Suicide

Women have very low death rates from suicide, and this is true in prison as well. Correctional facilities have clear guidelines to prevent any opportunity or means to suicide (Hayes 1995). For example, any inmate who is considered a high risk is housed in a "safe room" near the staff office or in the clinic. All pens, pins, matches, glass, belts, and sometimes bed linens and the bed are removed. Although it is rare that institutions meet all guidelines, they are expected to have a written policy; perform an intake assessment to determine risk; train their staff to recognize warning signs, to become certified in CPR, and to practice levels of observation appropriate for high-risk inmates; offer safe housing to inmates; and conduct a mortality review procedure.

However, the case of Caroline Wood, aged nineteen, exemplifies this unusual event. When Caroline was admitted to prison, records noted that she was addicted to heroin. Despite this fact, she was given no methadone treatment or counseling. On the day of her death, there was only one officer, who was busy with other administrative duties, on her ward. An earlier officer had noted that she was depressed, but nothing was done (Coles and Ward 1994).

Incarcerated women may rarely die from suicide, but dying from AIDS is much more likely.

HIV/AIDS

According to the National AIDS Advisory Council report on HIV in correctional facilities (1991, 8), the prison system could become "a charnel house in which inmates sentenced to reform and punishment are consigned to a tragic and hastened death, in pain and isolation." The HIV/AIDS epidemic has increasingly infiltrated the prison system, and little has changed since the above quote was written. The New York Department of Corrections is probably the largest single provider of health care to HIV-positive patients in the United States (Berkman 1995). AIDS is the second leading cause of death among prison inmates in the United States, after all other natural causes combined (Maruschak 2002, 2004), and AIDS-related deaths among black inmates account for two-thirds of all AIDS-related deaths (Maruschak 2004). As discussed earlier, this high prevalence rate of HIV/AIDS among prisoners, especially among black and Hispanic women, echoes the inequities of an entire social system in which the poor die before the rich.

■ Institutional Responses to Dying Inmates

With longer life expectancies and improved technologies, the public has become more aware of the dying process. Most agree that it is possible and advisable to improve the quality of death, making it more comfortable for dying individuals and less stressful for their families. Although the "good death" is incompletely realized by many in the community, Box 7.3 lists some of the principles of a good death that are even more unreachable for those dying in prison. Applying these principles to women suggests that although the expe-

---

Box 7.3   The Good Death

- To know that death is coming and to understand what can be expected
- To retain reasonable control of what happens
- To be afforded dignity and privacy
- To have adequate control over pain relief and other symptoms
- To choose where death occurs
- To have access to needed information and expertise
- To have access to desired spiritual and emotional support
- To have access to hospice or palliative care in any location
- To have a say about who is present during the final days
- To issue advance directives that ensure wishes are respected
- To have time to say goodbye
- To leave when it is time to go and not have life prolonged pointlessly

Source: Adapted from Rich Smith. 2000. "A Good Death," *British Medical Journal* 320 (January 15): 129–130.

---

rience of dying in prison may be rare, the experience of having a "good death" by community standards is probably even more unusual.

Prisons are not designed to address the physical symptoms, mental states, and social needs that patients exhibit at the end of life. Many prisons consolidate care for terminally ill inmates in one or more facilities within a state; some use contracted beds, in local hospitals for example. Others simply place terminally ill women in regular infirmaries. The two most humane approaches to caring for terminally ill inmates are compassionate release programs and hospices.

Compassionate Release

Compassionate release (often called early release or medical parole) programs allow terminally ill inmates to return home for the last months of their lives if they do not pose a threat to society. Motivated by the high costs of caring for dying individuals, prisons increasingly use parole boards and special committees to decide who is allowed to go home. New York, under Governor Mario Cuomo, estimated that their early release program saved nearly $2 million in its first year. A California assemblyman sponsored a bill to establish firm timetables and procedures for compassionate release after one terminally ill prisoner remained in prison despite his vegetative state, costing the state nearly $890,000 in the last six months of his life (AIDS Policy and Law 1997). Other states, however, have been reluctant to establish or even consider such programs.

Despite their financial savings, releases, as well as the numbers of applications, are uncommon. In the year 2000 in New York, for example, out of 170 prison deaths, eighty-one inmates had applied for compassionate release, but only twelve were granted. The obstacles to early release include complicated eligibility requirements and elaborate, time-consuming review processes. In addition, determinate sentencing that requires prisoners to serve their designated time makes early release impossible under any condition. These barriers help explain the fact that more than twice as many inmates died during the review process as were granted release (Quinn 2001) and negate any incentive prisoners and medical personnel might have to initiate applications. Legislative efforts are underway to streamline compassionate release policies to make this option more feasible for terminally ill prisoners (Do Valle 2003). Because of the excessive paperwork and wasted time, prison medical staff often turn to more available alternatives to cope with their dying patients.

Prison Hospices

One success story in the grim anthology of prison health care is the introduction of the prison hospice. The term "hospice" is rooted in the Latin term *hospitium*, meaning a place that receives guests, and originally referred to places where weary and sick pilgrims could rest on their way to the crusades in the Holy Land. The first present-day hospice was founded in 1967 by Cicely Saunders to introduce an element of dignity into the dying process. The emphasis in hospice is on palliative care (the control of pain and other symptoms), rather than treatment or cure. According to the National Prison Hospice Association, hospice is "an interdisciplinary, comfort-oriented care that allows seriously ill and dying patients to die with dignity and humanity with as little pain as possible in an environment where they have mental and spiritual preparation for the natural process in dying" (National Institute of Corrections 1998, 1).

The first prison hospice was founded by a paraplegic wheelchair-bound prisoner in Missouri after he became concerned that so many men were dying alone (Maull 1991). He began visiting them, and his efforts, reinforced and supported by prison staff, led to a movement that is becoming more common. The Public Policy on Correctional Health Care from the American Correctional Association (2001) encourages prison health care programs to establish hospice services for terminally ill offenders and compassionate release programs for those who qualify.

The first prison hospices dealt mainly with deaths due to the HIV/AIDS epidemic. Now the programs are used by inmates dying from other causes as well, which is becoming more common because longer sentences have resulted in aging prison populations. Regardless of the cause of death, prison hospices must deal with a "double whammy" (Maull 1998); their patients are facing not only death but also death in prison, considered the ultimate indignity by many inmates.

All formal prison hospice programs are governed by specific policies and procedures that address such issues as criteria for admission, special privileges for patients, use of pain medication, use of volunteers, requirements for housing in hospice settings, and "do not resuscitate" (DNR) orders.[4] Admissions policies are set by a combination of medical staff, hospice coordinator, and security personnel. As in the community, admission to hospice requires a physician's certification that the individual is terminally ill and has a life expectancy of approximately six months or less.

Special privileges are generally allowed for hospice patients. The most common is relaxed visitation policies. Because women in prison are generally so far from their own families, hospices may allow a fairly broad definition of family for visitation purposes. In the Louisiana Department of Corrections, for example, the inmate herself defines her "family," and it may include "persons within or without the prison who are not related to the patient by blood" (National Institute of Corrections 1998). Prison hospices have often found that until inmates feel confident that they will not be separated from their prison families, they are not willing to leave their usual housing situations (Seidlitz 1999). Many hospice programs also attempt reconciliation with estranged family members. Other privileges include allowing additional personal property, special diets, smoking, and visits from clergy and social workers. In addition, hospice programs typically offer a variety of programs and services, including counseling, assistance with funeral planning, peer support, and bereavement counseling for the family.

Hospices are designed for palliative care that eases the suffering of the dying patient. Until fairly recently, however, physicians were reluctant to prescribe adequate doses of pain medication to terminally ill patients for fear of addiction. Now most community hospice workers are allowed to give terminally ill patients sufficient painkillers to make them comfortable. This lenient use of pain medication is more suspect in prison, however, for fear that inmate volunteers with easy access will steal and use or sell the drugs. Special policies are still being developed on the use of pain medications for terminally ill inmates (National Institute of Corrections 1997).

Hospices, both inside and outside prisons, make heavy use of volunteers. In prison, volunteers usually must go through intensive training, and they are dropped from the program for any violation of prison rules. Most successful programs draw from the patient's circle of prison "family members," individuals with whom they have significant ties. These volunteers help care for the patient in different ways, from simply visiting to being involved in the actual care of the patient.

Housing options vary from prison to prison. Some hospice programs are offered in the prison itself; some are offered in publicly funded and some in privately funded locations in the community (National Institute of Corrections 1997). One study of state and federal prisons (Young and Reviere 2001) reported that 28 percent offered hospice services onsite, and 23 percent offered them offsite. (Forty-nine percent, however, had no hospice services available at all.) Other prisons provide hospice care only if the inmate or her family pay or have insurance to pay for the services.

The "do not resuscitate" order is required by some hospices as a condition of participation in the program (National Institute of Corrections 1998), but it is not as straightforward in a prison setting as in the community. First, women in prison may not feel they have the autonomy necessary to make such a serious decision (Cohn 1999). Second, African American women are overly represented in prison populations and, for a variety of valid historical reasons, are less likely to sign DNR orders than white women (Burrs 1995).

■ "Oh, Lady, Your Husband Just Died": Dealing with Loss in Prison

Grieving and dealing with loss are never easy; for those in prison it may be "mission impossible" (Schetky 1998). Many women in prison have accumulated numerous losses before even coming to prison; once in prison they have to deal with further losses, such as loss of freedom, privacy, and their children. And because many women in prison come from families where violence and poor health are facts of life, the ongoing tales of pain and death may only intensify their feelings of bereavement. Worries about their children's susceptibility to injury, drugs, or even murder are common. A diagnosis of HIV can trigger a profound sense of grief: women may feel the impending loss not only of their own lives but also of a mother for her children (Lawson and Fawkes 1993). These multiple losses take a heavy psychic toll and may never be completely resolved without time and counseling.

Add to these losses the death of a family member or friend while a woman is incarcerated. There is little women in prison can do if a loved one on the outside is dying. They may be allowed only a few telephone calls to a terminally ill loved one. Inmates are rarely able to pay their last respects (Aday 1994); if allowed to go to the funeral, they may be kept in shackles. Away from their families, these women feel not only their own grief but also guilt at not being able to help, anger at life's circumstances, and depression at being so helpless in the face of difficulties. This grief, complicated by mental health problems and unresolved loss and stress, may create further adjustment issues for inmates (DeSpelder and Strickland 2005). Although in one study (Young and Reviere 2001), 92 percent of prisons reported offering bereavement counseling on-site, it is hard to imagine its efficacy since regular mental health services are often unsuccessful. Few studies are available that report on grief and loss in prison, but as the population of inmates continues to grow and to age, the issue will become more relevant.

Conclusion

Dying in prison is considered by many prisoners and community individuals alike as the ultimate failure. Although one might draw parallels with dying in another institution, the hospital, clearly there are important physical and psychological differences.

Death is a difficult topic in any setting. Whether we are discussing the death penalty or organ transplants for prisoners, the emotion attached to dying is more volatile when the subjects are incarcerated. Because prisoners are seen as having forfeited their rights, they are also seen as less deserving of compassion. Yet of all the stages of life, the end is perhaps the most compelling time to consider the human right to dignity. Most women in prison have suffered lives of desperation. It seems that if they are dying or are afflicted with a serious disease, they are condemned to die under the same circumstances.

Notes

1. Eighth Amendment: Excessive bail shall not be required, nor excessive fines imposed, nor cruel and unusual punishments inflicted.

2. Fourteenth Amendment, Section 1: No State shall make or enforce any law which shall abridge the privileges or immunities of citizens of the United States; nor shall any State deprive any person of life, liberty, or property, without due process of law; nor deny to any person within its jurisdiction the equal protection of the laws.

3. Mitigating factors: (1) The defendant's capacity to appreciate the wrongfulness of the defendant's conduct or to conform conduct to the requirements of law was significantly impaired, regardless of whether the capacity was so impaired as to constitute a defense to the charge. (2) The defendant was under unusual and substantial duress, regardless of whether the duress was of such a degree as to constitute a defense to the charge. (3) The defendant is punishable as a principal . . . in the offense, which was committed by another, but the defendant's participation was relatively minor, regardless of whether the participation was so minor as to constitute a defense to the charge. (4) The defendant could not reasonably have foreseen that the defendant's conduct in the course of the commission of murder, or other offense resulting in death for which the defendant was convicted, would cause, or would create a grave risk of causing, death to any person. (5) The defendant was youthful, although not under the age of eighteen. (6) The defendant did not have a significant prior criminal record. (7) The defendant committed the offense under severe mental or emotional disturbance. (8) Another defendant or defendants, equally culpable in the crime, will not be punished by death. (9) The victim consented to the criminal conduct that resulted in the victim's death. (10) That other factors in the defendant's background or character mitigate against imposition of the death sentence.

Aggravating factors for homicide: (1) The defendant (a) intentionally killed the victim; (b) intentionally inflicted serious bodily injury which resulted in the death of the victim; (c) intentionally engaged in conduct intending that the victim be killed or that lethal force be employed against the victim, which resulted in the death of the victim; (d) intentionally engaged in conduct which (i) the defendant knew would create a grave risk of death to a person, other than one of the participants in the offense; and (ii) resulted in the death of the victim. (2) The defendant has been convicted of another federal offense or a state offense resulting in the death of a person, for which a sentence of life imprisonment or a sentence of death was authorized by statute. (3) The defendant has previously been convicted of two or more state or federal offenses punishable by a term of imprisonment of more than one year, committed on different occasions, involving the infliction of, or attempted infliction of, serious bodily injury upon another person. (4) The defendant has previously been convicted of two or more state or federal offenses punishable by a term of imprisonment of more than one year, committed on different occasions, involving the distribution of a controlled substance. (5) In the commission of the offense or in escaping apprehension for a violation, the defendant knowingly created a grave risk of death to one or more persons in addition to the victims of the offense. (6) The defendant procured the commission of the offense by payment, or promise of payment, of anything of pecuniary value. (7) The defendant committed the offense as consideration for the receipt, or in the expectation of the receipt, of anything of pecuniary value. (8) The defendant committed the offense after substantial planning and premeditation. (9) The victim was particularly vulnerable due to old age, youth, or infirmity. (10) The defendant had previously been convicted of a violation for which a sentence of five or more years may be imposed or had previously been convicted of engaging in a continuing criminal enterprise. . . . (12) The defendant committed the offense in an especially heinous, cruel, or depraved manner in that it involved torture or serious physical abuse to the victim (U.S.C., Section 3592, Title 18).

4. The DNR order is intended to inform medical or nursing staff that the terminally ill patient does not want life-saving measures in the event of cardiac or respiratory failure. These orders are usually written by the physician after consultation with the patient and detail what procedures should be undertaken in these cases.

We Want You Back:
The Return to Society

Intellectual and public policy discussions regarding prisoner reentry, probation or parole services, and the impact of incarceration on community life
more generally, have failed to incorporate the specific challenges that incarcerated women face as they return to their communities. (Richie 2001, 368)

Ann Jacobs (2000, 44) describes female offenders as women with a multi-
plicity of problems:

They are overwhelmingly poor and substance abusers. They are also victims
of abuse and violence. Many are depressed and suffer from various forms of
mental illness. They experience a high rate of HIV infection, other sexually
transmitted diseases, tuberculosis, and untreated chronic diseases. A high
percentage are homeless or marginally housed. Typically, they are undereducated, unemployed, and have minimal legitimate work histories. On average, 75 to 80 percent of them are mothers.

These are the women who will be returning to the community to begin their
lives anew. Allen Beck (2000) projected that 585,400 state and federal prisoners would be released in the year 2000. In 2001 about 600,000 state inmates
were released to the community after serving time in prison. It is estimated that
650,000 state and federal prisoners will be released in 2004. That number is
larger than the population of a number of our major urban areas, including
Washington, D.C., Boston, Baltimore, Las Vegas, and Denver. If other things remain equal, 12 percent or about 78,000 of these returning prisoners, will be
women. As indicated in Chapter 3, the female inmate population is increasing,
which suggests that the number of women inmates who will be returning to the
community will also be increasing.

Changes in both sentencing and release policies mean that the offender
returning to the community today differs in many ways from the offender who

returned in the past. First, as a result of mandatory sentencing, sentencing guidelines, determinate sentencing, and truth-in-sentencing policies, offenders are serving longer periods of time incarcerated. This increase in the time served corresponds to an increase in the time away from family, community, and the larger society. James Lynch and William Sabol (2001) argue that this increase in time served results in less frequent contact with family members, which is believed to make reintegration into the community easier. Their examination of Bureau of Justice Statistics indicated that calls, letters, and visits became more infrequent the longer inmates were incarcerated. For example, in 1997 about 18 percent of those who were expecting to be released after serving one year or less reported at least weekly visits from their children. This decreased to about 13 percent among those to be released after serving one to five years, and to 10 percent among those to be released after serving more than five years. Coincidentally, the GAO reported (1999) that the maximum median sentence for female offenders was five years, and the New York State Department of Correctional Services (2001) reported that women served an average minimum of fifty-four months and a maximum of 110 months.

We must add to the general increase in time served the introduction of harsh drug laws, which also led to longer sentences. The 1986 Anti–Drug Abuse Act imposes a much harsher sentence for the possession and distribution of crack cocaine than for the possession and distribution of powder cocaine. More specifically, a five-year minimum sentence is imposed for 5 grams of cocaine base (crack cocaine) or 500 grams of cocaine powder, thus creating a 100 to 1 ratio (see Chapter 4). As noted earlier, minority female offenders, especially African Americans, are more likely to be arrested and convicted of crack cocaine offenses.

Second, as a result of changes in the approach to incarceration, a large number of offenders are returning without having had access to rehabilitation programs that focused on education and training (Lynch and Sabol 2001). In 1965 Congress passed Title IV of the Higher Education Act, which authorized the federal Pell Grant program. This program, introduced to provide assistance to low-income undergraduate students with a high school degree or its equivalent, supported postsecondary academic and vocational studies. Student eligibility was based on financial need and included prisoners. Even though studies indicated that the recidivism rates for those in education programs were much lower than rates for those not in such programs, a number of moves were made to cut off these funds (Taylor 1993; Gaes et al. 1999).

In 1992 Congress reauthorized the Higher Education Act but restricted Pell Grants for prisoners to tuition and fees; death-row and life-without-parole inmates were ineligible for the grants. Just two years later, in 1994, the Violent Crime Control and Law Enforcement Act ended prisoners' eligibility for federal Pell Grants. A number of states also cut back on vocational training programs, which included hairstyling, flower arranging, and nurses' aide training, as well as heavy equipment operation, welding, and computer maintenance (Gehring and Eggleston 1996).

A national survey by the Criminal Justice Institute (CJI 1999) found that 25 percent of the prison population were not participating in any meaningful work or education programs and less than 15 percent of inmates were in mental health or drug treatment programs. This means that these inmates are returning to a much-changed economy without any appreciable change in their education or skills level.

Traditionally, parole involved the supervision of alcohol and drug use, employment status, personal associations, and travel, but significant changes in postprison supervision have occurred. In those jurisdictions that have truth-in-sentencing or that have abolished parole, there is little, if any, postprison supervision. Therefore, resources that were used to help inmates find housing and employment and maintain connections to the treatment programs that may have been available to them during their incarceration are no longer available. Still, although parole has been abolished in sixteen states, almost all states maintain some form of postprison supervision. Even so, Travis (2001, 3) noted that "the phenomenon of prisoner reentry is fundamentally different today. These prisoners have been incarcerated for longer periods of time. Fewer of them have participated in education, job training, or drug treatment programs as corrections agencies have scrambled to pay for new prisons and new corrections officers."

Moreover, Stephanie Covington (2002) argued that the planning for a woman's successful reentry should begin when the woman begins her sentence. The lack of rehabilitation programs that focus on education and training makes planning for reentry very difficult. Therefore, many incarcerated women are returning to the community with no prerelease plan and no plan for reintegration; they are no better off than when they left.

Those returning to the community have a number of concerns to handle (see Box 8.1). Most will want to reunite with their children and other family members, so they will need to regain custody and find child care. They will be released with no job, no housing, and no money and will need to find housing and employment. They will need to continue to address personal problems that are related to their health and substance abuse.

■ Reunification

National and state reforms in welfare and adoption laws have made it easier to eliminate welfare benefits for women offenders, and have created nearly insurmountable barriers for inmate mothers who want to be eventually reunited with their children. (Krisberg and Temin 2001, 4)

The majority of incarcerated women with children expect to be reunited with their children once they are released from prison (Bloom and Steinhart

---

Box 8.1   Elise's Journey

Elise walked the winter streets, her hands and face bitterly cold; her mind filled and distracted; her heart brittle. No one had prepared her for the enormity of the challenges she faced—no place to live; no money; her children scattered and angry; no true friends; and that burning desire to get back to (and at the same time avoid) the "people, places, and things" that had landed her in jail in the first place. Just when success was so important, all she could think of was failure.

Source: Catherine Conly. 1998. "The Women's Prison Association: Supporting Women Offenders and Their Families." Washington, DC: National Institute of Justice, US Department of Justice (NCJ 172858).

1993; Immarigeon 1994). Many incarcerated mothers are likely to be the sole guardians of their children upon their return. These women will return to their families and their communities with little change in their educational level or their employment skills. They will need job training, support to improve their educational status, and help in providing adequate housing their families. Unfortunately, there are a number of pieces of federal legislation or regulations that negatively affect female offenders and their families (the Higher Education Act of 1998; the Personal Responsibility and Work Opportunity Reconciliation Act of 1996; the One Strike and You're Out Policy, which is part of the 1988 Anti–Drug Abuse Act).

Henriques (1996) suggested that the success of reunification efforts depended upon the age of the children at the time of incarceration, the nature of the relationship the children had with their mothers prior to incarceration, the experiences of children during their mother's incarceration, and the length of time that the mother was incarcerated. One of the first obstacles to successful reunification involves trying to regain custody of the children left behind. Recall that for most incarcerated mothers, the maternal grandparent cares for their children. In most of these cases, the expectation is that the mother will be able to resume custody of her children.

Many women, however, have lost custody of their children as a result of their incarceration. Some states even passed legislation that would make incarceration paramount to neglect on the part of the mother. However, efforts to use incarceration as the only factor to deny a mother her parental rights have not met with widespread success. For example, although a felony conviction and incarceration is included among the grounds for termination of parental rights in Florida, there are a number of other factors (Florida Statutes

Section 39.806). These factors include the period of time the parent will be incarcerated relative to the child's age of majority, the type of offense, and the best interest of the child.

Gentry (1995) reported that more than twenty-five states had termination of parental rights statutes or adoption statutes that were specific to incarcerated parents. An incarcerated parent who has not had contact with his or her child for six months can be charged with "abandonment," and steps to terminate parental rights can be taken. By 1998, felony convictions/incarceration were among the grounds for termination of parental rights in thirty-nine states (National Clearinghouse on Child Abuse and Neglect 1998).

As noted in Chapter 6, the federal Adoption and Safe Families Act of 1997 increased the likelihood that women will lose their parental rights entirely as a consequence of serving long prison terms (Acoca and Raeder 1999). Gentry (1998) reported that before this federal legislation was passed, incarcerated women nationwide were serving an average of fifteen months in prison; however, the average for black women was greater, at about twenty-two months. At the same time, in New York State, women were serving an average of almost eighteen months in prison. Nevertheless, the act required states to initiate or join termination of parental rights proceedings for children who had been in the custody of the state, in foster care, for fifteen of the most recent twenty-two months. Gentry (1998, 152) argued that "the new federal 15-month rule will mandate that termination proceedings be brought in the overwhelming majority of out-of-home cases involving incarcerated parents." The situation is even more hurtful when we take note of a recent report presented by the Women's Prison Association (WPA 2003), which indicated that women were serving an average of nineteen months in prison. This increase in the average sentence of four months in less than five years makes it even more likely that incarcerated women will lose their parental rights.

ASFA comes down especially hard on those inmates whose children are placed in foster care, serving to increase the number of women who will lose the right to reunite with their children. John Hagan and Juleigh Coleman (2001) pointed out that the time a female inmate spends away from her children is lengthened by the time involved in pretrial detainment, custody hearings and trials, and the actual criminal trial.

Over the years, the average sentence for incarcerated women has increased significantly, which does not augur well for incarcerated mothers with children in foster care. ASFA also mandates that once termination has been granted, the agency is required to find a permanent placement for the child. Finding such a placement, however, is often fraught with difficulties. It depends upon the race, ethnicity, sex, age, and physical and mental condition of the child. Even if the child is not adopted, the initiation of this process makes reunification between the mother and her child unlikely.

■ **Employment**

The road to reentry is complicated by the fact that those released from prison must address a number of survival issues simultaneously. The female ex-offender with children will need to have a job and housing in place before she can realistically reunite with her children, but many inmates have very erratic and poor job histories, making them marginally employable. According to the BJS survey (1999b), half of all incarcerated mothers were unemployed at the time of their arrest, which means many incarcerated mothers will not be eligible to apply for unemployment benefits, which could possibly tide them over until they could find gainful employment (Petersilia 2000). In the District of Columbia, unemployment benefits last a maximum of twenty-six weeks. If the former employee/ex-offender collected unemployment benefits for less than twenty-six weeks prior to incarceration, then she is only eligible to collect benefits for the number of weeks remaining. However, if she has exhausted her entitlement or was fired from her place of employment, she is ineligible for unemployment benefits.

Furthermore, because the profile of the incarcerated female is that of a woman with a minimal legitimate work history and few marketable job skills, the legitimate jobs available are unlikely to provide a living wage (Lynch and Sabol 2001). These individuals are included among the working poor. In addition, congressional changes to the Higher Education Act in 1998 affected eligibility for federal financial aid programs such as Perkins loans, Pell Grants, Supplemental Education Opportunity Grants, PLUS loans, and work-study programs. This act disqualifies those who have been convicted of any offense under any federal or state law involving the possession or sale of a controlled substance from receiving any grant, loan, or work assistance (Allard 2002). This aid is suspended on the date of conviction, and reinstatement depends on the type of offense and criminal history of the offender. Paul Samuels and Debbie Mukamal (2004) advise that this restriction applies even if the person was not receiving assistance at the time of conviction. This legislation closes another door to those women who leave prison without marketable job skills, since these women are likely to have been convicted for a drug offense.

For those with the requisite skills and good job histories, finding a job takes a considerable amount of time and effort. These conditions are compounded for the returning prisoner. Looking for a job requires money. The job hunter must be mobile, and either access to a car or the use of public transportation requires funds. The job seeker must be able to garner information about job openings, which requires access to a telephone and the newspaper. The job seeker must also have appropriate clothing for the initial interview and for the job, if the interview is successful. Those who have children must secure child care. Ironically, looking for a job to provide the monies needed to support a family requires monies that the individual just released from prison may not have. This adds to the burden of satisfying the conditions of release and reintegrating into the family and the community.

What's more, individuals who are banned from Temporary Assistance for Needy Families (TANF) because of their criminal conviction also lose access to a wide range of employment-related services provided by states through TANF programs (Hirsch 2002). At the state level, recipients of TANF are eligible to participate in a job-training partnership program, an employment service that provides information from a number of state agencies on job openings, and adult education programs. When ex-offenders are banned from TANF assistance, they also lose access to these services, which would help them to improve their education and employment skills, thereby making the hunt for a job easier. Having access to state job listings would also open up the possibility of employment in a better-paying job.

Finally, a number of employment restrictions go along with having been convicted of a crime. A felony conviction may negatively affect federal employment and result in the loss of a federal license. Some restrictions also exist at the state level. Lynch and Sabol (2001) reported that California parolees were barred from the fields of law, real estate, medicine, nursing, physical therapy, and education, whereas Colorado prohibited them from becoming dentists, engineers, nurses, pharmacists, physicians, or real estate agents. Even though most incarcerated women may not be affected by these restrictions, it is likely that some will be. Sharon Dietrich (2002) found that in some states, ex-offenders are barred from employment in nursing homes, in-home health care, and in-home child care facilities, occupations that many would qualify for without the criminal record.

Because of the employment-at-will laws common in the United States, a number of employers refuse to hire or retain persons with criminal records, even though typically they are not prohibited from doing so (Dietrich 2002). Since there is no contract in these settings, the presumption is that employment is voluntary and can be terminated by both employees and employers. A review of state laws by Samuels and Mukamal (2004) indicates the magnitude of the impact of a criminal record on employment opportunities. In twenty-nine states there were no standards governing the relevance of conviction records to licenses; in thirty-six states there were no standards governing a public employer's consideration of criminal records, and in forty-five states there were no standards governing private employers. Without standards, employers and licensees are free to allow their prejudices to enter into their selections for employment.

Jeremy Travis, Amy Solomon, and Michelle Waul (2001) reviewed an earlier survey by Harry Holzer, who found that two-thirds of all employers in five major cities indicated that they would not knowingly hire an ex-prisoner and that about one-third of the employers surveyed checked the criminal histories of their new employees. Amy Hirsch (2002) reported that research indicated that over 60 percent of employers probably would not hire an ex-offender. Moreover, there were differences by race, with a criminal record being more detrimental to the job prospects of African American applicants than white applicants. More specifically, the research indicated that a criminal record reduced employment opportunities for white applicants by 50 percent and those for African American applicants by 64 percent. Although these studies did not examine differences by gender or by race and gender, there is little reason to believe that female ex-offenders are looked upon more favorably than male ex-offenders or that black female ex-offenders get a fairer shake than white female ex-offenders.

Dina Rose and Todd Clear (2002) described additional barriers uncovered in interviews with ex-offenders employed in Florida. They recounted being offered too few hours, which did not qualify them for benefits such as health care. Consequently, one job was insufficient to provide a living wage, and many had to work multiple jobs. This complicates the situation even more for inmate mothers, who have children for whom they must provide financial support and supervision.

Clearly, for the returning offender, the job of finding a job is very challenging. The ex-offender brings a number of personal deficiencies to the employment setting, including a poor job history, lack of a high school diploma, and few marketable skills. The ex-offender may also bring a number of situational deficits to the employment setting, such as poor provisions for child care and inadequate access to transportation. Add to these obstacles the designation of ex-offender, and the search for a job may seem as difficult as running against a 30-mile-per-hour crosswind.

Bruce Western, Jeffrey Kling, and David Weiman (2001) examine the labor market consequences of incarceration for men. They found that those who had been incarcerated earned between 10 and 30 percent less than those who had never been incarcerated. Since women as a group make significantly less than men, it can be hypothesized that women who have been incarcerated will make less than women who have not been incarcerated. Moreover, it is expected that the gap between the earnings for the two groups of women will be at least equal to the differential found for the men.

The fact that releasees may be under the jurisdiction of multiple agencies whose policies and practices conflict and who fail to communicate with each other adds to the quagmire. Most states require that TANF recipients work between twenty and thirty hours per week, depending in part on whether they have school-age children. In addition to the twenty-four-month work requirement, there is also a two-month community service requirement. Hirsch (2002) argued that the requirements of TANF, the food stamp program's work requirements, and probation and parole requirements often conflict. Participants in TANF and food stamp programs must attend welfare-to-work programs during particular hours. Unfortunately, these times often conflict with the conditions of release placed upon those on probation or parole. For example, parolees are required to check in with their supervisors, and many must attend drug, individual, and family counseling sessions, which often are held during traditional work hours. The often-used excuses, "I have a doctor's appointment" or "I have to meet with my child's teacher," have a very limited life expectancy. The dilemma should be clear. On the one hand, missing work or training could result in the denial of TANF and food stamp benefits. On the other hand, missing counseling sessions or meetings with the parole supervisor could result in revocation of parole. The releasee is stuck between the proverbial rock and a hard place.

■ Welfare

Federal and state governments offer assistance to individuals and families who have insufficient income to provide for their necessities. However, national legislators have moved to restrict these benefits for those who have been incarcerated. In 1996 the federal government introduced legislation aimed at reforming the welfare system in the United States. The Personal Responsibility and Work Opportunity Reconciliation Act (see Box 8.2) replaced welfare with Temporary Assistance to Needy Families (TANF), a block grant to individual states (Krisberg and Temin 2001; Rubenstein and Mukamal 2002). This legislation, which made it easier to drop families from welfare rolls if the parents had criminal convictions for a drug offense, applies to any person convicted of a state or federal felony offense for using or selling drugs. It directly affects roughly one-third of female inmates and indirectly affects their children (Gaouette 1997).

Welfare reform places a five-year lifetime limit on benefits and requires welfare recipients to work to receive benefits. The act also permanently bars anyone with a drug-related felony conviction from receiving cash assistance and food stamps during her lifetime (Jacobs 2000), thus prohibiting states from providing TANF benefits and food stamps. There seems to be some confusion with respect to other categories of benefits. Jacobs (2000) reports that the legislation also bars those with drug-related felony convictions from receiving Supplementary Security Income (SSI). Hirsch (1999), in a study of the impact of welfare reform in Pennsylvania, argued that although the ban does not apply to SSI, Medicaid, or Medicare, many women indicated that they were denied such benefits by Department of Public Welfare caseworkers who were confused about the provisions.

Thirty-nine states have eliminated or modified the lifetime ban (see Box 8.3). In 1997, one year after the legislation creating the lifetime ban was introduced, Washington State passed legislation that modified the ban. New York, New Jersey, Illinois, Connecticut, Oklahoma, and Ohio, states with sizable female prison populations, are included among those who have eliminated or

162

> ### Box 8.2 Highlights of the Personal Responsibility and Work Opportunity Reconciliation Act of 1996
>
> *Work requirements.* Recipients must work after two years on assistance. Single parents must participate for at least twenty hours per week the first year, increasing that number of hours to at least thirty per week by year two. Two-parent families must work thirty-five hours per week by July 1 of year one.
>
> *Support for families transitioning into jobs.* The new welfare law provides funding for child care to help more mothers move into jobs. The new law also guarantees that women on welfare continue to receive health coverage for their families, including at least one year of transitional Medicaid when they leave welfare for work.
>
> *Work activities.* To meet their state work requirements, recipients will be required to participate in unsubsidized or subsidized employment, on-the-job training, work experience, community service, or twelve months of vocational training or provide child care services to individuals who are participating in community service. Up to six weeks of job search (no more than four consecutive weeks) would count toward the work requirement. However, no more than 20 percent of each state's caseload may count toward the work requirement solely by participating in vocational training or by being a teen parent in secondary school. Single parents with a child under six who cannot find child care cannot be penalized for failure to meet the work requirements. States can exempt from the work requirement single parents with children under age one and disregard these individuals in the calculation of participation rates for up to twelve months.
>
> - *A five-year time limit.* Families who have received assistance for five cumulative years (or less at state option) will be ineligible for cash aid under the new welfare law.
> - *Job subsidies.* The law also allows states to create jobs by taking money now used for welfare checks and using it to create community service jobs or to provide income subsidies or hiring incentives for potential employers.
>
> *Source:* "Fact Sheet." 1996. Administration for Children and Families, US Department of Health and Human Services. www.acf.dhhs.gov/programs/ofa/prwora96.htm.

Box 8.3   Ban on Drug Felons Receiving TANF and Food Stamps

Adopted Federal Ban	Opted Out of Federal Ban Entirely	Opted Out of Food Stamps and Modified Ban on TANF	Modified Ban by Requiring Treatment	Modified Ban by Completion of Sentence or Treatment	Other Modifications[a]
Alabama	Idaho	Illinois	Colorado	Connecticut	Arkansas
Alaska	Maine	Massachusetts	Hawaii		Delaware
Arizona	Michigan		Iowa		Florida
California	New Hampshire		Kentucky		Louisiana
Georgia	New Mexico		Nevada		Maryland
Indiana	New York		South Carolina		Minnesota
Kansas	Ohio		Tennessee		New Jersey
Mississippi	Oklahoma				North Carolina
Missouri	Pennsylvania[b]				Rhode Island
Montana	Oregon				Washington
Nebraska	Utah				Wisconsin
North Dakota	Vermont				
South Dakota					
Texas					
Virginia					
West Virginia					
Wyoming					

Source: "After Frison: Roadblocks to Reentry." 2004. Legal Action Center, www.lac.org/roadblocks.html.

Notes: a. Limiting ban to distribution or sale offenses or requiring submission to drug testing.

b. The new statute opting out specifically requires the department to follow preexisting procedures for referral for assessment and treatment if available and appropriate.

modified the ban (Hirsch 1999). Unfortunately, in seventeen states women convicted of drug felonies are still permanently ineligible for public assistance (Samuels and Mukamal 2004; Allard 2002). Furthermore, this restriction applies to cases in which the crime occurred in previous years and in situations in which the person has been treated and rehabilitated. Texas and California, which together hold almost one-quarter of all female prisoners, and Mississippi, which has the second-highest female incarceration rate in the country, are all among this second group.

In seven states (Alabama, Delaware, Illinois, Mississippi, Virginia, Pennsylvania, and Texas) that implement the ban in part or in full, African American and Latinas represent the majority of women subject to the ban. Patricia Allard (2002) estimated that this ban affects over 92,000 women, including nearly 35,000 African American women (and almost 10,000 Latinas) and places over 135,000 children at risk of coming in contact with child welfare services and the criminal justice system due to reduced family income support. The ban endangers basic needs of low-income women and their children, including housing, food, job training, education, and drug treatment. A number of drug treatment programs depend on food stamps and cash assistance to feed and house women and children in treatment programs.

Hirsch (1999) suggested that the introduction of the ban focused on an image of "drug felons" that does not align with the actual drug felon, especially not women with felony drug convictions. According to Hirsch (1999, v), based on the women that she interviewed in Pennsylvania: "The overwhelming majority of the women had no prior drug convictions, and their felony convictions are for *very* small quantities of drugs (often only $5 or $10 worth)."

Finally, it is important to keep in mind that this ban is only on the person with the drug conviction. Hirsch (1999) stresses that other household members can still be eligible. However, any income or resources that the barred individual may earn will be counted against the rest of the family's benefits. In the case of women with felony drug convictions, this can prove to be an unbearable burden. If they return to the household and are capable of providing some resources, they place their families in a zero-sum situation. If they return and are incapable of providing resources, then they are adding to the size of the family and siphoning off what are probably the bare subsistence resources of their family members.

For those women who have been incarcerated for other types of offenses, the situation is not much better. The Personal Responsibility and Work Opportunity Reconciliation Act of 1996 also subjects TANF recipients to a five-year limit on the length of time they can receive benefits over their lifetimes (Jacobs 2000). The profile of the typical female inmate indicated that a number of them had received benefits prior to incarceration. If no extensions are available, then benefits either may not be available for some returnees or available for a very limited time. Either case may jeopardize reconciliation and "promote" recidivism.

Workfare requirements on public assistance recipients can also be problematic. If the participant misses an appointment, her benefits may be terminated. The behavior of their children may also jeopardize their benefits. For example, if a child is truant, the parents may risk the termination of their benefits.

Another obstacle that confronts eligible applicants is the time required to complete the application process. Jacobs (2000) reports that there may be significant delays between the time a woman applies for benefits and the time she is declared eligible. For example, Jacobs reports that in New York City, the mandated waiting period is forty-five days, but the actual wait is often longer.

■ Housing

Offenders returning to the community must first find shelter. It may be a condition of release. Often, they are able to return to their homes or can find shelter with family or friends. If not, they may find emergency shelter or transitional housing (Rossman 2002). Emergency shelters are used by a significant number of ex-offenders and provide little stability. Travis, Solomon, and Waul (2001) found that in New York State, 11 percent of released prisoners entered homeless shelters within two years after release, with one-third reincarcerated within two years. These shelters should be considered stopgap measures; alternative arrangements must still be made. In the case of transitional housing, the returning offender is usually provided with housing assistance, job placement assistance, and residency credentials, which help them to gain access to other services (Rossman 2002).

In addition, the federal government has a long history of providing housing for those without resources. Since the 1970s, a number of changes have been made to these programs. Prominent among them have been restrictions on those who may participate in these programs. One group that has been targeted for exclusion is drug offenders. Unfortunately, a large number of those returning to their communities in need of housing are drug offenders.

Since the 1930s, the federal government has created housing assistance programs to help provide low-income housing to families needing assistance. In 1974 Congress passed the Housing and Community Development Act, creating the Section 8 program that provides subsidies to help low-income families pay their rent. Under Section 8, tenants pay between 30 and 40 percent of their income for rent, and the remainder is paid with federal money. Over the years, this legislation has undergone numerous revisions.

In 1988 the second federal Anti–Drug Abuse Act was passed, which included the "One Strike and You're Out" policy (see Box 8.4). It was designed to curb drug-related crime in public housing projects and to protect tenants by

Box 8.4   US Department of Housing and
Urban Development (HUD) "One-Strike" Policy

This policy originated in the Anti–Drug Abuse Act of 1988. Congress found that "the Federal Government has a duty to provide public and other federally assisted low-income housing that is decent, safe, and free from illegal drugs" and that "public and other federally assisted low-income housing in many areas suffers from rampant drug-related crime." Congress required that public housing authorities (PHAs) use leases

> which prohibit any drug-related criminal activity on or near the premises by a resident, any member of the household, guest, or another person under the resident's control, provide that a public housing tenant, any member of the tenant's household, or a guest or other person under the tenant's control shall not engage in criminal activity, including drug-related criminal activity, on or near public housing premises, while the tenant is a tenant in public housing, and such criminal activity shall be cause for termination of tenancy.

In 1990, Congress revised the language of the statute without substantive effect. Congress amended this statute again in 1996, replacing the phrase "on or near public housing premises" with "on *or off* such premises" (emphasis added).

In 1991, HUD issued regulations implementing the statute. One regulation, 24 C.F.R. § 966.4(f)(12), requires the lease to include language that obligates the tenant

> (i) [t]o assure that the tenant, any member of the household, a guest, or another person under the tenant's control, shall not engage in:
> . . . (B) Any drug-related criminal activity on or near such premises. Any criminal activity in violation of the preceding sentence shall be cause for termination of tenancy, and for eviction from the unit.

HUD rejected comments opposing the "strict liability" policy in developing these rules, providing PHAs the discretion to evict a tenant whose household members or guests use or sell drugs on or near public housing premises, regardless of whether the tenant knew or should have known of such activity. In exercising that discretion, the rules also recognize the importance of giving each case individualized consideration in light of the inequities presented and evaluating the propriety of alternative remedial measures.

In his 1996 State of the Union speech, President Clinton gave new emphasis to enforcement of this policy, and HUD followed up with issuance of its "One Strike" notice soon afterward. In 1998, Congress elsewhere added other duplicative provisions requiring leases to permit eviction for drug use by household members that threatens other tenants' health and safety.

Source: "Ninth Circuit Panel Upholds 'One Strike' Evictions." *National Housing Law Project: Housing Law Bulletin.* www.nhlp.org/html/hlb/200/ninthcircuit.htm.

forbidding "any member of the tenant's household, or a guest or other person under the tenant's control" from engaging in drug-related criminal activity on or near public housing. In 1996 the "One Strike" was enacted as part of the Housing Opportunity Extension Act (P.L. 104-120; 110 Stat. 834). This extension was much more expansive. The "new" policy allowed public housing authorities (PHAs) to evict not only residents who committed a felony but also residents whose friends or relatives were suspected of using drugs, even if the suspect was not arrested in the tenant's home, the charges were dropped, or the suspect was found innocent. In addition, eviction can result from activity on or off the premises by tenants, household members, or guests and on the premises of persons under the tenant's control (Landau 2002). The measure also allowed federal housing administrators to reject housing applicants who had already been convicted of felonies.

It is important to stress that although the emphasis has been on drug offenses because this group of offenses accounts for the largest percentage of convictions, the legislation covers a much broader range of offenses. According to Rue Landau (2002), "In general, a PHA can deny admission to adult applicant family members who have a history of crimes of physical violence to people or property, or of other criminal acts that would adversely affect the health, safety, and welfare of other tenants." Landau (2002) points out that in Philadelphia, disorderly conduct is included among the list of offenses that could lead to a denial of admission to subsidized housing.

First, under this legislation women incarcerated for drug offenses, who may have been living with relatives or even visiting relatives in public housing, may place their family members in jeopardy (US Housing Act, Title 42 U.S. C. Section 1437d). In *Department of Housing and Urban Development v. Rucker et al.* (2002), the U.S. Supreme Court upheld a provision that permits public housing authorities to evict longtime tenants for drug-related activity of family members or guests (see Box 8.5). This provision also applies to alcohol abuse. Those evicted are ineligible for three years. These no-fault evictions extend to drug activity off the premises as well (Extenders Act, Section 9, 1996). In the court case mentioned above, two grandmothers were ordered out of their homes because their children or grandchildren were seen outside the house with drugs (marijuana and cocaine) and drug paraphernalia (a crack pipe). Not only were those family members left without subsidized housing, but also the housing options for their children or grandchildren returning from prison may be restricted.

The Extenders Act (Section 9, 1996) also provides for access to criminal records for screening people applying for Section 8 certificates. This effectively bars people with drug convictions from living in federally funded public housing and precludes many women offenders from a tool available for securing affordable permanent housing.

Box 8.5   "One Strike and You're Out"

■ The Plaintiffs

Pearlie Rucker, sixty-three, resided at her home for twelve years. Living with her is her daughter, two granddaughters, and one great-grand-daughter. Pearlie is the primary caregiver for the entire family. Her daughter is incapable of caring for herself due to mental disability.

Herman Walker is seventy-five years old and disabled. He has lived in his home for eight years. He is partially paralyzed, has problems walking, usually needs a cane, is hard of hearing, and is periodically put on oxygen. He is no longer capable of living independently and requires in-home health care.

Willie Lee is seventy-one years old and has resided in her home at the Oakland Housing Authority for twenty-five years.

Barbara Hill is sixty-three years old and has lived at her premises for approximately thirty years.

■ The Eviction Offenses

Rucker

Approximately three blocks from the Rucker home, the disabled daughter was arrested for being drunk in public. A search of the young woman revealed one rock of suspected cocaine and a crack cocaine pipe. The woman gave Rucker's address as her own. Another family member was arrested about eight blocks away on a warrant and for possession of rock cocaine. Although the latter family member did not live with the other Ruckers, he gave their address as his. Pearlie testified that she had searched the room of her daughter looking for evidence of alcohol and drug use but had never found any drugs or drug paraphernalia, nor had her daughter ever shown any sign of drug use. She said she warned her daughter and others that any drug use or criminal activity on the premises could result in eviction.

Walker

Three women and a child, none of whom are on the lease but who shared the unit nonetheless, had various narcotic arrest records in the complex. Two of those women, upon searches, were arrested when officers found one rock of cocaine, a cocaine pipe, and narcotics paraphernalia. As officers searched the unit, they recovered a cardboard

continues

Box 8.5   continued

box inside Herman Walker's bedroom containing a plate with suspected rock cocaine chips and four metal crack cocaine pipes. Two subsequent searches of the unit, one a week later and another two months later, uncovered additional drug paraphernalia on both occasions. Walker revealed that one of the women in the apartment was his in-home caregiver, whom he fired once he learned she was accused of drug activity in his unit. Walker's eviction suit is awaiting trial.

Lee

A grandson listed as a resident on the lease was cited in the parking lot area of the complex for possession of marijuana. Lee said she had warned household members that any drug use or criminal activity on the premises could result in eviction. The eviction suit against Lee is awaiting trial.

Hill

A grandson listed as resident on the lease was cited in the parking lot area of the complex for smoking marijuana. Hill warned her household that any drug use or criminal activity on the premises could result in eviction. The eviction suit against Ms. Hill awaits trial.

Public and other forms of assisted housing in the United States are slowly evolving from a "take it or leave it" approach to management to a market approach embracing Standard and Poor's evaluation of the facility's curb appeal, efficiency, and competitiveness, as well as the "corporate" balance sheet. Persons and families receiving Section 8 rental assistance vouchers or living in publicly assisted housing need no longer endure criminal activity inside or outside their homes. The federal government, through its housing managers, is determined to provide decent, safe, affordable housing to people who need it.

This long-awaited Supreme Court decision is meant to help residents of all assisted housing take a 'bite out of crime', and to help management maintain safe environments for all their tenants' families. Residents are encouraged to report suspected criminal conduct to their management office.

Source: Michael Cummings, "'One Strike and You're Out' of Rent Assisted Housing." *Step Up* 6 (2), www.housingall.com/housing/OneStrike.htm.

▪ Drug Treatment

Beth Richie (2001) identified a number of challenges that face women returning to their communities from prison. Included among these challenges is the need for treatment for substance abuse problems, health care, and mental health issues (see Chapters 4 and 5).

As we reported earlier in this book, many incarcerated women have alcohol and drug addiction problems. In the late 1980s harsh drug sentences were introduced at the federal level. The crack cocaine sentencing policy resulted in what has been called the 100 to 1 ratio. A conviction for possession of 500 grams or more of powder cocaine with intent to distribute carried a five-year sentence, whereas a conviction of possession with intent to distribute 5 grams of crack cocaine carried the same penalty. Crack also carries a mandatory sentence for first offense simple possession. According to the US Sentencing Commission (1995), black men and women are serving longer prison sentences than white men and women. Largely the result of approaches to enforcement, this policy has led to incarceration of more drug offenders and now release of more of those who entered prison with drug problems.

Research indicates that institutionalized prisoners do not have access to the type and number of drug treatment programs that would reduce or eliminate their drug abuse problems (Mears et al. 2003). Without any treatment in prison, these women return to the communities with their drug problems latent. Participation in drug treatment programs upon release (at their own expense) is often a condition of release, however. Hagan and Coleman (2001) noted that successful completion of such a program is often a condition of reunification.

A number of residential drug treatment programs depend on food stamps and cash assistance to feed and house women and children in treatment programs. Rukaiyah Adams, David Onek, and Alissa Riker (1998) reported that a survey of fourteen residential treatment programs in California indicated that 69 percent of the programs' food expenses were covered by food stamps. Without this support, the programs would have a difficult time surviving. It is believed that this is the case beyond California. Unfortunately, the releasees who are most in need of access to these programs will be ineligible due to their drug convictions. As a result, these offenders are at high risk of both relapse and participation in crimes aimed at supporting their illegal drug use (GAO 2001).

▪ Health Care

Richie (2001, 373) reported that the formerly incarcerated women that she interviewed described their health care needs as "treatment related to complications of HIV, asthma, diabetes, hypertension, and reproductive health problems." Upon their return to the community one issue of major concern is access to benefits programs that will cover health care needs. Theodore Hammett, Cheryl Roberts, and Sofia Kennedy (2001) noted that ex-offenders are not eligible for Medicaid, SSI, or the AIDS Drug Assistance Program (ADAP). Laura Maruschak (2004) reported that at the end of 2002, there were 19,297 male inmates and 2,053 female inmates in state prisons who were HIV-positive (see Chapter 7). Upon their return to the community, they would not be eligible to receive free medications through ADAP. Hammett, Roberts, and Kennedy (2001) go on to say that few releasees have health insurance through a family member. Furthermore, since most do not have jobs upon their release, they do not have health insurance through an employer. Gerald Gaes and Newton Kendig (2002, 105) concede: "Even with aggressive discharge planning, certain offenders will not qualify for either private or publicly funded medical insurance and will fall to the bottom rung of available medical care, typically community health care networks and local emergency rooms." Consequently, many conditions will be neglected until releasees gain access to benefits. Unfortunately, without attention these conditions may deteriorate.

This suggests that these returnees will have to rely on the public sector for health care services. Without adequate finances or access to health care through others, finding health care services will be very difficult. Lois Davis and Sharon Pacchiana (2003) added that the situation is complicated by the fact that these ex-offenders return to communities in which health care resources are limited. As a result, returnees must seek services elsewhere. Sadly, without monies for transportation, doctors' bills, and prescription fees, health care needs will go untreated, and existing conditions will probably get worse.

Hammett, Roberts, and Kennedy (2001, 392) also identified another issue, that of "discharge planning, community linkages, and continuity of care." The authors noted that past research indicated that the majority of state and federal prison systems and large city and county jail systems provide some discharge planning. However, upon closer examination, they discovered that more systems provided referrals for services than actually making appointments for releasees for specific services. The suggestion was that providing appointments increased the likelihood that releasees would actually receive services.

As noted earlier, ex-offenders often suffer from a number of chronic health problems. If these problems go untreated, it may be difficult for the ex-offender to look for a job or to work. It will also create difficulties when the ex-offender has to attend postrelease meetings.

■ Voting

Box 8.6 offers just two examples of state laws governing the disenfranchisement of convicted felons. In forty-eight states and the District of Columbia, inmates may not vote while incarcerated for a felony offense. Prohibitions are in effect for felons on parole in thirty-two states, for those who are on probation

---

Box 8.6   Sample Disenfranchisement Statutes

New Mexico: A person convicted of a felony or infamous crime for-feits the rights to vote and to hold public office. N.M. Const. art. VII Section, 1, 2; N.M. Stat. Ann. Sections 10-1-2, 31-13-1.

A person convicted under New Mexico law may regain his civil rights by presenting the certificate of discharge he receives upon com-pletion of sentence to the Governor, who has the power to pardon . . . or to issue a certificate restoring the person to full rights of citizenship. N.M. Const. art. V. Section 6; N.M Stat. Ann, Section 31-13-1.

District of Columbia: A felon's right to vote is suspended only during imprisonment. D.C. Code Section 1-1302(7) A.

The rights to vote and to hold many public offices are restored upon release from imprisonment. D.C. Code Sections 1-225; 1-241(c); 1302(7) A.

---

in twenty-eight states, and for ex-felons who have completed their sentences in thirteen states (Simson 2002). Just two states, Maine and Vermont, have no re-strictions on the right to vote by people with felony convictions (Samuels and Mukamal 2004). Mississippi, which has the second-highest female incarcera-tion rate in the country, has a lifetime ban on voting for those convicted of a felony. In Louisiana, Okalahoma, Texas, and Florida, four jurisdictions with large numbers of incarcerated females, people are barred from voting while they are incarcerated or serving parole or probation sentences. Prior to 1996, convicted felons in Texas had to wait two years after completing their sentence before they were eligible to vote (Kalogeras 2003).

Marc Mauer (2002) revealed that almost 5 million Americans have cur-rently or permanently lost the right to vote because they were either serving a felony sentence or had previously been convicted of a felony. He contended that "whether the *intended* effect of disenfranchisement policies today is to re-duce minority voting power, it is inescapable that this impact could have been predicted as a logical consequence of the nation's wars on crime and drugs" (2002, 52). Furthermore, 1.4 million of those who are disenfranchised as a re-sult of felony convictions are African American males, accounting for 13 per-cent of the adult black male population (Mauer 2002).

Of course, disenfranchisement also affects the female population. Women make up a small proportion (over 500,000) of the remaining 2.6 million Americans who are disenfranchised. It is expected that just about one-half of them are black females. When we add the number of black females to the 1.4 million black males, the consequences for democratic participation on the part of the black community become even more unsettling. Factor in the number of other minorities, especially Hispanic males and females, who also suffer from disenfranchisement, and the magnitude of the problem balloons. Still, the actual number and the relative impact, as it relates to the number of people who are likely to vote, is unknown.

Furthermore, Mauer (2002) argued, in part, that these laws are counterproductive because they conflict with the goals of promoting public safety. Joan Petersilia (2000, 5) added: "denying large segments of the minority population the right to vote is likely to cause further alienation. Disillusionment with the political process also erodes citizens' feeling of engagement and makes them less willing to participate in local political activities and to exert informal social control in their community."

Simson (2002) underscored that in 2000, just 537 votes in Florida decided the winner of the presidential election at the same time that 647,100 Floridians were prohibited from voting as a result of disenfranchisement laws. Moreover, 436,000 of these ex-felons have successfully completed their sentences. Since that time, Allard and Mauer (2000) have reviewed the policy changes introduced by thirteen jurisdictions that have revisited their disenfranchisement laws. Although Massachusetts voted to strip persons incarcerated for a felony offense of their right to vote and Kansas added probationers to the category of excluded felons, most of the policy changes extended voting rights to ex-felons. It is expected that this debate will intensify as the number of disenfranchised continues to grow, and the political consequences for minority communities are acknowledged.

▧ Stigma

> One of the problems that all ex-offenders face is the stigma of their criminal history, which affects the ex-offenders, their families, and the communities they are entering after serving prison terms. (Celinska 2000, 100)

When offenders return to their homes and their communities from prison, they face a dilemma. Should they tell those outside the family about their ex-offender status? This decision may have a negative impact on access to housing and employment. It may also strain relationships between community members, neighbors, and other family members.

Mary Dodge and Mark Pogrebin (2001, 50) related the consequences of the stigma of the criminal label respondents in two settings, one with parents of other children and the other in a religious environment. According to one respondent:

> I became friends with some other mothers at my kid's school. They were really nice. I joined the PTA and it was going good. Then I told someone, I

don't know how it came up, that I was in prison. Now, some of them won't talk to me, and they won't let their kids play with mine. So I learned my lesson. I don't really care what people think of me. Well, I kind of do, but I just don't want my kids to suffer.

Rose and Clear (2002) present four possible solutions to dealing with stigma: actively trying to change the other's opinions, going on about their business (living with other's opinions of you), isolating from others who may judge them, and moving to a new community to start over. These authors contend that changing the opinions of others promotes a sense of reconnectedness at the family level and enhances a sense of belonging and trust at the community level. The other options seem less positive in terms of social capital. They promote alienation and undermine a feeling of belonging, which in turn diminish participation in community activities and lead to increases in crime (Rose and Clear 2002). Finally, relocating is costly. Offenders incur financial costs when moving and setting up new households. They also increase the distance from long-term social supports and enter a new community in which they must forge new relationships.

The task ahead of them involves destigmatizing, or at least lessening, the stigma of what has long been viewed as a "master status," the status or label that supersedes all other statuses. It requires that people in the United States take action to (1) fund and evaluate programs aimed at habilitating or rehabilitating offenders, (2) educate the public as to the success of these programs, and (3) encourage family and community members to extend their friendship and acceptance to returning offenders.

■ Conclusion

The typical returning woman faced with multiple and competing demands "may be simultaneously attempting to regain custody of her children, looking for an apartment and a job, and trying to get into a substance abuse treatment program as a condition of her probation or parole" (Richie 2001, 380).

Each of the areas reviewed above has been identified as a roadblock to reentry. There have been efforts to assess the far-reaching impact of these impediments. Samuels and Mukamal (2004) graded the states on the extent to which their laws and policies created roadblocks in a number of areas, including employment, public assistance and food stamps, access to criminal records, voting, and public housing. Texas and Mississippi were rated thirty-fifth and thirty-eighth, respectively, out of the fifty states and were ranked among the worst in terms of these roadblocks.

There are also efforts afoot to change public policy. The Supreme Court struck down the Washington State sentencing guidelines in *Blakely v. Washington* (2004). The Court ruled that in order to increase the penalty attached to a crime beyond the prescribed statutory minimum, the defendant's Sixth Amendment right to trial by jury required that the jury must find all facts proved beyond a reasonable doubt. This ruling called into question the stability of the sentencing guidelines, one factor accounting for the longer prison terms. Months later in *United States v. Booker* (2005) and *United States v. Fanfan* (2005), the Supreme Court ruled that federal sentencing guidelines were no longer mandatory. As a result of these rulings, sentencing guidelines for federal and state courts have been invalidated. Other sentencing schemes, including "three strikes and you're out," are also under review.

The Second Chance Act of 2004: Community Safety Through Recidivism Prevention was also introduced in the US House of Representatives. This bill would earmark monies for drug treatment and mentoring programs to help newly released felons. It would also repeal the provision in the Higher Education Act that denies college loans to applicants with drug offenses (*Washington Times* 2004). The bill was reintroduced in 2005.

Whether these efforts are undertaken to ease the burden on an overcrowded corrections system or to lessen the financial drain on state and federal budgets, the result will be the same. The removal of these roadblocks will facilitate the successful reintegration of ex-offenders into their families and into the larger society. The sustained success of these ex-offenders will depend on our joint efforts.

PART 3

Conclusion

Still More Problems
Than Solutions

Assumptions about the nature of the raw materials for women's prisons—criminal women—and about their ideal end products—normatively feminine women—have tended to both soften the regimes imposed upon women and deny women's prisons certain resources. . . . The history of women's imprisonment is, of course, much more complex than this statement conveys. Neglect and inadequate resources, punitive treatment of nonwhite and poor women, long sentences for relatively minor crimes are important aspects of this history. (Gartner and Kruttschnitt 2004, 267)

The United States has more women behind bars than any other developed country. Our "corrections" policies and programs are, in reality, "punishment" policies and programs. Women, particularly women of color, are crowded into facilities—designed for and by men—before they are returned, with old problems intact, and probably new ones, to a community ill-equipped to ease the transition. This lack of sensitivity to the gendered nature of the problems that women face before, during, and after incarceration reduces opportunities for rehabilitation and reform and thus results in an additional burden of punishment for women. This additional burden affects not only these women but ultimately the larger society.

When we began the book, we asked, "How did it come to this?" We examined the history of the prison system, characteristics of prisons and prisoners, and issues with distinct meaning for and impact on incarcerated women. No doubt there have been some improvements in prisons for women over time. For example, women are no longer punished for gossiping or adultery, housed with men, and segregated by race. Women are now in top management positions and provide frontline care in a number of facilities. Prisons are beginning to recognize the need for and to introduce programs specifically for women. In the grand scheme of things, there has been progress, but the journey to a prison system free from gender or racial inequalities is far from over.

As indicated earlier, changes in criminal justice policies, rather than criminal behavior, account for the increasing number of women of color behind bars. The wars on crime and on drugs—introduced in the 1960s, 1970s, 1980s, and 1990s, and still waged today—focused on punitiveness. The resulting policies and practices were initially aimed at serious offenders, such as those who committed violent crimes, who were repeat and habitual offenders, who were major drug distributors, and whose offenses involved the use of guns. Since these "wars" began, offenders have been sentenced more frequently and more severely for all types of offenses, but especially for drug offenses, and more women are sent to prison now than at any time in US history. Some of these women are serving very long prison terms because of the type of drug they were convicted of selling or using. For example, the differences in sentencing for crack versus powder cocaine offenses and the differential involvement of women by race have been well documented. And despite the general knowledge of these facts, there is little support for changing the laws to make penalties for crack cocaine and powder cocaine equivalent. This bias remains because of a reluctance to acknowledge the institutional racism behind these policies and a lack of political will for change. With the present policies in place, crime has become a code word for race (Chesney-Lind 1998).

In a society still permeated with sexism and racism, we have to consider how the present punishments relate to women. Traditionally, there are assumed to be four purposes of corrections: retribution—exacting "an eye for an eye"; deterrence—teaching offenders that criminal behavior has steep negative consequences; incapacitation—making it impossible to commit future offenses; and rehabilitation—correcting deviant behavior. Nowhere in these four stated purposes is there the recognition of the diversity of individuals to whom punishment is directed or the context of the offending behavior, issues that are particularly important for the present cohort of incarcerated women.

■ Equal Rights Are Lost Opportunities for Women

Historically, women have been punished for different crimes than men: men have rarely been put to death or imprisoned for adultery, witchcraft, or gossip, for example. We find that again today there are attempts to criminalize behavior that is unique to women, supporting the argument that rights and opportunities are gendered. For example, some jurisdictions have introduced legislation that criminalizes pregnant women who use illegal drugs. This legislation has been premised on the danger to unborn children, although researchers have found no significant differences in IQ scores at age four between cocaine-exposed and similar unexposed children (Hurt et al. 1997). But factors (such as poor nutrition or lack of available prenatal care) that are known to affect the health of the unborn child are largely ignored in this debate, just as the offending male was usually ignored in the adultery suit.

Clearly, standards for acceptable behavior for women are still more stringent than they are for men.

Below we summarize issues discussed earlier. Problems that disproportionately affect women in prison ultimately have an impact on their families, communities, and the larger society. Without significant changes, opportunities for improving their lives and the lives of their families are wasted.

Families

Gender and racial differences are apparent in family arrangements for incarcerated individuals. The gender difference is especially apparent in dealing with children and their care while mothers are in prison. Worries about their children, such as the uncertainties and lack of information on child care arrangements, can aggravate or precipitate mental and physical health problems. Rarely is this true for incarcerated men; they can rely on the child's mother for care—a woman can rarely depend on the child's father. Further, social class differences are seen in caregiver arrangements and the ties between mothers and their children. Mothers can only maintain good relationships with their children with the cooperation of the caregiver. If the caregiver has no money for prison visits or is burdened with other responsibilities, the mother-child bond is bound to weaken. The fear of losing one's child, either literally or emotionally, is an additional burden that men do not usually share.

Because most incarcerated women are mothers, the impact of incarceration reaches far beyond the individual in prison. But despite the importance of mothers to their children, children to their mothers, and the pro-family public opinion of the early twenty-first century, policies at the state and federal levels have made it difficult for inmates to return to the community and reunite with intact families. Children may be in foster care, family members may be unwilling to allow the renewal of relationships with the returnees, or reunification may lead to the loss of needed housing and maintenance benefits for the family of the returning inmate. Program managers and policymakers must address the gendered nature of these issues if efforts toward reunification and a corresponding reduction in the rate of recidivism are to be successful.

Health

As we have said many times, healthy, well adjusted women rarely enter prison; women who end up behind bars have a multitude of interconnected substance abuse, medical, and mental health problems. And these problems differ by race and gender.

Substance abuse. Many women are in prison because of drug offenses; gender, race, and class differences are obvious in the types of drug problems they have, their arrest and incarceration rates, and their access to drug treatment programs. Quality substance abuse treatment designed for women must be available during their imprisonment—it is the logical and practical time for intervention. For example, treatment must consider the role of domestic violence as one aspect of women's involvement with drugs. The erosion in the number and variety of drug treatment programs available before and after incarceration makes getting and staying clean cumbersome, if not impossible, for someone who has no insurance, no transportation, and no child care. We know that different types of drug treatment programs work for different types of offenders, but there are still too few attempts to apply this knowledge in designing gender-specific programs and even fewer to consider the roles of race and ethnicity. Lack of appropriate, available treatment increases the likelihood of relapse and recidivism.

Physical health problems. Physical health problems also plague these inmates and are integrally related to mental health and substance abuse problems. Women, particularly women of color, have higher rates of medical disorders and disabilities than men, which suggests differential histories of poverty and violence. High rates of HIV/AIDS are a prime example. Women in prison have higher rates of this disease than men in prison or women in the community. There is no better time for implementing treatment regimes and educational programs that deal with both the disease and the complicating factor of substance abuse. Infected inmates who are released with access to alcohol and drug awareness programs should be given immediate access to necessary medications and to residential or outpatient drug treatment facilities. But HIV/AIDS cannot be treated in isolation: currently, some jurisdictions expedite insurance services available for HIV-positive inmates, but for other chronic disorders that complicate this disease, these services may not be available. There is an obvious need for mandatory treatment for such problems as substance abuse and HIV/AIDS; however, mandating treatment when there is no treatment available is mandating failure.

Mental health problems. Since the move to deinstitutionalization, corrections facilities have housed an increasingly large proportion of the mentally ill population. The most common treatment for this troubled population is psychotropic medication; most women in prison are simply drugged until they can take their problems home. Medication certainly is useful, but alone it is not the answer. Neither are traditional individual and group therapies, however, if they ignore the codependence and the co-occurring problems of drug use and mental illness and their context in the community. Mental health treatment in prison must start with a detailed assessment and build from there; for many, the first step is simply to learn to trust themselves. Developing and building self-esteem and addressing feelings of powerlessness and hopelessness after lives of neglect, violence, and betrayal are not easy. To this end, some prisons have successfully implemented therapies in which inmates garden or tend to pets. The success achieved in prison, however, can only be maintained by bridging the gap between services available during incarceration and services available upon release. Addressing mental health concerns with the dynamics of women's lives as the theoretical and practical basis could go a long way toward helping offenders cope with and resolve the underlying issues that contribute to their criminal behavior.

Tackling only one aspect of women's complicated and interconnected health problems is not a solution: If a car has four flat tires, we do not fix only one if we want to drive. Personnel trained in the overall constellation of problems that women present must be readily available; individualized assessment and treatment programs must be designed and implemented upon entry; and plans to provide treatment, transportation, and financial support after release must be addressed. Health education is perhaps the easiest entrée to improving health for women and, ultimately, their families. The federal government is advancing the Healthy People 2010 program, which sets health goals for individuals and communities; many of them, such as targets for diet and exercise, could easily be implemented in prison. Achieving and maintaining success in one health behavior might give prisoners a sense of confidence, competence, and control that could generalize to other health behaviors.

> "Many [prisoners] never manage to navigate the public health system—because they do not know how to fill in application forms for Medicaid, because they lack the necessary identification to apply, because they have no permanent address. And even those who do successfully complete the process generally have to wait several months before their benefits kick in" (Abramsky 2002, 29).

The public pays the bill for prisoners' health, either directly while a woman is incarcerated or indirectly when she returns home, unable to work or care for her children. Prevention, coordination, and health insurance can lessen the financial load. If diseases and problems are treated earlier, the cost is usually considerably less. Universal vaccinations against hepatitis B would help to serve this purpose, for example. Coordination between prisons, public health agencies, and mental health agencies reduces the number of those who fall between the bureaucratic cracks. When women have to make choices about allocation of their time and money, they will usually not choose health care for themselves; they will make spending choices that favor their children.

End-of-life issues. Just as life is different for women and men and for different racial and ethnic groups, so are dying and death. Most individuals in prison are given no resources to deal with the grief that has compounded their lives. They are left to cope with the memories of their pasts, the pain of their own illnesses, the hardships of their families, and the worries over reentry. In addition to the losses of their everyday lives, many will become terminally ill themselves or will face the death of someone they love. The larger society is still struggling with the ethical and practical dilemmas that emerge at the end of life; for prisoners they are magnified. Therapies that allow for working through grief can reduce the pressure on other mental health services; expanded hospice and compassionate release programs can alleviate the costs and the indignities of dying in prison. Even in death, the role of gender must be considered.

Reentry

If returning to homes and communities is vastly different for women and men, it is also different for women of different social classes. If a woman has a husband, an education, and a home, reentry may be embarrassing and reintegration slow, but there is usually little worry of recidivism. But most incarcerated women are *not* middle class and face numerous economic challenges. We know that poor women account for the largest proportion of the incarcerated female population. Recent federal policies have created barriers to finding homes and jobs. Also, racial and ethnic differences in access to these resources prior to conviction are only compounded by the addition of a criminal record. There has been little improvement in the employment and education picture for these women. Institutional job and education programs have been cut, and those employment programs still available provide little in the way of increased salaries or upward mobility. The "welfare-to-work" opportunities disappear for those convicted of drug offenses; for others the income is minimal, while the work takes them away from child care responsibilities. In addition, ex-inmates are permanently locked out of certain jobs, such as those in education, child care, transportation, and nursing homes; in many states, they cannot earn licenses for even basic jobs such as in beauty salons or barbershops.

Programs that provided federally subsidized housing are off limits to many returnees because of their drug convictions and the ease with which potential landlords can access their criminal records. Further, many communities where these inmates lived prior to their incarceration have been gentrified, decreasing the number of available rental properties and increasing the rents on those that remain. These hardships complicate relocation and community reintegration and add to the stresses related to children, safety, finances, and health that female returnees already face.

Almost all the women who are incarcerated will return to the communities and families that they left behind. Benefits must be available to those who return. Many of the solutions are obvious and have been suggested before: more money for drug treatment that is designed for women, more job training for jobs that actually exist for women with a history of drug violations, and a coordinated network of community services waiting when a woman leaves prison.

▨ Prison Staff

In addition to those problems that we discussed earlier in the book, there are others that are uniquely relevant to women. Prison personnel play a crucial role in the everyday life of inmates; we consider the importance of gender and race and ethnicity.

Gender and Guards

One area in which there is a particular dearth of information is the impact of males attending to women in prison. The United States is fairly unusual among developed countries in allowing men to work as prison guards in women's prisons (Amnesty International 1999). Many of these women have been physically, sexually, and verbally abused and, as a result, do not trust men. Guards in US prisons sometimes touch women's bodies; perform cavity searches; and watch them shower, dress, and use the toilet. In addition, they may use language that is inappropriate, degrading, disrespectful, unduly familiar, or threatening (Bloom, Owen, and Covington 2003). This "sexual misconduct" is inappropriate anywhere, but especially in this setting, where women struggle for self-respect and self-esteem.

Women do hold custody positions in women's prisons. There is, however, a great deal of variability: Thigpen and Hunter's (1998) survey of departments of corrections found that male staff held from 3 to 82 percent of custody positions, whereas female staff predominated in program and administrative positions. Hiring practices and policies differ according to institutional circumstances that determine the assignment of custody officers. For example, in Vermont a labor union contract forbids assignments on the basis of gender (Thigpen and Hunter 1998). In this case again, gender neutrality works against women.

Raeder (2003) suggested that same-sex supervision could lessen the likelihood of sexual misconduct and violations of privacy. She contended that such supervision could be legally justified in certain settings. In the best of circumstances, men are probably not appropriate to oversee women who are vulnerable. But in this case, when most women have been victims of abuse by men, the hiring of male guards, counselors, and health care workers seems particularly inappropriate, however small the numbers may be. Although there is little empirical research to document the effects of male guards on women prisoners and their mental health, common sense and empathy suggest that women in these positions would likely be better choices.

These policies might be informed by those from shelters for battered women. Most shelters train their counselors in aspects of abuse as well as basic principles of working with vulnerable women. Importantly, some shelters give abuse victims an opportunity to select the gender of their initial counselors and, as they gain trust and confidence, to phase in contact with male counselors. Such an approach would be difficult to implement in a correctional facility, but if the long-term goal is the increased well-being of these prisoners, then the coordination required might be worth it.

Staff Sensitivity to Race and Ethnicity

Another overlooked and underresearched issue is the race and ethnicity of inmates and staff. At this point most correctional officers are white and rural, whereas most prisoners are dark and urban; before their contact in the institution, they may have had little contact with each other. The very personal nature of custody and programming requires sensitivity to racial, ethnic, and cultural differences among inmates and between inmates and service providers. In addition to training on issues specific to women, staff should receive basic education on racial and cultural issues, including basic language skills. Failure to acknowledge the existence of these differences, to address ways of overcoming biases, and to develop mutual respect can contribute to institutional discord and affect the quality and safety of prison life.

■ Violence Against Women

Male violence toward women is perhaps the most striking and devastating example of the different lives of women and men. Women in prison generally do not come from stable, healthy families; both their families of origin and the families they formed are characterized by violence, particularly from the men in their lives. Many of their crimes stem directly from this abuse. For example, women often use illegal drugs or legal drugs illegally as a form of self-medication, to deal with the depression, fear, and anger resulting from a lifetime of victimization. Some women tend to use drugs with and because of the men in their lives, but when they need help with drug abuse or addiction, those same men largely ignore their efforts to change. Further, as we have repeatedly discussed, many of their health, grief, and family problems result from exposure to violence.

In addition, those few women who have been incarcerated for violent crimes are more likely than men to have victimized someone they know, generally someone who abused them or their children. Although both the battered woman syndrome and the battered child syndrome are considered in court, many of these women have never considered themselves victims of violence. As one woman put it, "I just thought I lost every fight." Many have never looked for help or told anyone about the violence. Over time the violence escalates, contributing to a host of other problems.

Recent actions in Illinois and Maryland to pardon those women who have been incarcerated for crimes stemming from domestic abuse have highlighted the need to consider the impact of these factors earlier in the system. The question arises: should these women be in prison at all (Albor 1995)? What steps can the police, the courts, and social service agencies take to prevent the escalation of these violent encounters? Measures that prevent the injury or death of an abuser, the incarceration of the victim/offender, and the disruption of the family should be further explored and supported.

Women must be free from gender-based violence all their lives; abused children grow up to be prison inmates. Legislation that purports to address the serious nature of violence against women and children but does not address the root social causes of this violence serves more as symbolic politics than as a programmatic solution. When programs are made for political rather than humane or scientific reasons, individuals suffer. In our society that glorifies violence and objectifies women, policies alone are not enough; systemic changes in the acceptance and disapproval of aggression toward women are requisite before women and children will be safe.

■ Looking at Options

Prison and prison conditions make headlines in extreme cases. The treatment of inmates at the Abu Ghraib prison in Iraq by US guards has led to more general questions about the physical and psychological treatment of the incarcerated. Moreover, the media coverage of white-collar criminals going to prison—women like Martha Stewart—has caught the attention of the public and legislators. This publicity has added to the debate about the nature of the present forms of punishment and pushed some to call for reevaluation of the use of incarceration for various categories of offenses and consideration of alternatives to incarceration.

Public Opinion

There is a growing recognition that the United States has passed the point of benefit from increased criminal penalties and higher levels of incarceration (Besteman 1991) Clearly, mandatory minimums are not going away in the near future, but many states are overwhelmed with the growing numbers and costs of inmates generated by sentencing requirements. Hopefully, the attitudes that made possible the harsh approaches of past decades are fading. Public opinion polls (Hart Research Associates 2003) conducted over the past years suggest several trends:

1. Americans list prevention as the best way to fight crime, far ahead of punishment or reinforcement. Seventy-six percent believe that the US currently puts too little emphasis on crime prevention.
2. Americans strongly believe that the best way to ensure public safety is through rehabilitation and reentry programs rather than incapacitation. Nearly two-thirds believe that the best way to reduce crime is to require education and job training of prisoners to give them the tools to turn away from crime.
3. Support for mandatory minimum sentences has eroded significantly since the mid-1990s, and now the majority of Americans no longer believe than mandatory sentences are a good idea. Instead, most Americans see drug abuse as a medical problem to be handled with treatment and counseling, rather than a serious crime to be handled with courts and prisons.
4. Roughly 70 percent of Americans believe the war on drugs has been more of a failure than a success.
5. Over one-half of Americans believe that the nation's approach to crime is on the wrong track; just a little over one-third believe that it is on the right track.
6. Over three-fourths favor mandatory treatment for minor drug crimes, as opposed to mandatory prison sentences.

Alternatives to Prison

These polls suggest that the public is interested in alternatives to incarceration for those who commit nonviolent crimes, and women commit very few violent crimes. Alternatives to prison, such as those introduced in the mid-1980s, include probation, intensive probation, home confinement, day fines, and boot camps; the available research particularly favors alternatives to prison for those who are mentally ill. The wisdom of coordination of services is especially salient when the alternatives are considered. Joan Petersilia (1998) concluded in her review of these programs that "no agency is an island." She suggested that crime is a complex, multifaceted problem that requires the combined efforts and involvement of surveillance, rehabilitation, police, probation, mental health, and schools.

However, evaluation of these alternatives often determines whether or not they are continued. When intermediate sanctions are introduced, the simple evaluation focuses on average rather than individual effectiveness. If they do not work for all, we tend to conclude that they do not work for any. Until the differential imposition of these penalties by gender, by gender and race, or by gender, race, and type of offense are explored, we cannot determine their effectiveness. At this point, although the public seems interested in alternatives, they are often ignored; the cost of design, evaluation, and implementation seems too steep to give them a chance of success, despite possible savings in the long run.

Privatization

Budget shortages coupled with public opinion could force legislators to shift monies from prison spending to prevention programs and alternatives to incarceration. Instead, the government is cutting costs by contracting with private businesses to take over prison construction, ownership, and control as profit-generating enterprises (Chandler 2003). For example, Corrections Corporation of America (CCA) operates sixty-four facilities and owns thirty-nine across the country.[1] Companies like CCA charge a fee for each inmate; to make money, their costs must be less than those paid by the government. All costs, such as food, health care, drug treatment, housing, and staff, are kept as low as possible. Prison diets are heavy in cheap foods, loaded with starch and carbohydrates; these menus may save money on food but do little to improve the physical health of inmates. This trend toward focusing on profits rather than prisoners has led, in part, to what Angela Davis and others have termed "the prison industrial complex."[2]

Private prisons are expected to earn money for their stockholders but are less accountable and less transparent in their functioning than government-operated prisons. Privatizing prisons and/or prison services allows the government to further ignore and deny the increasingly expensive prison buildup at the same time it ignores and denies the unique aspects of prison life for women.

■ Methodological Issues

Planning for programs and policies is only possible if it is grounded in sound research, using quality data and a solid theoretical base. Both data and theory are in short supply for examining issues relevant for women in prison.

The Lack of Data

Many times in this book, we have mentioned differences in estimates from different sources or questions that remain because of a lack of information. There is a clear and compelling need for valid, reliable, and generalizable data that give us more specific detail about these women before, during, and after prison. Individual-level data and data from private prisons are almost completely unavailable now.

We miss opportunities to improve conditions until we know who is in prison and what their needs are. Detailed data are crucial because we know little about minority women other than African Americans in prison. The lack of real information about smaller subgroups of women is particularly pressing;

for example, as the number of incarcerated Hispanic women increases, the need for translators may increase—without data on language; the problem may be undocumented and unmet. Another relatively straightforward example of a needed improvement is a massively expanded data collection system that would allow public health officials to track and treat infectious diseases among the prison population (Abramsky 2002) and to follow their progress when they leave. Minority communities already are overburdened with health problems; HIV/AIDS is the most obvious example. Ignoring illness and other needs will ultimately cost more than any data collection system.

Data gathering should be based on the real lives and needs of women rather than precoded, simplistic categories. Further, gathering data to support a particular political agenda does not necessarily result in viable solutions to the actual difficulties of these women. Clearly though, numbers must be coupled with action before they become dynamic and useful to the prisoners themselves.

The Need for Theory

Data without theory are simply numbers; theory gives meaning to statistics. Although there is a wealth of theories from psychology, criminology, sociology, women's studies, and social work that are relevant for women in prison, few efforts have been made to construct a unified theory of the individual and social worlds of women whose lives spiral downward to prison. Violence, poverty, sexism, and racism are as important to theoretical construction as are social control and individual agency. We suggest that efforts to prevent and punish crime will continue to lurch along without an integrated theoretical framework from which to interpret the numbers agencies now use to design prisons for women. The challenge for theoretical development relevant to incarcerated women is still unmet.

■ Conclusion

Incarcerating large numbers of women has not worked to improve their lives, cut costs of corrections, or strengthen families. It is time to reevaluate past efforts in light of the specific population of interest, namely the actual female offender population, rather than the stereotypical image of the female offender that has been projected by presentations in the media, on the floors of the House and the Senate, and in our attributions of male offender characteristics to the female offender population. Programming based on these preconceived ideas represents two basic failures: it ignores both gender differences and differences within the population of incarcerated women. Because of these failures, many of the current programs are not relevant to the increasing number of women behind bars. Trying to fit all prisoners into one model increases women's disadvantage upon their return to the community.

Recognizing the diversity of the population, we have repeatedly described the typical woman in prison: a poor, unskilled woman of color, with small children, health problems, and a history of abuse, who is incarcerated for low-level drug or property offenses. This descriptive mantra gives us a picture, but despite this clear and compelling portrait, policies and policymakers have refused to think about the long-term social implications of repeatedly denying these women even access to, much less assistance on, the road to rehabilitation and social reintegration. Even more importantly, although we talk about the intersection of gender, race, ethnicity, and class, as a society, we have been unable or unwilling to translate the ramifications of these factors into policies sensitive to the daily lives and needs of women and their children.

Although there are research projects documenting the need for gender-specific programming, there is little momentum to take the next step—to implement programs that are designed specifically for the women who are actually incarcerated. Race and class differences may ultimately be as relevant to successful programming as gender differences, but policies have completely ignored these crucial dimensions of the lives of these women. There have been few specific policies and programs for women, much less the diversity that women present, and as a result, their basic concerns—family, health, drug problems—have not been fully addressed.

Policies that affect prisoners have an impact on us all; societies suffer when prisoners suffer. The costs are simply transferred from one social agency to another. These inmates have been removed from their children, their families, their communities, and the normal progression of their lives. Through their incarceration, we allege that they have paid their debts to society. Unfortunately, the sole emphasis on punishment has stymied efforts to habilitate or rehabilitate these offenders. For a considerable period of time, these offenders are held at bay without the programs that would help them to develop and maintain a crime-free lifestyle. Moreover, the barriers that are in place now so constrain the choices women have that for some a violation of the conditions of release is a given. If we continue along the present path, the future of thousands of poor women and their children becomes even bleaker.

The US prison system does not exist in isolation; it exists in a country where sexism, racism, poverty, and violence are woven into everyday life. Most of the conversation in this book has focused on prisons and prisoners, but they are simply products of our larger society. It is only by addressing the most basic social problems that we can address the problems of our institutions of social control. Women, particularly women of color, are not simply victims of these various forms of oppression; they are also active agents, trying to fashion workable solutions to survival within a patchwork of problems. Until we recognize as a society that equal rights must be coupled with equal opportunities, we can expect only continued failure. If women could live in a society without prejudice, pain, and poverty, then we could expect their efforts to be geared toward health, family, education, and work rather than toward crime. Equal rights cannot exist in a society without equal opportunities; women in prison epitomize the failure of our society and evoke the possibilities for change.

■ Notes

1. Michael Erskine reported in the *Memphis [Tennessee] Commercial Appeal* about CCA's plan to take over the Shelby County and Memphis corrections facilities. CCA promised $30 million in cash to the county, a new $200 million facility, a fifty-year contract, and, subject to negotiation, jobs for current jail employees. This is an appealing offer to a cash-strapped county.

2. For more information on the "prison industrial complex," see Angela Y. Davis's article in *ColorLines*, "Masked Racism: Reflections on the Prison Industrial Complex."

References

AACP. 1999. "Position Statement of the AACP on the Mentally Ill Behind Bars." *American Association of Community Psychiatrists Newsletter.* 13th ed., Spring. www.comm.psych.pitt.edu/vol-13-2/bars.html.

Abramsky, Sarah. 2002. "The Shame of Prison Health Care." *Nation,* July 1, 28–34.

Acoca, Leslie. 1998. "Defusing the Time Bomb: Understanding and Meeting the Growing Health Care Needs of Incarcerated Women in America." *Crime and Delinquency* 44: 49–69.

Acoca, Leslie, and Myrna Raeder. 1999. "Severing Family Ties: The Plight of Nonviolent Female Offenders and Their Children." *Stanford Law Policy Review* 11 (1): 133–151.

Adams, Rukaiyah, David Onek, and Alissa Riker. 1998. *Double Jeopardy: An Assessment of the Felony Drug Provision of the Welfare Reform Act.* San Francisco: Justice Policy Institute.

Aday, Ronald H. 1994. "Aging in Prison: A Case Study of New Elderly Offenders." *International Journal of Offender Therapy and Comparative Criminology* 38 (1): 79–91.

Aid to Children of Imprisoned Mothers (AIM). 2004. "Facts About Mothers in Prison." www.takingaim.net/facts.asp.

Albor, T. 1995. "The Women Get Chains." *Nation,* February, 234–237.

Allard, Patricia. 2002. *Life Sentences: Denying Welfare Benefits to Women Convicted of Drug Offenses.* Washington, DC: Sentencing Project.

Allard, Patricia, and Marc Mauer. 2000. *Regaining the Vote: An Assessment of Activity Relating to Felon Disenfranchisement Laws.* Washington, DC: Sentencing Project.

American Correctional Association. 1998. "Health Care for Women Offenders." *Corrections Today* 60 (7): 122–128.

———. 2001. *Public Correctional Policy on Health Care.* Philadelphia: Congress of Corrections.

———. 2003. "Directory of Adult and Juvenile Correctional Departments, Institutions, Agencies, and Probation and Parole Authorities." Lanham, MD: American Correctional Association.

American Psychiatric Association. 1994. *Diagnostic and Statistical Manual of Mental Disorders* 4th ed. Washington, DC: American Psychiatric Association.

———. 2003. *Public Information: The Insanity Defense.* Washington, DC: American Psychiatric Association.

———. 2004. *Mental Illness and the Criminal Justice System: Redirecting Resources Toward Treatment, Not Containment.* Washington, DC: American Psychiatric Association.

Amnesty International. 1999. *Not Part of My Sentence: Violations of the Human Rights of Women in Custody.* Washington, DC: Amnesty International.

Ancar, Katina. 2003. "Ninth Circuit Hands Long-Awaited Victory to Children Living with Relatives." *Journal of the National Center for Youth Law* 24 (12): 1–3.

———. 2004. "Federal Officials Seek to Derail Benefits for Child in Kinship Foster Care." *Journal of the National Center for Youth Law* 25 (2).

Anderson, Tammy L., Andre B. Rosay, and Christin Saum. 2002. "The Impact of Drug Use and Crime Involvement on Health Problems Among Female Drug Offenders." *Prison Journal* 82 (1): 50–68.

Andrews, William. 1899. *Bygone Punishments.* London: W. Andrews.

Anno, B. J. 2001. *Correctional Health Care: Guidelines for the Management of an Adequate Delivery System.* Washington, DC: National Commission on Correctional Health Care and the US Department of Justice, National Institute of Corrections.

Associated Press. 1999. "More Women Are in Prison for Drugs." *Philadelphia Inquirer,* November 18.

———. 2002. "South Carolina's 'Crack Mom' Law Faces Another Challenge." *Charleston Post and Courier,* November 4.

Atwood, J. E. 2000. *Too Much Time: Women in Prison.* London: Phaidon Press.

Auerhahn, Kathleen, and Elizabeth Dermody Leonard. 2000. "Docile Bodies? Chemical Restraints and the Female Inmate." *Journal of Criminal Law and Criminology* 90 (2).

Austin, J. 2001. "Prisoner Reentry: Current Trends, Practices, and Issues." *Crime and Delinquency* 47 (3): 314–334.

Bacon, Margaret. 2000. *Abby Hopper Gibbons: Prison Reformer and Social Activist.* Albany: State University of New York Press.

Baillargeon, J., and S. A. Contreras. 2001. "Antipsychotic Prescribing Patterns in the Texas Prison System." *Journal of the American Academy of Psychiatry and the Law* 29 (1): 48–53.

Baker, D. V. 1999. "A Descriptive Profile and Socio-Historical Analysis of Female Executions in the US: 1632–1997." *Women and Criminal Justice* 10 (3): 57–93.

Barnhill, Sandra. 1996. "Three Generations At Risk: Imprisoned Women, Their Children, and Grandmother Caregivers." *Generations* 20 (Spring): 39–40.

Bartlett, Rini. 2000. "Helping Inmate Moms Keep in Touch: Prison Programs Encourage Ties with Children." *Corrections Today* 62 (7): 102–104.

Baskin, Deborah, Ira Sommers, Richard Tessler, and Henry J. Steadman. 1989. "Role Incongruence and Gender Variation in the Provision of Prison Mental Health Services." *Journal of Health and Social Behavior* 30: 305–314.

Beck, Allen J. 2000. "State and Federal Prisoners Returning to the Community: Findings from the Bureau of Justice Statistics." Paper Presented at the First Reentry Courts Initiative Cluster Meeting, Washington, DC.

Beck, Allen J., and Darrell Gilliard. 1995. *Prisoners in 1994.* Washington, DC: Bureau of Justice Statistics (NCJ 151654).

Beck, Allen J., and Paige M. Harrison. 2001. *Prisoners in 2000*. Washington, DC: Bureau of Justice Statistics (NCJ 188207).

Beck, Allen J., and Laura M. Maruschak. 2001. *Mental Health Treatment in State Prisons, 2000*. Washington, DC: Bureau of Justice Statistics (NCJ 188215).

Beck, Allen J., J. Karberg, and P. Harrison. 2002. *Prison and Jail Inmates at Midyear 2001*. Washington, DC: Bureau of Justice Statistics (NCJ 191702).

Bedard, Kelly, and Eric Helland. 2000. "The Location of Women's Prisons and the Deterrence Effect of 'Harder' Time." Claremont College Working Papers in Economics. Claremont, CA.

Behrendt, C., N. Kendig, C. Dambita, J. Horman, J. Lawlor, and D. Vlahov. 1994. "Voluntary Testing for HIV in a Prison Population with a High Prevalence of HIV." *American Journal of Epidemiology* 139 (9): 918–926.

Belknap, Joanne. 2000. "Programming and Health Care Responsibility for Incarcerated Women." In Joy James, ed., *States of Confinement: Policing, Detention, and Prisons*. New York: St. Martin's Press.

———. 2001. *The Invisible Women: Gender, Crime and Justice*. 2nd ed. Belmont, CA: Wadsworth.

Benjamin, Elizabeth. 2004. "Drug Law Deal Raises Debate: Even as State Lawmakers Tout Assembly, Senate's Passage of Bill to Ease Harsh Rockefeller-Era Penalties, Some Say It Doesn't Go Far Enough." *Albany Times Union*, December 8.

Berkman, A. 1995. "Prison Health: The Breaking Point." *American Journal of Public Health* 85 (12): 1616–1618.

Bernstein, M. 2002. "A New Liver for a Prisoner." *Hastings Center Report* 32 (4): 12–13.

Besteman, K. J. 1991. "War Is Still Not the Answer." Pp. 151–156 in J. A. Inciardi, ed., *The Drug Legalization Debate*. Newbury Park, CA: Sage Publications.

BJS (Bureau of Justice Statistics). 1997. *Correctional Populations in the United States, 1995*. Washington, DC: Bureau of Justice Statistics (NCJ 163916).

———. 1999a. *Correctional Populations in the United States, 1996*. Washington, DC: Bureau of Justice Statistics (NCJ 170013).

———. 1999b. *Women Offenders: Special Report*. Washington, DC: Bureau of Justice Statistics (NCJ 175688).

———. 2000. *Correctional Populations in the United States, 1997*. Washington, DC: Bureau of Justice Statistics (NCJ 177613).

———. 2001. *Correctional Populations in the United States. 1998*. Washington, DC: Bureau of Justice Statistics (NCJ 192929).

Blinn, C. 1997. *Maternal Ties: A Selection of Programs for Female Offenders*. Lanham, MD: American Correctional Association.

Bloom, Barbara, and D. Steinhart. 1993. *Why Punish the Children? A Reappraisal of the Children of Incarcerated Mothers in America*. San Francisco, CA: National Council on Crime and Delinquency.

Bloom, Barbara, Barbara Owen, and Stephanie Covington. 2003. *Gender-Responsive Strategies: Research, Practice, and Guiding Principles for Women Offenders*. Washington, DC: National Institute of Corrections, US Department of Justice.

Bohm, Robert M. 2003. *Deathquest II: An Introduction to the Theory and Practice of Capital Punishment in the United States*. Cincinnati: Anderson Publishing.

Bonczar, Thomas P., and Tracy M. Snell. 2003. *Capital Punishment, 2000*. Washington, DC: Bureau of Justice Statistics (NCJ 201848).

Boudouris, J. 1996. *Parents in Prison: Addressing the Needs of Families*. Lanham, MD: American Correctional Association.

Brackett, Jeffrey. 1889. *Notes on the Progress of the Colored People of Maryland Since the War.* Baltimore: Johns Hopkins University Press.

Bresler, Laura, and Diane Lewis. 1984. "Black and White Women Prisoners: Differences in Family Ties and Their Programmatic Implications." *Prison Journal* 64 (1): 116–123.

Brewer, M. K., and D. Baldwin. 2000. "The Relationship Between Self-Esteem, Health Habits, and Knowledge of BSE Practice in Female Inmates." *Public Health Nursing* 17 (1): 16–24.

Brewer, V. E., J. W. Marquart, J. L. Mullings, and B. M. Crouch. 1998. "AIDS-Related Risk Behavior Among Female Prisoners with Histories of Mental Impairment." *Prison Journal* 78 (2): 101–109.

Briggs, John, Christopher Harrison, Angus McInnes, and David Vincent. 1996. *Crime and Punishment in England: An Introductory History.* New York: St. Martin's Press.

Brown, V. B., M. S. Ridgely, B. Pepper, I. S. Levine, and H. Ryglewicz. 1989. "The Dual Crisis: Mental Illness and Substance Abuse." *American Psychologist* 44 (3): 565–569.

Buck, Jeffrey. 2001. "Spending for State Mental Health Care." *Psychiatric Services* 52 (10): 1294.

Burford, E., and S. Shulman. 1992. *Of Bridles and Burnings: The Punishment of Women.* New York: St. Martin's Press.

Burkhart, Kathryn Watterson. 1973. *Women in Prison.* Garden City, NJ: Doubleday.

Burrs, F. A. 1995. "The African American Experience: Breaking the Barriers to Hospices." *Hospice Journal* 10 (2): 15–18.

Burton, L. 1992. "Black Grandparents Rearing Children of Drug-Addicted Parents: Stressors, Outcomes, and Social Needs." *Gerontologist* 32 (6): 744–751.

Buruma, Ian. 2005. "What Teaching a College-Level Class at a Maximum-Security Correctional Facility Did for the Inmates—and for Me." *New York Times Magazine*, February 20, 38–41.

Bush-Baskette, S. R. 1998. "The War on Drugs as a War Against Black Women." Pp. 113–129 in S. L. Miller, ed., *Crime Control and Women: Feminist Implications of Criminal Justice Policy.* Thousand Oaks, CA: Sage.

Butler, Anne M. 1989. "Still in Chains: Black Women in Western Prisons, 1865–1910." *Western Historical Quarterly*, 20–35.

———. 1997. *Gendered Justice in the American West: Women Prisoners in Men's Penitentiaries.* Urbana: University of Illinois Press.

Butzin, C. A., S. S. Martin, and J. A. Inciardi. 2002. "Evaluating Component Effects of a Prison-Based Treatment Continuum." *Journal of Substance Abuse Treatment* 22: 63–69.

"California Is Considering Early Release of Dying Inmates." 1997. *AIDS Policy and Law* 12 (17): 4.

Camp, Camille, and George Camp. 1997. *The Corrections Yearbook: Adult Corrections 1997.* New York: Criminal Justice Institute.

Camp, Scott D., and Gerald G. Gaes. 2002. "Growth and Quality of US Private Prisons: Evidence from a National Survey." *Criminology and Public Policy* 1 (3): 427–449.

CASA (National Center on Addiction and Substance Abuse at Columbia University). February 2003. *The Formative Years: Pathways to Substance Abuse Among Girls and Young Women Ages 8–22.* New York: CASA.

Casey-Acevedo, Karen, and Tim Bakken. 2002. "Visiting Women in Prison: Who Visits and Who Cares?" *Journal of Offender Rehabilitation* 34 (2): 67–83.

Cavan, R. S. 1987. "Is Special Treatment Needed for Elderly Offenders?" *Criminal Justice Policy Review* 2 (3): 213–224.

Cavanaugh, John C., and Fredda Blanchard-Fields. 2002. *Adult Development and Aging.* 4th ed. Belmont, CA: Wadsworth.

CCIP (Center for Children of Incarcerated Parents). 2001. "The Effects of Imprisonment on Families: Fact Sheet," www.correctionalassociation.org/images/Children-of-Incarcerated-Parents.pdf.

CDC (Centers for Disease Control and Prevention). 1992. "HIV Prevention in the US Correctional System, 1991." *Journal of the American Medical Association* 268 (1): 23–25.

———. 1999. "AIDS Rate in Prison Is Six Times National Rate." *CDC News.* Retrieved June 13, 2002, from www.hivdent.org/cdc/.

Celinska, Katarzyna. 2000. "Volunteer Involvement in Ex-Offenders' Readjustment Reducing the Stigma of Imprisonment." *Journal of Offender Rehabilitation* 30 (3–4): 99–116.

Center for Juvenile and Criminal Justice. 2001. *Cutting Correctly: New Prison Policies for Times of Fiscal Crisis.* San Francisco: Center for Juvenile and Criminal Justice.

Center for Public Representation. 1999. *The Legal Rights of Prisoners with Mental Disorders.* Newton, MA: Center for Public Representation.

Chandler, Cynthia. 2003. "Death and Dying in America: The Prison Industrial Complex's Impact on Women's Health." *Berkeley Women's Law Journal,* 37–57.

Chesney-Lind, Meda. 1998. "Women in Prison: from Partial Justice to Vengeful Equity." *Corrections Today* 60 (7): 66–72.

Child Welfare League of America. 1996–2005. "What Happens to Children." http://www.cwla.org/programs/incarcerated/whathappens.htm.

Church, C. and S. Browning. 1990. "The View from Behind Bars." *Time,* Nov. 1, 20–23.

Cohn, Felicia. 1999. "The Ethics of End-of-Life for Prison Inmates." *Journal of Law, Medicine, and Ethics* 27 (3): 252–259.

Coles, Deborah, and Tony Ward. 1994. "Failure Stories: Prison Suicides and How Not to Prevent Them." Pp. 127–142 in A. Liebling and Tony Ward, eds., *Deaths in Custody: International Perspectives.* London: Whiting and Birch.

Colvin, Mark. 1997. *Penitentiaries, Reformatories, and Chain Gangs: Social Theory and the History of Punishment in Nineteenth-Century America.* New York: St. Martin's Press.

Conly, Catherine. 1998. "The Women's Prison Association: Supporting Women Offenders and Their Families." Washington, DC: US Department of Justice, National Institute of Justice (NCJ 172858).

Cooper, Cynthia. 2002. "A Cancer Grows: Medical Treatment in Women's Prisons Ranges from Brutal to Nonexistent." *Nation,* May 6. Retrieved October 10, 2002, from www.indybay.org/news/2002/05/125643.php.

Correctional Association of New York. 2002. *Women in Prison Project.* New York: Correctional Association of New York.

Corwin, P. 2001. "Senioritis: Why Elderly Federal Inmates Are Literally Dying to Get Out of Prison." *Journal of Contemporary Health and Law Policy* 17 (2): 687–714.

Cote, G., A. Lesage, N. Chawky, and M. Loyer. 1997. "Clinical Specificity of Prison Inmates with Severe Mental Disorders: A Case-Control Study." *British Journal of Psychiatry* 170 (June): 571–577.

Cotten-Oldenburg, N., B. Jordan, S. Martin, and L. Kupper. 1999. "Women Inmates' Risky Sex and Drug Behaviors: Are They Related?" *American Journal of Drug and Alcohol Abuse* 25 (1): 129–149.

Coughenour, J. C. 1995. "Separate and Unequal: Women in the Federal Criminal Justice System." *Federal Sentencing Reporter* 8: 142–144.

Covington, Stephanie. 2002. "A Woman's Journey Home: Challenges for Female Offenders and Their Children." Paper prepared for the "From Prison to Home" Conference, sponsored by the Urban Institute and funded by the US Department of Health and Human Services, www.urban.org/uploadedpdf/410630_female offenders.pdf.

Craddock, Amy. 1996. "Classification Systems." Pp. 87–95 in Marilyn McShane and Frank Williams III, eds., *Encyclopedia of American Prisons*. New York: Garland.

Craig, Robert J. 2004. *Counseling the Alcohol and Drug Dependent Client: A Practical Approach*. Boston: Pearson Education.

Criminal Justice Institute. 1999. *Corrections Yearbook, 1998*. Middleton, CT: Criminal Justice Institute.

Cummings, Michael. "'One Strike and You're Out' of Rent Assisted Housing." *Step Up* 6 (2), www.housingall.com/housing/OneStrike.htm.

Davis, Lois, and Sharon Pacchiana. 2003. "Health Profile of the State Prison Population and Returning Officers: Public Health Challenges." *Journal of Correctional Health Care* 10, no. 3.

Day, Dawn. 2003. *Health Emergency 2003: The Spread of Drug-Related AIDS and Hepatitis C Among African Americans and Latinos*. Princeton, NJ: Dogwood Center.

Dean-Gaitor, H. D., and P. L. Fleming. 1999. "Epidemiology of AIDS in Incarcerated Persons in the United States, 1994–1996." *AIDS* 13 (17): 2475–2476.

DeGroot, A. S. 2001. "HIV Among Incarcerated Women: An Epidemic Behind Walls." *Corrections Today* 63 (1): 77–81.

DeSpelder, Lynne Ann, and Albert Lee Strickland. 2005. *The Last Dance*. New York: McGraw-Hill.

Devine, K. 1997. "Family Unity: The Benefits and Costs of Community-Based Sentencing Programs for Women and Their Children in Illinois." Chicago Legal Aid to Incarcerated Mothers. www.claim-il.org/.

Dietrich, Sharon. 2002. "Criminal Records and Employment: Ex-Offenders Thwarted in Attempts to Earn a Living for Their Families." In Amy Hirsch et al., *Every Door Closed: Barriers Facing Parents with Criminal Records*. Community Legal Services and the Center for Law and Social Policy, http://www.clasp.org/publications/every_door_closed.pdf.

Ditton, Paula M. 1999. *Mental Health and Treatment of Inmates and Probationers*. Washington, DC: Bureau of Justice Statistics (NCJ 174463).

Dobash, Russell, R. E. Dobash, and Sue Gutteridge. 1986. *The Imprisonment of Women*. New York: Basil Blackwell.

Dodge, L. Mara. 2002. *Whores and Thieves of the Worst Kind: A Study of Women, Crime, and Prisons, 1835–2000*. DeKalb: Northern Illinois University Press.

Dodge, Mary, and Mark Pogrebin. 2001. "Collateral Costs of Imprisonment for Women: Complications of Reintegration." *Prison Journal* 81 (1): 42–54.

Do Valle, Alice. 2003. "Three Deaths at Chowchilla Prison Spark Compassionate Release Debate." Retrieved May 28, 2004, from http://sf.indymedia.org.

Dowden, C., and D. C. Andrews. 1999. "What Works for Female Offenders: A Meta-Analytic Review." *Crime and Delinquency* 45 (4): 438–452.

Dressel, Paula, Jeff Porterfield, and Sandra Barnhill. 1998. "Mothers Behind Bars: Incarcerating Increasing Numbers of Mothers Has Serious Implications for Families and Society." *Corrections Today* 60 (7): 90–94.

Drummond, Tammerlin. 2000. "Mothers in Prison." *Time,* Nov. 6, 3–5.

Earle, Alice. 1969. *Curious Punishments of Bygone Days*. Montclair, NJ: Patterson Smith. http://www.getchwood.com/punishments/curious/index.html.

Enos, S. 1998. "Managing Motherhood in Prison: The Impact of Race and Ethnicity on Child Placements." *Women and Therapy* 20 (4): 57–73.

Feinman, Clarice. 1983. "An Historical Overview of the Treatment of Incarcerated Women: Myths and Realities of Rehabilitation." *Prison Journal* 63 (2): 12–26.

Flanigan, T. P., J. Y. Kim, S. Zierler, J. Rich, K. Vigilante, and D. Bury-Maynard. 1996. "A Prison Release Program for HIV-Positive Women: Linking Them to Health Services and Community Follow-Up." *American Journal of Public Health* 86 (6): 886–887.

Florida House of Representatives Justice Council. Committee on Corrections. 1998. *Maintaining Family Contact When a Family Member Goes to Prison: An Examination of State Policies on Mail, Visiting, and Telephone Access*. .

Freedman, Estelle B. 1981. *Their Sisters' Keepers: Women's Prison Reform in America, 1830–1930*. Ann Arbor: University of Michigan Press.

———. 2002. *No Turning Back. The History of Feminism and the Future of Women*. New York: Ballantine Books.

Frontline. 2005. "Thirty Years of America's Drug War: A Chronology." http://www.pbs.org/wgbh/pages/frontline/shows/drugs/cron/.

Fuller, Lisa. 1993. "Visitors to Women's Prisons in California: An Exploratory Study." *Federal Probation* 57 (4): 41–47.

Gabel, Katherine, and Denise Johnston, eds. 1995. *Children of Incarcerated Parents*. New York: Lexington Books.

Gabel, Stewart. 1992. "Behavioral Problems in Sons of Incarcerated or Otherwise Absent Fathers: The Issue of Separation." *Family Process* 31 (September): 303–314.

Gaes, Gerald, Tim Flanagan, Larry Motiuk, and Lynn Stewart. "Adult Correctional Treatment," in Michael Tonry and Joan Petersilia, eds., *Prisons, Crime, and Justice: A Review of Research*. Vol. 26. Chicago: University of Chicago Press, 1999.

Gaes, Gerald, and Newton Kendig. 2002. "The Skill Sets and Health Care Needs of Released Offenders." Paper prepared for the "From Prison to Home" Conference, sponsored by the Urban Institute and funded by the US Department of Health and Human Services, www.urban.org/uploadedpdf/410629_releasedoffenders.pdf.

Gaouette, Nicole. 1997. "Prisons Grapple with Rapid Influx of Women and Mothers." *Christian Science Monitor*, May 19.

Gartner, Rosemary, and Candace Kruttschnitt. 2004. "A Brief History of Doing Time: The California Institution for Women in the 1960s and the 1990s." *Law and Society Review* 38 (2).

Geen, Rob. 2003. *Foster Children Placed with Relatives Often Receive Less Government Help*. New Federalism: Issues and Options for States. Series A, No. A-59. Washington, DC: Urban Institute.

Gehring, Thom, and Carolyn Eggleston. 1996. "Vocational Programs." Pp. 479–482 in Marilyn McShane and Frank Williams III, eds., *Encyclopedia of American Prisons*. New York: Garland.

"Gender Differences in Drug Abuse Risks and Treatment." 2000. *NIDA Notes* 15 (4). www.nida.nih.gov/NIDA_Notes/NNvol15n4/tearoff.html.

Gentry, Philip. 1995. "Termination of Parental Rights Among Prisoners: A National Perspective." Pp.167–182 in Katherine Gabel and Denise Johnston, eds., *Children of Incarcerated Parents*. New York: Lexington Books.

———. 1998. "Permanency Planning in the Context of Parental Incarceration: Legal Issues and Recommendations." *Child Welfare* 77 (5): 543–559.

Gettleman, Marvin E. 1992. "The Maryland Penitentiary in the Age of Tocqueville, 1828–1842." Pp. 271–292 in M. Tonry, ed., *Crime and Justice in American History*. New York: K. G. Saur.

Gillece, Joan B., and Betty G. Russell. 2001. "Maryland's Programs for Women Offenders with Mental Illness and Substance Abuse Disorders: Incarcerated and in the Community." *Women, Girls, and Criminal Justice* 2 (6): 89–95.

Gillespie, L. Kay. 1997. "Dancehall Ladies: The Criminal Executions of America's Condemned Women." Lanham, MD: University Press of America.

Gilliard, D. K., and Allen J. Beck. 1998. *Prison and Jail Inmates at Midyear, 1997*. Washington, DC: Bureau of Justice Statistics (NCJ 167247).

Goebel, Julius, and T. R. Naughton. 1944. *Law Enforcement in Colonial New York: A Study of Criminal Procedure, 1664–1776*. New York: Commonwealth Fund.

Grana, Sheryl. 2002. *Women and (in)Justice: The Criminal and Civil Effects of the Common Law on Women's Lives*. Boston: Allyn and Bacon.

Grant, B. A., and L. Lefebvre. 1994. "Older Offenders in the Correctional Service of Canada." *Forum on Corrections Research* 6 (2): 10–13.

Greene, Susan, Craig Haney, and Aida Hurtado. 2000. "Cycles of Pain: Risk Factors in the Lives of Incarcerated Mothers and Their Children." *Prison Journal* 80 (1): 3–23.

Greenfeld, Lawrence A., and Tracy L. Snell. 1999. *Women Offenders*. Washington, DC: Bureau of Justice Statistics (NCJ 175688).

Greenstein, Robert, and Isaac Shapiro. 2003. *The New Definitive CBO Data on Income and Tax Trends*. Washington, DC: Center on Budget and Policy Priorities, September 23.

Guyon, L., S. Brochu, I. Parent, and L. Desjardins. 1999. "At-Risk Behaviors with Regard to HIV and Addiction Among Women in Prison." *Women and Health* 29 (3): 49–66.

Hagan, John, and Juleigh Coleman. 2001. "Returning Captives of the American War on Drugs: Issues of Community and Family Reentry." *Crime and Delinquency* 47 (3): 352–367.

Hahn, Nicole. 1985. *Partial Justice: Women in State Prisons, 1800–1935*. Boston: Northeastern University Press.

Hairston, C. Finney. 1995. "Fathers in Prison." Pp. 31–40 in Katherine Gabel and Denise Johnston, eds., *Children of Incarcerated Parents*. New York: Lexington Books.

———. 2002. "Prisoners and Families: Parenting Issues During Incarceration." Paper prepared for the "From Prison to Home" Conference, sponsored by the Urban Institute and funded by the US Department of Health and Human Services.

Hall, Elizabeth A., Michael Prendergast, Jean Wellisch, Meredith Patten, and Yan Cao. 2004. "Treating Drug-Abusing Women Prisoners: An Outcomes Evaluation of the Forever Free Program." *Prison Journal* 84 (1): 81–105.

Hammett, Theodore, Cheryl Roberts, and Sofia Kennedy. 2001. "Health-Related Issues in Prisoner Reentry." *Crime and Delinquency* 47 (3): 390–409.

Hankins, C. A., S. Gendron, M. A. Handley, C. Richard, M. T. Lai Tung, and M. O'Shaughnessy. 1994. "HIV infection Among Women in Prison: An Assessment of Risk Factors Using a Nonnominal Methodology." *American Journal of Public Health* 84 (10): 1637–1640.

Harlow, Caroline Wolf. 1999. *Prior Abuses Reported by Inmates and Probationers*. Washington, DC: Bureau of Justice Statistics (NCJ 172879).

Harris, J. 1993. "Comparison of Stressors Among Female v. Male Inmates." *Journal of Offender Rehabilitation* 19 (1–2): 43–56.

Harrison, Paige M., and Allen J. Beck. 2002. *Prisoners in 2001.* Washington, DC: Bureau of Justice Statistics (NCJ 195189).

———. 2004. *Prisoners in 2003.* Washington, DC: Bureau of Justice Statistics (NCJ 205335).

Harrison, Paige, and Jennifer Karlberg. 2003. *Prison and Jail Inmates at Midyear 2002.* Washington, DC: Bureau of Justice Statistics (NCJ 198877).

Harrison Ross, P., and J. Lawrence. 1998. "Health Care for Women Offenders." *Corrections Today* 60: 579–587.

Hart Research Associates. 2003. *Changing Public Attitudes Toward the Criminal Justice System: Summary of Findings.* New York: Open Society Institute.

Hawkes, Mary. 1994. *Excellent Effect: The Edna Mahan Story.* Laurel, MD: American Correctional Association.

Hayes, Lindsey. 1995. *Prison Suicide: An Overview and Guide to Prevention.* Mansfield, MA: National Center on Institutions and Alternatives.

Heffernan, Esther. 1992. "The Alderson Years." *Federal Prisons Journal* (Fall): 21–26.

Heise, L., M. Ellsberg, and M. Gottemoeller. 1999. "Ending Violence Against Women." Population Reports, Series L, no. 11. Baltimore: Johns Hopkins University School of Public Health, Population Information Program.

Henderson, D. 1998. "Drug Abuse and Incarcerated Women: A Research Review." *Journal of Substance Abuse and Treatment* 15 (6): 579–587.

Henriques, Zelma. 1996. "Imprisoned Mothers and Their Children: Separation-Reunion Syndrome Dual Impact." *Women and Criminal Justice* 8 (1): 77–95.

Hester, Tom. 2005. "Group to Urge Expanding State Drug Courts." *Newark State Ledger,* January 26.

"High Phone Costs Sock Inmates' Family, Friends." 2002. *Manitowoc Herald Times Reporter.*

Hirsch, Amy. 1999. "'Some Days Are Harder Than Hard': Welfare Reform and Women with Drug Convictions in Pennsylvania." Center for Law and Social Policy, www.clasp.org/publications/some_days_are_harder_than_hard.pdf.

———. 2002. "Parents with Criminal Records and Public Benefits: 'Welfare Helps Us Stay in Touch with Society.'" In Amy Hirsch et al., *Every Door Closed: Barriers Facing Parents with Criminal Records.* Community Legal Services and the Center for Law and Social Policy, www.clasp.org/publications/every_door_closed.pdf.

Holley, Philip D., and Dennis Brewster. 1997–1998. "A Brief History of Women in Oklahoma Corrections: Inmates and Employees." *Journal of the Oklahoma Criminal Justice Research Consortium* 4: 1–8.

Howell, N. 1992. "Special Problems of Female Offenders." *Corrections Compendium: The National Journal for Corrections Professionals* 17 (9).

Huffington, Ariana. 2000. "New Drug Laws Strip Minority Rights." http://www.alternet.org/story/98711.

Hungerford, Gregory. 1996. "Caregivers of Children Whose Mothers Are Incarcerated: A Study of the Kinship Placement System." *Children Today* 24 (1): 23–27.

Hunt, H., E. Malmud, L. Betancourt, L. E. Braitman, N. L. Brodsky, and J. Giannetta. 1997. "Children with in Utero Cocaine Exposure Do Not Differ from Control Subjects on Intelligence Testing." *Archives of Pediatrics and Adolescent Medicine* 151 (12): 1237–1241.

Immarigeon, Russ. 1994. *Reconciliation Between Victims and Imprisoned Offenders: Programs and Issues.* Akron, Ohio: Mennonite Central Committee, US Office on Crime and Justice.

Ingram-Fogel, C. 1991. "Health Problems and Needs of Incarcerated Women." *Journal of Prison and Jail Health* 10: 43–57.

"Inmates Sue over High Phone Costs: Some States Profit in Collect Calls." 2000. *Crimnews* 4 (28).

Institute of Medicine. 2004. *Public Financing and Delivery of HIV/ AIDS Care: Securing the Legacy of Ryan White.* Washington, DC: National Academies Press.

Jacobs, Ann. 2000. "Give 'Em a Fighting Chance: The Challenges for Women Offenders Trying to Succeed in the Community." In Morris L. Thigpen and George Keiser, eds., *Topics in Community Corrections, Annual Issue 2000: Responding to Women Offenders in the Community.* www.nicic.org/pubs/2000/period190. pdf#search.

Jacoby, J., and B. Kozie-Peak. 1997. "The Benefits of Social Support for Mentally Ill Offenders: Prison-to-Community Transitions." *Behavioral Science Law* 15 (4): 483–501.

James, J. F., D. Gregory, R. Jones, and O. Rundell. 1985. "Mental Health Status of Prisoners in an Urban Jail." *Criminal Justice and Behavior* 12: 29–53.

Janusz, Luke. 1991. "Separate but Unequal: Women Behind Bars in Massachusetts." *Odyssey* (Fall): 6–17.

Johnson, Bruce D., Eloise Dunlap, and Sylvie C. Tourigny. 2000. "Crack Distribution and Abuse in New York." Pp. 19–57 in Mangai Natarajan and Mike Hough, eds., *Illegal Drug Markets: From Research to Prevention Policy.* Vol. 11 in the Crime Prevention Studies series. Monsey, NY: Criminal Justice Press.

Johnston, Denise. 1992. *Report No. 6: Children of Offenders.* Pasadena, CA: Center for Children of Incarcerated Parents.

———. 1995. "Effects of Parental Incarceration." Pp. 59–88 in Katherine Gable and Denise Johnston, eds., *Children of Incarcerated Parents.* New York: Lexington Books.

———. 2001. "Prisons and Child Custody." FCN Report 22: 1–9.

Jones, R. 1993. "Coping with Separation: Adaptive Responses of Women Prisoners." *Women and Criminal Justice* 5 (1): 71–97.

Jose-Kampfner, Christina. 1995. "Post-Traumatic Stress Reactions in Children of Imprisoned Mothers." Pp. 89–100 in Katherine Gabel and Denise Johnston, eds., *Children of Incarcerated Parents.* New York: Lexington Books.

Justice Now. 2003. *Compassionate Release Law in California: The Facts.* Oakland, CA: Justice Now.

Kalogeras, Steven. Edited by Marc Mauer. 2003. *Legislative Changes on Felony Disenfranchisement, 1996–2003.* Washington, DC: Sentencing Project, www.sentencingproject.org/pdfs/legchanges-report.pdf.

Kauffman, Kelsey. 2001. "Mothers in Prison." *Corrections Today* 63 (1): 62–65.

Kealey, Linda. 1986. "Patterns of Punishment: Massachusetts in the Eighteenth Century." *American Journal of Legal History* 30: 163–186.

Kerr, D. 1998. "Substance Abuse Among Female Offenders." *Corrections Today* 60 (7): 114–119.

Keve, Paul. 1986. *The History of Corrections in Virginia.* Charlottesville: University of Virginia.

———. 1991. *Prisons and the American Conscience: A History of US Federal Corrections.* Carbondale: Southern Illinois University Press.

Kiser, George. 1991. "Female Inmates and Their Families." *Federal Probation* 55 (3): 56–63.

Koss, M. P. 1990. "The Women's Mental Health Research Agenda: Violence Against Women." *American Psychologist* 45: 374–380.

Kratcoski, Peter, and Susan Babb. 1990. "Adjustment of Older Inmates: An Analysis by Institutional Structure and Gender." *Journal of Contemporary Criminal Justice* 6 (4): 264–281.

Krisberg, Barry, and Carolyn Temin. 2001. "The Plight of Children Whose Parents Are in Prison." NCCD Focus, www.nccd-crc.org/nccd/pubs/2001_focus_plightofchildren.pdf.

Kupers, T. A. 1999. *Prison Madness: The Mental Health Crisis Behind Bars and What We Must Do About It.* San Francisco: Jossey-Bass.

Kurshan, Nancy. 1996. "Behind the Walls: The History and Current Reality of Women's Imprisonment." http://prisonactivist.org/women/women-and-imprisonment.htm.

Landau, Rue. 2002. "Criminal Records and Subsidized Housing: Families Losing the Opportunity for Decent Shelter." In Amy Hirsch et al., *Every Door Closed: Barriers Facing Parents with Criminal Records.* Community Legal Services and the Center for Law and Social Policy, www.clasp.org/publications/every_door_closed.pdf.

Langan, N., and B. Pelissier. 2001. "Gender Differences Among Prisoners in Drug Treatment." *Journal of Substance Abuse* 13 (3): 291–301.

LaPoint, Velma. 1980. "The Impact of Separation on Families: Presence and Policy Issues." Paper presented at the Research Forum on Family Issues, National Advisory Committee of the White House Conference on Families, Washington, DC.

Lawson, W. Travis, and Lena Sue Fawkes. 1993. "HIV, AIDS, and the Female Offender." *Female Offenders: Meeting the Needs of a Neglected Population.* Laurel, MD: American Correctional Association.

Lekkerkerker, Eugenia. 1931. *Reformatories for Women.* The Hague-Batava: J. B. Woeters Groningen.

Lewis, Orlando. 1922. *The Development of American Prisons and Prison Customs, 1776–1845.* New York: Prison Association of New York.

Liebling, A., and Tony Ward. 1994. *Deaths in Custody: International Perspectives.* London: Whiting and Birch.

Lindquist, C., and C. Lindquist. 1999. "Health Behind Bars: Utilization and Evaluation of Medical Care Among Jail Inmates." *Journal of Community Health* 24: 285–303.

Longest, B. B. 1998. *Health Policy Making in the United States.* 2nd ed. Chicago: Health Administration Press.

Lundberg-Love, P. 1999. "The Resilience of the Human Psyche: Recognition and Treatment of the Adult Survivor of Incest." Pp. 3–22 in M. Paludi, ed.. *The Psychology of Sexual Victimization: A Handbook.* Westport, CT: Greenwood Press.

Lynch, James P., and William J. Sabol. 2001. "Prisoner Reentry in Perspective." *Crime Policy Report* 3. Washington, DC: Urban Institute.

Mackey, Philip English. 1982. *Hanging in the Balance: The Anti–Capital Punishment Movement in New York, 1776–1861.* New York: Garland.

Mann, Coramae. 1984. *Female Crime and Delinquency.* Tuscaloosa: University of Alabama Press.

Marble, M. 1995. "Suit Challenges Women's Health Care in Prisons." *Women's Health Weekly*, April 17, 11–13.

———. 1996. Half of California's Female Prison Inmates Infected with Hepatitis B. *Women's Health Weekly,* October 28, 1–4.

Marshall, Helen E. 1937. *Dorothea Dix: Forgotten Samaritan.* New York: Russell and Russell.

Martin, Sandra, and Niki Cotton. 1995. "Literacy Intervention for Incarcerated Women." *Corrections Today* 57 (7): 120–122.

Maruschak, Laura M. 2002. *HIV in Prisons, 2000*. Washington, DC: Bureau of Justice Statistics (NCJ 196023).

———. 2004. *HIV in Prisons and Jails, 2002*. Washington, DC: Bureau of Justice Statistics (NCJ 205333).

Maruschak, Laura M., and Allen J. Beck. 2001. *Medical Problems of Inmates, 1997*. Washington, DC: Bureau of Justice Statistics (NCJ 181644).

Mauer, Marc. 2001. "The Causes and Consequences of Prison Growth in the United States." *Punishment and Society: The International Journal of Penology* 3 (1): 9–20.

———. 2002. "Disenfranchisement of Felons: The Modern-Day Voting Rights Challenge." *Civil Rights Journal: US Commission on Civil Rights* 6 (1): 40–43.

Mauer, Marc, Cathy Potler, and Richard Wolf. 1999. "Gender and Justice: Women, Drugs and Sentencing Policy." Washington, DC: Sentencing Project staff@sentencingproject.org.

Maull, F. W. 1991. "Dying in Prison: Sociocultural and Psychosocial Dynamics." *Hospice Journal* 7 (1–2): 127–142.

———. 1998. "Issues in Prison Hospice: Toward a Model for the Delivery of Hospice Care in a Correctional Setting." *Hospice Journal* 13 (4): 57–82.

McBride, D. C., Y. M. Terry, and J. A. Inciardi. 1991. "Alternative Perspectives on the Drug Policy Debate." Pp. 9–54 in J. Inciardi, ed., *The Drug Legalization Debate*. Newbury Park, CA: Sage.

McDonald, Lawrence Herbert. 1974. "Prelude to Emancipation: The Failure of the Great Reaction in Maryland, 1831–1850." PhD diss., University of Maryland.

McGowan, Brenda, and Karen Blumenthal. 1978. *Why Punish the Children? A Study of Children of Women Prisoners*. Hackensack, NJ: National Council on Crime and Delinquency.

McKelvey, Blake. 1968. *American Prisons: A Study in American Social History Prior to 1915*. Montclair, NJ: Patterson Smith.

McManus, Edgar. 1993. *Law and Liberty in Early New England: Criminal Justice and Due Process, 1620–1692*. Amherst; University of Massachusetts Press.

McQuaide, S., and J. H. Ehrenreich. 1998. "Women in Prison: Approaches to Understanding the Lives of a Forgotten Population." *Affilia: Journal of Women and Social Work* 13 (2): 233–247.

Mears, Daniel P., Laura Winterfield, John Hunsaker, Gretchen E. Moore, and Ruth M. White. 2003. *Drug Treatment in the Criminal Justice System: The Current State of Knowledge*. Washington, DC: Urban Institute.

Mechanic, David. 1999. "Mental Health and Mental Illness: Definitions and Perspectives." Pp. 12–28 in Allan V. Horwitz and Teresa L. Scheid, eds., *A Handbook for the Study of Mental Health: Social Contexts, Theories, and Systems*. Cambridge: Cambridge University Press.

Menard, Russell. 1993. "Whatever Happened to Early American Population History?" *William and Mary Quarterly* 1 (2): 356–366.

Merlo, Alida, and Joycelyn Pollock. 1995. *Women, Law, and Social Control*. Boston: Allyn and Bacon.

"Methamphetamine Use Takes Major Toll on Inmates' Dental Health." 2004. *Drug Week* 129, April 30.

Miller, Inga. 2000. "Paying Their Debt: Prisoner Advocates Say Inmates Charged Too Much." *Fairfield Daily Republic,* July 21, www.geocities.com/capitolhill/parliament/2398/memberspublished5.html.

Minkler, M., and K. Roe. 1996. "Grandparents as Surrogate Parents." *Generations* 2: 34–38.

Minkoff, K. 1987. "Resistance of Mental Health Professionals to Working with the Chronic Mentally Ill." Pp. 3–20 in A. Myerson, ed., *Barriers to Treating the Chronic Mentally Ill.* San Francisco: Jossey-Bass.

Morton, Joann. 1992. *An Administrative Overview of the Older Inmate.* Washington, DC: National Institute of Corrections.

Morton, Joann, and Deborah Williams. 1998. "Mother-Child Bonding." *Corrections Today* 60 (7): 98–103.

Moses, Marilyn. 1995. "A Synergistic Solution for Children of Incarcerated Parents." *Corrections Today* 57 (7): 124–127.

Moynahan, J. M., and E. Stewart. 1980. *The American Jail: Its Development and Growth.* Chicago: Nelson-Hall.

Muckenhoupt, Margaret. 2003. *Dorothea Dix: Advocate for Mental Health Care.* Oxford: Oxford University Press.

Mumola, Christopher J. 2002. *Incarcerated Parents and Their Children.* Washington, DC: Bureau of Justice Statistics (NCJ 182335).

Murphy, Kate. 2004. "After Enron, a Sunless Year in a Tiny Cell." *New York Times*, June 20, BU5.

Murphy, Sheigla, and Karina Arroyo. 2000. "Women as Judicious Consumers of Drug Markets." Pp. 101–120 in Mangai Natarajan and Mike Hough, eds., *Illegal Drug Markets: From Research to Prevention Policy.* Volume 11 of the Crime Prevention Studies series. Monsey, NY: Criminal Justice Press.

National AIDS Advisory Council. 1991. *HIV in Correctional Facilities.* Report no. 4. Washington, DC: National Commission on AIDS.

National Center for Health Statistics. 1999. *Health, United States, 1998.* Washington, DC: National Center for Health Statistics.

National Clearinghouse on Child Abuse and Neglect Information. "Statutes-at-a-Glance 1998: Grounds for Termination of Parental Rights." Washington, DC: Administration for Children and Families.

National Coalition of Hispanic Health and Human Services Organizations. 1998. *HIV/AIDS: The Impact on Minorities.* Washington, DC: National Coalition of Hispanic Health and Human Services Organizations.

National Commission on Correctional Health Care. 2002. *The Health Status of Soon-to-Be-Released Inmates: A Report to Congress.* Chicago: National Commission on Correctional Health Care.

"National Drug Control Strategy." 2003. www.whitehousedrugpolicy.gov/publications/policy/04budget/.

National Institute of Corrections. 1997. *Prison Medical Care: Special Needs Populations and Cost Control.* Longmont, CO: LIS.

———. 1998. *Hospice and Palliative Care in Prisons.* Longmont, CO: LIS.

Neeley, Connie L., L. Addison, and D. Craig-Moreland. 1997. "Addressing the Needs of Elderly Offenders." *Corrections Today* 59 (5): 120–124.

Neto, Virginia V., and LaNelle Marie Bainer. 1983. "Mother and Wife Locked Up: A Day with the Family." *Prison Journal* 63, no. 2: 124.

Newburger, Eric. 2001. *Home Computers and Internet Use in the United States: August 2000.* Special Studies. Washington, DC: US Department of Commerce.

Newman, Graeme. 1978. *The Punishment Response.* Philadelphia: J. B. Lippincott.

———. 1983. *Just and Painful: A Case for the Corporal Punishment of Criminals.* New York: Macmillan.

New York State Department of Correctional Services. 2001. "Female Offenders: 1999–2000." wpaonline.irg/website/focus/wpa _trends_focus_newlogo.pdf.

NIAID (National Institute of Allergy and Infectious Disease). 1999. *NIAID Fact Sheet: An Introduction to Sexually Transmitted Diseases.* Washington, DC: US Department of Health and Human Services.

Novick, L. F., and E. Remmlinger. 1978. "A Study of 128 Deaths in New York City Correctional Facilities (1971–1976): Implications for Prisoner Health Care." *Journal of Medical Care* 16 (9): 749–756.

Obeidallah, Dawn A., and Felton J. Earls. 1999. *Adolescent Girls: The Role of Depression in the Development of Delinquency.* Washington, DC: National Institute of Justice.

O'Brien, Patricia. 2001. *Making It in the "Free World": Women in Transition from Prison.* Albany: State University of New York Press.

Office of Research on Women's Health. 1998. *Women of Color Health Data Book: Adolescents to Seniors.* Bethesda, MD: National Institutes of Health (98-4247).

Okie, S. 1998. "Inmates with Kidney Disease Call Transplant Policy Cruel." *Washington Post*, October 12, A1.

O'Shea, Kathleen. 1993. "Women on Death Row." Pp. 75–89 in Beverly R. Fletcher, Lynda Dixon Shaver, and Dreama G. Moon, eds., *Women Prisoners: A Forgotten Population.* Westport, CT: Praeger.

———. 1999. *Women and the Death Penalty in the United States, 1900–1998.* Westport, CT: Praeger.

Owen, B., and B. Bloom. 1995. "Profiling Women Prisoners: Findings from National Surveys and a California Sample." *Prison Journal* 75 (2): 165–185.

Palen, J. John. 2002. *The Urban World.* 6th ed. Boston: McGraw-Hill.

Peters, Roger H., Anne L. Strozier, Mary R. Murrin, and William D. Kearns. 1997. "Treatment of Substance-Abusing Jail Inmates: Examination of Gender Differences." *Journal of Substance Abuse Treatment* 14 (4): 339–349.

Petersilia, Joan. 1998. "A Decade of Experimenting with Intermediate Sanctions: What Have We Learned?" *Federal Probation* 62 (2): 3–9.

———. 2000. "When Prisoners Return to the Community: Political, Economic, and Social Consequences." *Research in Brief: Issues for the Twenty-first Century. Papers from the Executive Sessions on Sentencing and Corrections.* Washington, DC: Office of Justice Programs, National Institute of Justice (NCJ 184253).

Petras, D. D. 1999. "The Effect of Caregiver Preparation and Sense of Control on Adaptation of Kinship Caregivers." Pp. 233–255 in P. Gleeson and C. F. Hairston, eds., *Kinship Care: Improving Practice Through Research.* Washington, DC: CWLA Press.

Peugh, Jordon, and Steven Belenko. 1999. "Substance-Involved Women Inmates: Challenges to Providing Effective Treatment." *Prison Journal* 79 (1): 23–44.

Phillips, Susan, and Nancy Harm. 1997. "Women Prisoners: A Contextual Framework." *Women and Therapy* 20 (4): 1–9.

Pollack, Joycelyn. 2002. "Parenting Programs in Women's Prisons." *Women and Criminal Justice* 14 (1): 131–154.

Pomeroy, E. C., R. Kiam, and E. Abel. 1998. "Meeting the Mental Health Needs of Incarcerated Women." *Health and Social Work* 23 (1): 71–76.

Potter, Joan. 1978. "In Prison, Women Are Different." *Corrections Magazine* 4: 14–24.

Preyer, Kathryn. 1982. "Penal Measures in the American Colonies: An Overview." *American Journal of Legal History* 26, 326–353.

Quinn, Nina. 2001. "Medical Parole: Politics vs. Compassion." *Prison Hospice* 7 (1): 1.

Raeder, Myrna. 2003. "Gendered Implications of Sentencing and Correctional Practices: A Legal Perspective." Pp. 173–208 in Barbara Bloom, ed., *Gendered Justice: Addressing Female Offenders.* Durham, NC: Carolina Academic Press.

Rafter, Nicole. 1985. *Partial Justice: Women in State Prisons, 1800–1935*. Boston: Northeastern University Press.

Randa, Laura. 1997. *Society's Final Solution: A History and Discussion of the Death Penalty*. Lanham, MD: University Press of America.

Rapaport, Elizabeth. 1991. "The Death Penalty and Gender Discrimination." Law and Society Review 25: 367–368.

Reilly, Jackie, and Sally Martin. 1998. "Children of Incarcerated Parents: What Is the Caregiver's Role?" National Network for Child Care. www.canr.uconn.edu/ces/child/newsarticles/ccc743.htm.

Reviere, Rebecca, and Vernetta D. Young. 2004. "Aging Behind Bars: Health Care for Older Women in Prison." *Journal of Women and Aging* 16 (1–2): 55–67.

Richardson, Hester. 1903. *Side-Lights on Maryland History with Sketches of Early Maryland Families*. Baltimore: Williams and Wilkins.

Richie, Beth E. 2001. "Challenges Incarcerated Women Face as They Return to Their Communities: Findings from Life History Interviews." *Crime and Delinquency* 47 (3): 368–389.

Rierden, Andi. 1997. *The Farm: Life Inside a Women's Prison*. Amherst: University of Massachusetts Press.

Rigert, Joe. 1997. "Sentencing Guidelines of Drug Laws Frustrate Many Judges." *Minneapolis Star*, December 14.

Riley, M. 1998. "Successful Aging." *Gerontologist* 38 (2): 151.

Rogers, Joseph. 2000. "Mary Belle Harris: Warden and Rehabilitation Pioneer." *Women and Criminal Justice* 11 (4): 5–27.

Rose, Dina, and Todd Clear. 2002. Incarceration, Reentry and Social Capital: Social Networks in the Balance. Paper prepared for the "From Prison to Home" Conference. Sponsored by the Urban Institute and funded by the US Department of Health and Human Services.

Rosefield, H. A. 1993. "The Older Inmate: Where Do We Go from Here?" *Journal of Prison and Jail Health* 12 (1): 51–58.

Rossman, Shelli. 2002. "Services Integration: Strengthening Offenders and Families, While Promoting Community Health and Safety." Paper prepared for the "From Prison to Home" Conference.

Rothman, David. 1971. *Discovery of the Asylum: Social Order and Disorder in the New Republic*. Boston: Little, Brown.

Rubenstein, Gwen, and Debbie Mukamal. 2002. "Welfare and Housing: Denial of Benefits to Drug Offenders." Pp. 37–49 in Marc Mauer and Meda Chesney-Lind, eds., *Invisible Punishment: The Collateral Consequences of Mass Imprisonment*. New York: New Press.

Ruiz, Dorothy. 2002. "The Increase in Incarceration Among Women and Its Impact on the Grandmother Caregiver: Some Racial Considerations." *Journal of Sociology and Social Welfare* 2 (3): 179–197.

Salganicoff, A., J. Z. Beckerman, R. Wyn, and V. D. Ojeda. 2003. "Women's Health Care in the United States: Health Coverage and Access to Care." Pp. 493–500 in Philip R. Lee and Carroll L. Estes, eds., *The Nation's Health*. 7th ed. Sudbury, MA: Jones and Barlett.

SAMHSA (Substance Abuse and Mental Health Services Administration). 2003. *Results from the 2002 National Survey on Drug Use and Health: National Findings*. Rockville, MD: Office of Applied Studies (NSDUH Series H-22, DHHS Publication No. SMA 03-3836).

———. 2004a. *Results from the 2003 National Survey on Drug Use and Health: Na-*

tional Findings. Rockville, MD: Office of Applied Studies (NSDUH Series H-25, DHHS Publication SMA 04-3964).

———. 2004b. *Treatment Episode Data Set (TEDS) Highlights—2002: National Admission to Substance Abuse Treatment Services*. Rockville, MD: Office of Applied Studies (NSDUH Series S-22, DHHS Publication No. SMA 04-3946).

———. 2005. *National Expenditures for Mental Health Services and Substance Abuse Treatment, 1991–2001*. Rockville, MD (DHHS SMA 05-3999).

Samuels, Paul, and Debbie Mukamal. 2004. *After Prison: Roadblocks to Reentry: A Report on State Legal Barriers Facing People with Criminal Records*. Washington, DC: Legal Action Center.

Schafer, N., and A. B. Dellinger. 1999. "Jailed Parents: An Assessment." *Women and Criminal Justice* 10 (4): 73–91.

Schetky, D. 1998. "Mourning in Prison: Mission Impossible?" *Journal of the American Academy of Psychiatry and the Law* 26 (3): 383–391.

Schiraldi, Vincent. 1995. "3-Strikes Crime Laws to Spur Aging of Prisons." *Aging Today* (March/April): 12.

Schneider, Peter. 2002. "Criminal Convictions, Incarceration, and Child Welfare: Ex-Offenders Lose Their Children." In Amy Hirsch et al., *Every Door Closed: Barriers Facing Parents with Criminal Records*. Community Legal Services and the Center for Law and Social Policy, http://www.clasp.org/publications/every_door_closed.pdf.

Schneider, V., and John Smykla. 1991. "A Summary Analysis of Executions in the United States, 1608–1987: The Epsy File." Pp. 1–19 in Robert Bohm, ed., *The Death Penalty in America: Current Perspectives*. Cincinnati, OH: Anderson.

Seidlitz, Anne. 1999. "Doing 'Family' in a Women's Hospice." *National Prison Hospice Journal* 6.

Semmes, Raphael. 1938. *Crime and Punishment in Early Maryland*. Baltimore: Johns Hopkins University Press.

Sentencing Project. 2002. *Mentally Ill Offenders in the Criminal Justice System: An Analysis and Prescription*. Washington, DC: Sentencing Project.

Seymour, Cynthia. 1998. "Children with Parents in Prison: Child Welfare Policy, Program, and Practice Issues." *Child Welfare* 77 (5):469–494.

Sheppard, Erica, as told to Patrice Gaines. 2003. "Backtalk: A Remorseful Mother of Three Reaches Out to Her Children from Her Cell on Death Row." *Essence*, April.

Shugg, W. 2000. *A Monument to Good Intentions: The Story of the Maryland Penitentiary, 1804–1999*. Baltimore: Maryland Historical Society.

Shurley, Traci. 2004. "Increasing Number of Women Straining Arkansas' Prisons." NWAnews.com, November 14. http://www.nwanews.com/story.php?paper=adg&section=News&storyid=98761.

Simmons, Charlene Wear. 2000. "Children of Incarcerated Parents." *California Research Bureau* 7 (2).

Simson, Elizabeth. 2002. *Justice Denied: How Felony Disenfranchisement Laws Undermine American Democracy*. Washington, DC: Americans for Democratic Action Education Fund.

Singer, M. I., J. Bussey, L.Y. Song, and L. Lunghofer. 1995. "The Psychosocial Issues of Women Serving Time in Jail." *Social Work* 40 (1): 103–113.

Slaght, E. 1999. "Family and Offender Treatment Focusing on the Family in the Treatment of Substance-Abusing Criminal Offenders." *Journal of Drug Education* 19 (1): 53–62.

SLC. 2000. *Female Offenders: Special Needs and Southern State Challenges*. A Special Series Report of the Southern Legislative Conference. Prepared by Todd Alan

Edwards, Regional Representative, Southern Legislative Conference of the Council of State Governments.

Smith, Perry F., Jaromir Mikl, Benedict I. Truman, Lawrence Lessner, J. Stan Lehman, Roy W. Stevens, Elaine A. Lord, Raymond K. Broaddus, and Dale L. Morse. 1991. "HIV Infection Among Women Entering the New York State Correctional System." *American Journal of Public Health* 81 (5): 35–41.

Smith, Rich. 2000. "A Good Death." *British Medical Journal* 320: 129–130.

Snell, Tracy L. 1994. *Women in Prison: Survey of State Prison Inmates, 1991: Special Report.* Washington, DC: Bureau of Justice Statistics (NCJ 145321).

Snell, Tracy L., and Laura M. Maruschak. 2002. *Capital Punishment 2000.* Washington, DC: Bureau of Justice Statistics (NCJ 197020).

Snyder, Howard J. 2003. *Juvenile Arrests, 2001.* Washington, DC: Office of Juvenile Justice and Delinquency Prevention (NCJ 201370), January.

Stahl, Anne L. 2003. *Drug Offense Cases in Juvenile Courts, 1990–1999.* Washington, DC: Office of Juvenile Justice and Delinquency Prevention (FS 200308).

Stana, Richard. 2000. "State and Federal Prisoners: Profile of Inmate Characteristics in 1991 and 1997." US GAO. Report to the Honorable Charles B. Rangel, House of Representatives.

"STDs in Incarcerated Women." 2000. *Family Practice News* 30 (January 1): 19.

Steadman, H. J., E. Holohean, and J. Dvoskin. 1991. "Estimating Mental Health Needs and Service Utilization Among Prison Inmates." *Bulletin of the American Academy of Psychiatry and the Law* 19 (3): 297–307.

Steadman, H. J., S. Morris, and D. L. Dennis. 1995. "The Diversion of Mentally Ill Persons from Jail to Community-Based Services: A Profile of Programs." *American Journal of Public Health* 85 (12): 1630–1635.

St. Lawrence, J. S., G. Eldridge, M. Shelby, C. Little, T. Brasfield, and R. E. O'Bannon. 1997. "HIV Risk Reduction for Incarcerated Women: A Comparison of Brief Intervention Based on Two Theoretical Models." *Journal of Consulting and Clinical Psychology* 65 (3): 504–509.

Strauss, S., and G. Falkin. 2000. "The Relationship Between the Quality of Drug User Treatment and Program Completion: Understanding the Perceptions of Women in a Prison-Based Program." *Substance Use and Misuse* 35 (12–14): 2127–2159.

Streib, Victor. 2003. "Death Penalty for Female Offenders, January 1, 1973 Through June 30, 2003." Retrieved March 15, 2004, from www.law.onu.edu/faculty/streib/femdeath.pdf.

Strickland, Katherine. 1967. *Correctional Institutions for Women in the United States.* PhD diss., Syracuse University.

"Suit Challenges Women's Health Care in Prisons." 1995. *Women's Health Weekly,* April 17, 11–13.

Swain, Ellen D. 2001. "From Benevolence to Reform: The Expanding Career of Mrs. Rhoda M. Coffin." *Indiana Magazine of History* 97 (3): 190–217.

Swan, Neil. 1998. "Drug Abuse Cost to Society Set At $97.7 Billion, Continuing Steady Increase." *NIDA Notes* 13 (4).

Sykes, Gresham. 1958. *The Society of Captives.* Princeton, NJ: Princeton University Press.

Szalavitz, M. 1998. "War on Drugs, War on Women." *On the Issues Magazine,* Winter.

Tappan, Paul. 1960. *Crime, Justice, and Correction.* New York: McGraw-Hill.

Taylor, Jon Marc. 1993. "Pell Grants for Prisoners." *Nation,* January 25.

Taylor, P. J., and J. M. Parrott. 1988. "Elderly Offenders." *British Journal of Psychiatry* 152 (June): 340–346.

Taylor, V. 1999. "Florida Law Requires Prisons to Improve Visiting Conditions." *Corrections Journal* 3 (21): 3–4.

Temin, Carolyn. 2001. "Let Us Consider the Children." *Corrections Today* 63 (1): 66–68.

Thigpen, Morris, and Susan Hunter. 1998. *Special Issues in Corrections: Current Issues in the Operation of Women's Prisons.* Longmont, CO: US Department of Justice, National Institute of Corrections Information Center (NICIC).

Thomas, C., and D. Petersen. 1977. *Prison Organization and Inmate Subcultures.* Indianapolis: Bobbs-Merrill.

Toch, Hans. 1977. *Living in Prison.* New York: Free Press.

Travis, Jeremy. 1995. "The Drug Court Movement." National Institute of Justice Update. Washington, DC: US Department of Justice, Office of Justice Programs.

———. 2000. *But They All Come Back: Rethinking Prisoner Reentry.* Washington, DC: Office of Justice Programs, National Institute of Justice (NCJ 181413).

———. 2001. "Prisoner Reentry Seen Through a Community Lens." Luncheon address at a Neighborhood Reinvestment Corporation Training Institute, Urban Institute.

Travis, Jeremy, Amy Solomon, and Michelle Waul. 2001. *From Prison to Home: The Dimensions and Consequences of Prisoner Reentry.* Washington, DC: Urban Institute.

US Census Bureau. 2002. *2002 Poverty Highlights.* Washington, DC: US Census Bureau.

US DEA (US Drug Enforcement Administration). 2004. *Drug Scheduling.* www.usdoj.gov/dea/pubs/scheduling/htm.

US Department of Justice, Bureau of Justice Statistics. 1997. *Survey of Inmates in Adult State and Federal Correctional Facilities.* Washington, DC: US Department of Justice, Bureau of Justice Statistics.

US Department of Justice. 1999. *Correctional Populations in the United States, 1996.* Washington, DC: Bureau of Justice Statistics (NCJ 171684).

US Department of Justice. National Institute of Corrections Information Center (NICIC). 1998. *Current Issues in the Operation of Women's Prisons.* Longmont, CO: National Institute of Corrections.

US DHHS (US Department of Health and Human Services). 1999. *Mental Health: A Report of the Surgeon General—Executive Summary.* Rockville, MD: US Department of Health and Human Services, Substance Abuse and Mental Health Services Administration, Center for Mental Health Services, National Institutes of Health, National Institute of Mental Health.

US GAO (General Accounting Office). 1999. *Women in Prison: Issues and Challenges Confronting US Correctional Systems.* Washington, DC: GAO (GAO/GGD-00-22).

———. 2000. *Managing Female Inmate Populations.* Washington, DC: GAO. (GAO/GGD-00-22).

———. 2001. *Prisoner Releases: Trends and Information on Reintegration Programs.* Washington, DC: GAO. (GAO-01-483).

US Sentencing Commission. 1995. *Special Report to Congress: Cocaine and Federal Sentencing Policy.* Washington, DC: Government Printing Office, February.

———. 2001. *Sourcebook of Federal Sentencing Statistics.* 6th ed. Washington, DC: US Sentencing Commission (USSCFY01), Table 35.

———. 2004. *Fifteen Years of Guideline Sentencing. An Assessment of How Well the Federal Criminal Justice System Is Achieving the Goals of Sentencing Reform.* Washington, DC: US Sentencing Commission.

Van Voorhis, Patricia, and Lois Presser. 2001. "Classification of Women Offenders: A National Assessment of Current Practices." Washington, DC: US Department of Justice, National Institute of Corrections.

Verbrugge, Lois. 1985. "Gender and Health: An Update on Hypotheses and Evidence." *Journal of Health and Social Behavior* 26 (3): 156–182.

"Virginia Corrections Chairman Concerned About Health Care for Women Inmates." 1998. *Women's Health Weekly*, February 2, 20–22.

"Wackenhut Corrections Corporation Announces Name Change to The GEO Group, Inc." 2003. http://www.prnewswire.com/cgi-bin/stories.

Wade, Richard. 1964. *Slavery in the Cities*. New York: Oxford University Press.

Wallich, P., and M. Mukerjee. 1996. "Regulating the Body Business." *Scientific American* 274 (3): 12–13.

Walsh, C. Eamon. 1992. "Aging Inmate Offenders: Another Perspective." Pp. 197–212 in Claton Hartjen and Edward Rhine, eds., *Correctional Theory and Practice*. Chicago: Nelson-Hall.

Walsh, Richard, and W. L. Fox. 1974. *Maryland: A History 1632–1974*. Baltimore: Maryland Historical Society.

Ward, D., and G. Kassebaum. 1965. *Women's Prison: Sex and Social Structure*. Chicago: Aldine-Atherton.

Washington Times. 2004. "A Matter of Public Safety." Editorials. www/washington times.com.

Weilerstein, R. 1995. "The Prison Match Program." Pp. 255–264 in K. Gabel and D. Johnson, eds., *Children of Incarcerated Parents*. New York: Lexington Books.

Welter, B. 1966. "The Cult of True Womanhood: 1820–1860." *American Quarterly* 18: 151–174.

Western, Bruce, Jeffrey Kling, and David Weiman. 2001. "Labor Market Consequences of Incarceration." *Crime and Delinquency* 47 (3): 410–428.

Williams, David R. 2003. "Racial/Ethnic Variations in Women's Health: The Social Embeddedness of Health." Pp. 516–536 in Philip R. Lee and Carroll L. Estes, eds., *The Nation's Health*. 7th ed. Sudbury, MA: Jones and Barlett.

Wisconsin. 2005. "Governor Doyle Announces Return of Last Remaining Wisconsin Inmates Housed in Out-of-State Facilities." www.wi-doc-com/index_news.htm.

Women in Prison Project. 2002. *Fact Sheets*. New York: Correctional Association of New York: Women in Prison Project.

Woodrow, J. 1992. "Mothers Inside, Children Outside." Pp. 29–40 in R. Shaw, ed., *Prisoner's Children*. New York: Routledge, Chapman and Hall.

Works, C. 2003. "REENTRY: The Tie That Binds Civil Legal Aid Attorneys and Public Defenders." *Clearinghouse Review Journal of Poverty Law and Policy* (September–October): 328–340.

WPA (Women's Prison Association). 1995. "Breaking the Cycle of Despair: Children of Incarcerated Mothers." WPA Focus on Women and Justice series, http://www.wpaonline.org/website/publications.htm.

———. 2003. "Barriers to Reentry." WPA Focus on Women and Justice series, www.wpaonline.org/website/home.htm.

Wright, Lois, and Cynthia Seymour. 2000. *Working with Children and Families Separated by Incarceration: A Handbook for Child Welfare Agencies*. Washington, DC: Child Welfare League of America.

Young, Diane S. 1996. "Contributing Factors to Poor Health Among Incarcerated Women: A Conceptual Model." *Affilia: Journal of Women and Social Work* 11 (4): 440–462.

Young, Diane, and Carrie J. Smith. 2000. "When Moms Are Incarcerated: The Needs of Children, Mothers, and Caregivers." *Families in Society: The Journal of Contemporary Human Services* 81 (2): 130–141.
Young, Vernetta D. 2001. "All the Women in the Maryland State Penitentiary: 1812–1869." *Prison Journal* 81 (1): 113–132.
Young, Vernetta D., and R. Harrison. 2001. "Race/Ethnic Differences in the Sequences of Drugs Used by Women." *Journal of Drug Issues* 31 (2): 293–325.
Young, Vernetta D., and Rebecca Reviere. 2001. "Meeting the Health Care Needs of the New Woman Inmate: A National Survey of Prison Practices." *Journal of Offender Rehabilitation* 32 (2): 31–48.
Zedner, Lucia. 1995. "Wayward Sisters: The Prison for Women." Pp. 329–361 in Norval Morris and David J. Rothman, eds., *The Oxford History of the Prison: The Practice of Punishment in Western Society*. New York: Oxford University Press.
Zickler, Patrick. 2000. "Gender Differences in Prevalence of Drug Abuse Traced to Opportunities to Use." *NIDA Notes* 15 (4).

■ Court Cases

Blakely v. Washington, 111 Wash. App. 851, 47 P.3d 149, Reversed and Remanded, 2004.
Department of Housing and Urban Development v. Rucker et al., 237 Fed 1113, 2002.
Estelle v. Gamble, 429 US 97 (1976).
Furman v. Georgia, 408 US 238 (1972).
Gregg v. Georgia, 428 US 153 (1976).
In Re Sabrina N. (1998), 60 Cal.App.4th 996 [70 Cal.Rptr.2d 603]. Court of Appeal, Second District, Division 5.
Rosales v. Thompson, 321 F. 3d 835 (9th Circ. 2003).
United States v. Booker, 2005 WL 50108 (US Jan. 12, 2005).
United States v. Fanfan, 2005.

■ Legislative Acts

Adoption and Safe Families Act of 1997 (ASFA) 20 U.S.C. Section 1091r.
Anti–Drug Abuse Act, 1986 PL No. 99-570.
California Welfare and Institutional Code Section 361(e)(1).
Extenders Act Housing Opportunity Program Extension Act of 1996, PL No. 104-120, 110 Stat. 834 (Mar. 28, 1996): 142 *Congressional Record* H1267 (Feb. 27, 1996).
Maryland Acts of 1793.
Maryland Acts of 1804.
Maryland Acts of 1809.
Maryland Laws of 1809, Chp. 138.
Violent Crime Control and Law Enforcement Act (42 USC Chapter 136), 1994.

Index

Abuse, physical and sexual, 7, 9, 67, 69, 72, 73, 78, 82, 101, 102, 106, 140. *See also* Violence against women
ACA. *See* American Correctional Association
Accidents, 84, 88
ADA. *See* Americans with Disabilities Act
ADAA. *See* Anti-Drug Abuse Act
Addiction, 69, 73, 149, 186
Adoption and Safe Families Act of 1997 (ASFA), 111, 112, 116, 138, 157
Aggravating circumstances, 140, 143, 151
AIM. *See* Aid to Children of Imprisoned Mothers
Aid to Children of Imprisoned Mothers (AIM), 111, 116, 118
Alcohol abuse, 69, 72, 86, 88, 102
Alcoholics Anonymous, 81
Alderson, West Virginia, 40, 41, 125
American Correctional Association (ACA), 89, 92, 101, 148
American Psychiatric Association (APA), 100, 103, 104, 107
Americans with Disabilities Act (ADA) 95, 107
Amnesty International, 1, 10, 79, 80, 81, 89, 96, 97, 103, 106
Anti–Drug Abuse Act (ADAA), 75, 76, 86, 154, 156

APA. *See* American Psychiatric Association
Arrestee Drug Abuse Monitoring Program (ADAM), 69
ASFA. *See* Adoption and Safe Families Act of 1997
Atkinson, Eudora, 35, 36
Auburn Prison System, 30
Average daily population (ADP), 54

Banishment, 25
Barfield, Margie Velma, 142
Barton, Clara, 36
Bennett, William, 77
Bias, Len, 76
Bilboes, 20, 22
BJS. *See* Bureau of Justice Statistics
Boguille, Monica, 79
Boredom, 85, 102
Branding, 20, 22
Branks and gags, 21
Breastfeeding, 89, 90
Bureau of Justice Statistics (BJS), 9, 59, 60, 69, 73, 80, 81, 88, 101, 106, 143, 144
Bureau of Prisons. *See* Federal Bureau of Prisons
Bush, President George H. W., 77

California Institution for Women, 124, 132, 133

About the Book

Today's prisons are increasingly filled with poor, dark-skinned, single mothers locked up for low-level drug involvement—with serious ramifications for the corrections system. *Women Behind Bars* offers the first comprehensive exploration of the challenges faced by incarcerated women in the United States.

Young and Reviere show conclusively that serving time in prisons designed by and for men not only does little to address what landed women, particularly women of color, there in the first place, but also undermines their prospects for an improved life on the outside. Using a multifaceted race/class/gender lens, the authors make a convincing argument that women in prison are punished twice: first by their sentences and again because the policies that govern time behind bars were not designed to address women's unique problems and responsibilities.

Vernetta D. Young is associate professor of sociology at Howard University. She is coeditor of *African American Classics in Criminology and Criminal Justice*. **Rebecca Reviere** is associate professor of sociology at Howard University, where she cofounded and directed the Graduate Certificate Program in Women's Studies.